HEROES OF THE INDIAN MUTINY

HEROES OF THE INDIAN MUTINY

STORIES OF HEROIC DEEDS, INTREPIDITY, AND DETERMINATION IN THE FACE OF FEARFUL ODDS DURING THE GREAT MUTINY

EDWARD GILLIAT

GYAN

Published by

Gyan Publishing House
5, Ansari Road
Daryaganj, New Delhi-110002
Phone: 011-47034999, 9811692060
E-mail: books@gyanbooks.com

Distribution Network
gyanbooks.com
India, USA, Canada, UK, Australia

ISBN: 978-93-7097-301-5 (HB)

First Published, 1914

2nd Impression 2025

Printed at: Gyan Press, Delhi.

HEROES OF THE INDIAN MUTINY
Author: EDWARD GILLIAT

HEROES OF
THE INDIAN MUTINY

JAMES HILLS' BRAVE CHARGE

Hills had ordered out his two guns for action, but the enemy were upon them before they could be fired. But Hills, in order to check the attack and to give his men time, charged the Sepoys single handed and cut down the leading men.

HEROES OF THE INDIAN MUTINY

STORIES OF HEROIC DEEDS, INTREPIDITY, AND DETERMINATION IN THE FACE OF FEARFUL ODDS DURING THE GREAT MUTINY

BY

EDWARD GILLIAT, M.A. (Oxon.)

SOMETIME MASTER AT HARROW SCHOOL

AUTHOR OF "FOREST OUTLAWS," "HEROES OF MODERN CRUSADES," &c. &c.

WITH ILLUSTRATIONS

1914

IN MEMORY OF

A GOOD WIFE & HONEST CRITIC

CONTENTS

CONTENTS

CONTENTS

CHAPTER IX

GENERAL SIR A. TAYLOR, G.C.B.: THE MAN WHO TOOK DELHI

CHAPTER X

SIR HENRY AND JOHN LORD LAWRENCE: THE GREAT TWIN BRETHREN

CHAPTER XI

FIELD-MARSHAL SIR HENRY WYLIE NORMAN: THE ORGANISER OF VICTORY

CHAPTER XII

THE HEROES OF CAWNPUR

CONTENTS

LIST OF ILLUSTRATIONS

HEROES OF THE INDIAN MUTINY

CHAPTER I

BEFORE THE MUTINY: MUTTERINGS OF THE STORM

BEFORE we begin to record some of the brave or patient deeds performed by heroes of the Indian Mutiny, it will make matters more clear if we dwell briefly on the history of our Indian Empire, and on the causes which led to the Sepoy Mutiny of 1857.

Soon after Vasco da Gama had found the shores of Hindostan on May 17, 1498, Indian goods and curios began to enter Europe through the agency of the Portuguese and Venetians: but it was not until September 1599 that the merchants of London formed a trading association, and received a charter, which gave them exclusive trade with the countries east of the Cape of Good Hope.

The first vessels returned laden with cargoes of pepper, cloves and cinnamon, on which enormous profits were made, to the natural jealousy of the Portuguese and Dutch, the prior traders in that region.

In 1612, Captain Best was attacked by a strong Portuguese fleet, and beat off his assailants with great gallantry in the roadstead of Surat. He landed his cargo and obtained a commercial treaty from the Mogul emperor: in 1634, the Great Mogul gave the British a firman, enabling them to trade in Bengal: this year the Portuguese retired from that province, and left the trade to their rivals.

In 1639, Fort St. George, or Madras, our earliest possession in India, was founded by Francis Day, and in 1661 Bombay was given to the British Crown as part of the dowry of Catherine of Braganza, and was shortly afterwards transferred by King Charles II. to the East India Company.

After fighting for this trade with the Portuguese and Dutch, we found ourselves in 1744 at war with the French, who also had established themselves in Pondicherry: Dupleix, the French governor, had the ambition of founding a French Empire in India, but the British, under Clive and Sir Eyre Coote, succeeded in expelling the French in 1760. We cannot follow the details of the many wars which followed the attempt to push trade into the interior of India.

The Mahrattas, who had been used to raid and ravage up to the walls of Calcutta, had to be quelled: Oude was reduced by Major Munro in 1764: Hyder Ali of Mysore gave trouble in the Carnatic and ravaged the country up to Madras, but was defeated by Coote.

A second Mysore War gave half the dominions of Tippoo, Hyder's son, to the British: Tippoo himself was finally defeated and killed at Seringapatam in 1799. In the second Mahratta War, Sir Arthur Wellesley and Lord Lake won great victories, and Orissa fell under our rule. The Gurkhas were defeated in 1814, and Nepaul sued for peace.

In 1823 the first Burmese War took place, and we lost many men from disease.

In 1828, Lord William Bentinck became Governor-General of India, and made many social reforms: some of these are said to have led to the Mutiny, as they touched on the religion of the natives. He abolished suttee, or the burning of widows upon the bier of their husbands: he put down thugs, or the hereditary assassins of India: he forbade the flogging of native soldiers by English officers, of which we will write more anon. Under Lord Auckland the disastrous Afghan War took place and at the same time Sir Charles Napier conquered the Ameers of Scinde: in 1845, Sir Hugh Gough defeated in four battles the brave fighting race of the Sikhs, and a British Resident was sent to the Punjab. Under Lord Dalhousie fresh territory was annexed in the Punjab, Burma, Nagpore and Oude: at the end of the second Sikh War the Punjab became a British Province, and under John Lawrence was so prosperous and contented that it effected much toward stemming the tide of mutiny. In 1852 the second Burmese War gave Britain the valley of the Irrawaddy, and since then that province has advanced amazingly in all material development.

This brief résumé serves to show us how to the Indian mind war after war, and annexation after defeat, must have excited patriotic feelings and alarmed the ruling powers of native states and the high-caste priesthood with regard to what might follow. But the causes of the Mutiny were so numerous that it is worth while to unravel them in some detail.

One influence which weighed heavily with the superstitious native was caused by a rumour circulating through all the bazaars that fate limited the English rule in India to one hundred years from the date of Clive's great victory at Plassey (1757). The sepoy troops, too, had learnt on many a battlefield to win great victories, and thought the time had come for them to recognise their own valour and secure a great destiny. Being most of them the younger sons of zemindars, or small landholders, the sepoys were full of pride and ambition: they believed that the treasures of India belonged by right to them; they were looking forward to founding a great military despotism, under which they were to be the spoilt children of fortune. It is true a sepoy's pay was only seven rupees a month, less than fourteen shillings at that period: but as a Brahmin his faith restrained him from wasting his money on gross appetite, and his simple mode of life left him a surplus from which he could help his needy relations: so that he felt himself a man of some importance. For the Hindoo possesses a strong sense of clanship, and is extremely generous in his dealings with poor kinsmen. But the Indian dustoor, or etiquette of the family, sometimes compels him to launch out into enormous expenses through which he falls deeply into debt and becomes the slave of a grasping, pitiless usurer. For instance, a private soldier has often been known to celebrate a marriage feast in such style as to necessitate the spending of three or four hundred rupees. By this means he achieves a temporary consideration amongst the native populace, while he loses permanently all peace of mind, grows discontented and infects his regiment with his own sense of wrong. For an Indian regiment was not composed of separate units like a British regiment: the soubahdar-major, or native colonel, allowed his havildar, or sergeant, to recruit as many natives as he liked from his own village: so that a sepoy regiment partook of the nature of a clan in which near relations stood shoulder to shoulder, and any grievance which hurt one sepoy affected all together: this made them strong as a fighting machine, but in time of mutiny proved to be fraught with danger to our Empire, for family ties held them together against us. Some historians give the annexation of Oude as a cause for the mutiny, on the ground that the sepoy lost land by the change. Others attribute it to Russian intrigue, or Persian interference, or Mahommedan conspiracy, things difficult to prove.

Officers who served in sepoy regiments give more probable causes of the discontent: they say frankly that the sepoy had been taught to believe that he was the mainstay of our power in India: he had been indulged and petted by successive governors-general and commanding officers, who could not believe that the sepoy was at heart unfaithful, and who shut their eyes to any evidence of his disaffection. The bonds of discipline had gradually been relaxed since Lord William Bentinck had put down flogging: then the Brahmin priests grew alarmed for their influence and prestige, as infanticide was stopped, suttee abolished, and the privilege of dying under the car of Juggernaut was forbidden. Besides all this, Lord Dalhousie made all sepoys pay postage for their letters, instead of letting them go free, as before, under the signature of their commanding officer. The ferries too were no longer free to them; but now, unless on duty, they had to pay toll. An officer, who had been away from his regiment for ten years, and had been home on sick leave, on returning to his old regiment as colonel noticed a marked change for the worse in the conduct of the sepoys towards their European officers.

The other officers, who had been with the same men continually, did not notice any difference. But the colonel remarked at once on the want of cordial respect towards officers which had formerly been the rule: he saw with dismay a swaggering, free and easy kind of air about the sepoys, and that they were quite careless about showing respect to officers of other regiments.

"Riding in uniform past the guards of other regiments, I constantly observed that the sepoys would stand with their arms folded, their legs straddled, their noses in the air; and that they would salute with mock respect, or purposely with the left hand, an Indian way of offering an affront. I never passed over such acts of disrespect, and in the course of a few weeks, as I became known, their conduct altered towards myself."

However, the colonel had a striking illustration of the increasing insolence of the native soldiers in his own regiment. For a man named Toofànee having a quarrel with a comrade lodged a complaint against him before the captain of his company. The captain gave his decision, but Toofànee appealed to the colonel. On proceeding to the mess-house after morning parade to hear the case, the colonel met the adjutant and began conversing with him: at this moment Toofànee was brought up by the orderly havildar, or sergeant of his company, and without waiting to be addressed, or until the colonel had done speaking to the adjutant, he saluted in an insolent manner and shouted out, "I shall get no justice here: I shall bring my captain before the supreme court in Calcutta." The native officers who heard this were highly indignant at the man's insubordination.

Toofânee was instantly ordered into confinement, tried and punished: but his case was no exceptional one. The discipline of the sepoys had fallen from its high standard.

Another officer accuses Lord William Bentinck of having given the Indian army the first and most serious push down the incline from discipline to anarchy. In the first place, that governor-general made a change which lowered the white officer in the eyes of his men. There had been an allowance made to each officer, called "batta"; Lord William, out of motives of economy, passed "the half batta retrenchment": thus a few thousand pounds were screwed out of the pockets of needy officers, who had left home and friends to serve in an Indian climate.

The sepoys immediately said, "Ah! the English dare not touch our pay," and they twirled their moustaches with overweening pride and insolence. For, as a rule, the two things which the natives of India value most are money and power.

Lord William Bentinck mulcted the British officer in both. When he wished to abolish corporal punishment in the native army, Lord William sent a circular letter to every commanding officer in the service, asking his opinion on the subject. As a rule the native officers were consulted, and very freely they expressed their opinions. Said one, "We hope the Hazoor will not abolish flogging: we don't care about it: only the badmashes (scoundrels) are flogged, if they deserve it: flog them and turn them out: you will find plenty of good men. But if you abolish flogging, the army will no longer fear, and there will quickly be a mutiny."

This prophecy came to pass, but how much influence the abolition of flogging had in causing a mutiny, it is difficult for us in England to say. Flogging seems a degrading punishment, and only the degraded should suffer it. But there is little doubt that when flogging is permitted, too many are forced to submit to it, and the punishment is far too severe. A young officer had just joined his regiment—it was in 1823—in the days of tights and hessians: on his first morning there was a parade for punishment, and he saw a sepoy get 800 lashes for some offence. He says, "The sight of such fearful punishment made me shudder, and I went home so saddened and sickened by the appalling sight I had seen, that my new uniform did not appear so bright that day as it had done when I first put it on. My dislike to corporal punishment has since increased with years, but at the same time I am compelled to avow the sad conviction that the power to inflict it, and its actual infliction in certain cases, are at times absolutely and imperatively necessary."

We must remember that the Indian sepoy does not drink; he can avoid committing many crimes for which drink is responsible. Most of the sepoys came from Oude and were of high caste and the sons of land-owners: they were not likely to offend in a way to deserve flogging: they knew that a certain number of badmashes could only be kept in order by flogging; hence they gave their opinion in favour of the lash, and as there was never any difficulty in obtaining recruits, we must infer that flogging had no terrors for the ordinary native. Corporal punishment was felt to be a powerful aid in the maintenance of discipline: orders were obeyed in those days with an alacrity and cheerfulness unknown to more recent times: then there was no inattention or talking in the ranks, for a man could be ordered out of the ranks to receive two or three cuts with a cane. He preferred this to being confined for hours in barracks.

It was from a proper feeling of humanity, suggested perhaps at Exeter Hall, that flogging was prohibited under Bentinck; and it was from a feeling of its absolute necessity that a certain amount of flogging in serious cases was re-established by Lord Dalhousie. But commanding officers never had the full powers restored to them, and discipline suffered: Sir Thomas Seaton has left on record his opinion about flogging, and he was both a merciful man and a real friend of the natives.

He wrote in his book *From Cadet to Colonel*: "In these latter days all useful power to control, punish or reward has been taken away. . . . As for captains commanding companies, they were mere nonentities, and were treated by the sepoys accordingly. . . . By order of Sir William Gomm, any man to whom punishment had been awarded by his commanding officer might appeal against it to a court-martial, a measure which put the finishing stroke to all semblance of power in regimental officers. . . . The weapon that kept the wild beast in awe was taken out of their hands: the beast rose up against them, and they were weaponless, prostrate and helpless." Humanitarians ignored the fact that in the composition of respect a very necessary ingredient is a certain amount of fear. Here is a case which illustrates the change in the method of dealing with the sepoy.

A native soldier, convicted of disreputable conduct, had his good-conduct pay stopped for a year. The colonel sent a report to headquarters, stating the sepoy's offences, and in the margin he wrote, "Furlough and all indulgence to this sepoy to be stopped for a period of twelve months."

By return of post back came the papers from the adjutant's office, calling upon the colonel to state by what authority he had stopped the sepoy's furlough.

Thus the colonel's authority was over-ridden by a man who was not face to face with the facts; the sepoy was leniently treated, and the discipline of the regiment was undermined.

When for many months the sepoys had been petted and spoilt and taught to feel that they were the real conquerors of Britain's foes, and their officers only the servants of men who wrote in offices, a simple act of carelessness on the part of an official in Calcutta supplied the spark which lit the flame of revolt.

It had been decided to introduce the Enfield rifle into the Indian Army. Now the cartridge for this rifle required a lubricating medium which was made up as follows: five parts tallow, five stearine, one part wax. In other words, the Hindoo sepoy was ordered to bite and handle a cartridge smeared with the fat of the cow, an animal which his religion bade him hold in great veneration.

The Mahommedans, so it was said, believed that the mixture contained hog's lard: thus we had touched on the tenderest spot of both races. The "greased cartridge" became known first to one of the guards in the arsenal at Fort William; and this man ran horror-stricken and told his comrades there was a plot to destroy caste.

The rumour flew on wings of fear: the news spread like fire among stubble from bazaar to bazaar: the authorities did not trouble to explain matters, and suspicion soon grew to conviction.

The Fakirs, those filthy, sensual hedge-priests of the East, clad in yellow or orange-tawny, but for the most part naked, slid snake-like through the lines and shook their matted locks as they hissed the venomous tale in listening ears. Indignation stirred the innermost heart of the sepoys: they met in council and concocted schemes of red revenge: bungalows were burnt and ugly faces breathing hate confronted the still unsuspecting Briton. The insolence of the soldier, his disrespect for his officers, his lust of power made him only too ready to catch fire when his religion and his cast were, as he believed, the object of our attack.

He knew on what slender supports our Empire in India was based: only twenty thousand white troops held him in check, and these were scattered at large over the continent of India: he knew that all the field-batteries in Oude were manned by native gunners and drivers: he knew that the roads were boggy and the rivers choked with sandbanks:

help could not easily be dispatched from garrison or fort. But he also was led to believe that nearly all the white soldiers that England possessed were on duty in India.

One ruler, the Mayor of the Palace of Nepaul, had gone over to England on purpose to find out the true state of affairs: he returned with the assurance that Britain's millions of money and thousands of men were not lightly to be attacked.

Yet, though colonels believed that their own men were staunch and faithful, the governor-general received warning after warning that deep disaffection prevailed thoughout the continent.

"My Lord," wrote a Hindoo, "this is the most critical time ever reached in the administration of British India. Almost all the independent native princes and rajahs have been so much offended at the late annexation policy, that they have begun to entertain deadly enmity to the British Empire in India. Moreover, as for the internal defences of the Empire, the cartridge question has created a strenuous movement in some portions of the Hindoo sepoys, and will spread it through all their ranks over the whole country to the great insecurity of British rule."

What no officer suspected soon came to pass.

On the 24th of January 1857 the telegraph office at Barrackpur was burnt down: this was the first act of open insubordination. On the 25th of February a guard of the 34th Native Infantry arrived at Bahanipur and talked with the men of the 19th Native Infantry who were stationed there. The greased cartridge question was discussed; next day at parade, when ordered to exercise with blank cartridge, the men all refused to touch the unclean thing! Next night they rose and seized their arms, drumming and shouting defiance. The Indian Mutiny had begun! Thus the circulation of the chupatties or Indian cakes, which seemed so mysterious months ago, had been explained. The sepoys looked upon the chupatty as the symbol of food: they believed that the Company meant to deprive them of their food as well as of their land. The chupatty was to remind them that the hundred years were up, and the power of the white man was tottering to its fall.

A short résumé of the events of the mutiny will make the sketches which follow more distinct.

On 10th May incendiary fires began at Meerut: then the sepoys massacred their officers and marched away to Delhi.

The people of Delhi rose, with the connivance of their king, and butchered the Europeans in the city: other regiments revolted and joined the rebels at Delhi.

In May, risings were attempted at Ferozepore, Lahore and Peshawur, but by the quick initiative of Montgomery and Sir John Lawrence the sepoys were disarmed and the Punjab was saved. Thus Lawrence was able to send a strong force of Sikhs to aid in the siege of Delhi: this practically enabled us to crush the mutiny.

Meanwhile, risings and massacres occurred throughout Oude and the Doab. In Rajputana the native princes were faithful, but the widowed Rani of Jhansi headed a rising against us.

At Cawnpur, Nana Sahib ordered a massacre of men, women and children after promising safe passage; while at Lucknow, Sir Henry Lawrence was, with wise forethought, preparing for a long siege. Lucknow was at length relieved by Havelock, Outram, and finally by Sir Colin Campbell. Delhi was not re-taken until 20th September, after hard fighting.

General Windham was driven into his entrenchments at Cawnpur by Tantia Topee, and only saved by Sir Colin making a forced march from Lucknow.

The Bombay division under Sir Hugh Rose fought their way to Jhansi and defeated Tantia Topee in April 1858. On 17th June, Sir Hugh Rose captured Gwalior, and Napier ended the campaign by the victory of Alipore. The mutiny was over, and the East India Company gave way to the British Crown.

CHAPTER II

SIR THOMAS SEATON, K.C.B.: A SOLDIER OF THE COMPANY

GENERAL SEATON in his entertaining book, *From Cadet to Colonel*, tells us of far-off times and strange customs; he saw the first beginnings of the Mutiny, and had always observed the native sympathetically. Training for the army was not very scientific in 1822: for, one day, a cousin called at Seaton's home and said:

"Tom, would you like to go to India as a cadet?"

"Yes, very much," replied the boy of sixteen: a sudden vacancy had occurred, Tom Seaton was rushed into a new uniform, and in a week was sailing from Spithead bound for Calcutta.

A small amount of Latin and Greek had been caned into him; a few months in a London school had brushed up his arithmetic and French, but of the world—its trials and temptations—he knew nothing, and still less of his new profession of Arms. The good ship *Thames* was in no hurry, she took nearly six months getting to Calcutta: Tom was completing his education in his own style and method. With three other cadets he sprang ashore, near Calcutta, at Chandpaul ghaut (steps), somewhere near midnight on the 1st of January 1823.

They were alone in the dark in a strange land, not knowing a word of the language: just as they were about to return to their boat a figure in white loomed up, and cried out in harsh, metallic voice:

"Master, where come from?"

"From England," replied one.

"Master belong ship? What business make?"

"We are officers."

"Oh! officers. Master, where go now?"

"Don't know: where is the fort? Is there any hotel?"

"Fort long way. All officer gentlemen's sleep; master go punch ghur."

"Punch ghur? what in blazes is that?"

"There master get some eaty-drinky, sleepy bed. Yes, I show way; master give a littil present—backshish! boatman—he carry things."

So they were personally conducted to a villainous tavern, where some sailors were drinking, smoking, and playing billiards: they were too sleepy to talk, and went off to bed.

Next morning they found the fort and were received by the superintendent of cadets and taken to the cadets' mess, which consisted of twenty young men, ensigns waiting to be posted to regiments, and cadets like themselves, serving the East India Company on the pay of ninety rupees a month.

"No care was in any way taken of us: we were neither sent to drill nor taught our duty, nor encouraged to study the native languages. The consequences may be imagined. A parcel of young lads, just released from the restraint of school, arriving in this country, green and ignorant,—many at once ran riot and commenced a career of debauchery and profligacy that speedily ended in ruin."

Fortunately young Seaton, having a brand-new gun, delighted to cross the river and shoot every bird he saw: so he was kept out of mischief. In a month or so he was promoted to the rank of ensign and sent to Barrackpur. A native boat took him lazily up river: on arrival he reported himself to the adjutant, who took him to call on the colonel. To the first question, "Have you any uniform?" Tom had to reply, "Not much, sir: I had no time to get it ready."

"Well, you have a sword, I suppose?"

"No, sir; it was in my list, but the outfitter forgot it, I expect."

The colonel and adjutant exchanged meaning glances; the result was that a new outfit had to be ordered from a Calcutta tailor. The bill that followed was prodigious! and alas! the letters from home, after its reception, scolded him for being a spendthrift and a scapegrace. Then came the learning of regimental drill—warm work in the new red coat—and days in the jungle with shot and gun. There was no common mess-room, but five or six officers living in bungalows would chum together, camp fashion.

In July, Seaton was posted to the 17th Native Infantry at Ludhiana, and went by water in a native budgerow with sixteen oars, having in tow a small boat for cooking in. For figure-head this clumsy craft had the figure of a European, black hat, blue coat and yellow waistcoat. The roof of the cabin was flat and formed a promenade. As the boat was flat-bottomed it steered very badly and would sheer out, or run ashore, in a way that tried the temper of the crew badly.

Arriving at Cawnpur, Seaton and his friend hired a bungalow whilst they bought camels, horses and tents for their forward march. They were advised to take a chokeg-dar, or watchman, to prevent being robbed. As they seemed to consider this a useless expense, being still "griffs" or newcomers, they were told of a young officer who defied all the thieves and found next morning that his boxes had been removed from his bedroom, his gun and pistols had been taken from his bed, and his sword had been stuck through his mattress. Thieving in India is a fine art.

Seaton then took a fine old Brahmin of sixty, and old Bhowanny took to his master and treated him like a boy of his own. For eleven years this faithful Indian clave to his master, scolding him heartily when he was imprudent, and not allowing the servants to cheat him.

In those days there was a continuous jungle from four miles out of Delhi to Kurnal: now it is all under good cultivation. Seaton arrived at Ludhiana in December 1823, and was warmly welcomed by his brother-officers. He soon engaged a moonshee (teacher) and studied Hindostanee, so that he could converse with the villagers.

Some of the native regiments at that period had a bhat, or bard, whose business it was to incite the men in action to deeds of valour. The bard in Seaton's regiment was a noble-looking fellow, six feet high, with a splendid head and patriarchal beard of grey. Every day after parade he used to plant the butt of his spear on the ground, raise his right hand, and roll out in deep sonorous tones the praises of the colonel and all his officers.

In October 1825, Seaton's regiment escorted the guns from Meerut which were being taken to the siege of Bhurtpur. The sepoys were then faithful to their salt, but the villagers predicted defeat to the gora log (white men): one wrinkled hag came from her hut and, raising skinny arms in the air, cried hoarsely, "Go to Bhurtpur! they'll split you up. Go and be killed, all of you."

At this a sepoy rushed out of the ranks, and flourishing his firelock over her head, exclaimed, "Get in, old hag: when we come back, the elephants shall serve you out: we'll pound you and your brats into mortar."

However, the strong walls succumbed to a mine, storming parties rushed through the breach, and the British took the stronghold.

In 1835, Seaton lost the wife he had married at Barrackpur and most of his fortune; he asked for three years' furlough and returned to England.

In 1838 he married again and sailed for Calcutta: a pilot came on board in the river, and on taking a newspaper the first thing Seaton read told him his regiment had marched for the campaign in Afghanistan. Husband and wife looked at each other in suspense: she knew no one in India: must she return to England, or live alone in a strange land?

It ended in Seaton leaving his wife at Simla, and by the kind help of Sir Henry Lawrence he secured a boat at Ferozepur and soon joined the convoy, carrying guns and stores to the army. In crossing a desert the sepoys suffered terribly from want of water, and camp-followers carrying infants excited great compassion: strong men fell and beat their breasts, the camels were exhausted and could only go two and a half miles in the hour.

Seaton and a sepoy were looking for water in a ravine: the latter could not speak, his tongue rattled in his mouth and his face was distorted with agony; yet he made no complaint, but struggled on.

Many died of brain fever, and cholera made its dread appearance. "My servant, Hyder, a descendant of the Prophet and entitled to wear a green turban, came a mile out of camp," writes Seaton, "and met me with a bottle of tea: I was very grateful to the good fellow." The roads were littered with dead and dying: the strong suffered from dust and myriads of flies and the stench of the dead camels.

At last the only white doctor died, and faces began to look grave. One of the native officers had a little girl, his only child, in camp with him. She was a pretty, lively prattling thing of about six years of age, the delight of everybody. Every day she would chatter to her father, help him to light his fire and cook his food. One morning at ten o'clock she was quite well, at 3 p.m. she was dead and laid out for burial. The day the convoy arrived at Baugh, the natives told them that a report had come that all had perished, as they had never heard of a convoy crossing the desert in June!

On reaching a large pool of water the sepoys and camp-followers rushed into the water with shouts of delight, and from that hour all began to mend. A hundred sepoys had died, 300 camp-followers, and 6 officers.

When a camel was exhausted he would suddenly stop and sit down: from that position no torture could make the poor animal budge. "His heart is broken," said the natives, and they left him to die alone. Sometimes an officer would try a gill of whisky and water, followed by good food mixed with warming spice: then the camel might recover, if rested for a fortnight.

At Quetta they found a climate as cool as that of an English summer, gardens and fruit trees and long-woolled sheep met their eyes, and if it had not been for the jessail, or long rifles, of the Beloochees, they would have enjoyed their marches towards Candahar.

They halted one day at Ghuznee, where our men had just recently blown in the gate under Captain Thomson of the Bengal Engineers. When the Ameer heard that Ghuznee had fallen, he lost heart: for his people said, "Who can stand before the dreaded English?"

But a terrible calamity overtook Colonel Herring, who, with Lieutenants Carlyon and Hawtry, had climbed a hill to get a view. For they were suddenly attacked by Afghans, and, being unarmed, had to run down the hill: the colonel was caught by an Afghan, but managed to seize him by the throat and strike him with his stick. But another Afghan came up and drew his knife over the colonel's loins. When his body was found, it was an awful sight, hacked and mangled out of recognition by sixteen or seventeen deep wounds.

When the convoy reached Cabul they delivered over the treasure and stores, and Seaton was kindly welcomed by his old comrades and Sir Robert Sale. But out of 5000 camels that started with the convoy, only 500 reached Cabul: the rest had died on the road.

In war, more men die of disease than by wounds, except in a Japanese army; for our friends have learnt the use of science. In war it is the patient animal that suffers most: yet it need not be so: the lives of camels, horses and mules are well worth a little thought before the campaign opens.

At Cabul, Seaton noticed how the British soldiers fraternised with the sepoys, and the sepoys would often relieve the sentries for an hour. It would be too long a task to describe how Sir Robert Sale marched from Cabul to Jellalabad in November 1841, how he held that city and repaired the fortifications and drove off the enemy by sorties, how on the 9th of January 1842 there came a letter from General Elphinstone, recounting the slaughter of the English Envoy and his own capitulation to Akbar Khan, and finishing by an order to Sale to retire to Peshawur. However, that order was never acted upon: the flag was kept flying on the crumbling ramparts.

"On the 13th of January," writes Seaton, "I was on guard at the south gate, when, a little after twelve o'clock, some one came rushing along the passage. The door was burst open and Lieutenant B—— threw himself into my arms, exclaiming, 'My God! Seaton, the whole of our Cabul army has been destroyed.'" Only Dr. Brydone had escaped, as Lady Butler's picture shows us. The flag was hoisted at the west gate as a sign to fugitives, should there be any, cavalry were sent out, and at night buglers were posted to sound the advance every quarter of an hour: but the dreadful dirge brought no single soldier out of the Cabul Pass, the Afghans had shot all who had not died of cold and fatigue. This was the first catastrophe at Jellalabad.

The second occurred on the 19th of February: a little after eleven in the morning came a shock of an earthquake and a rumbling noise: this noise went on and grew louder, till it surpassed in volume the loudest thunder. The ground heaved in waves like a sea, one could not stand up without clutching at something for support: the walls and bastions began to rock and reel and crumble into dust and ruin. Then came a dead silence and men's faces were green with fear, while horses sweated and groaned and put their muzzles to the ground. Happily only three men were crushed, in the cavalry hospital.

"A month's cannonading with a hundred pieces of heavy artillery could not have produced the damage that the earthquake had effected in a few seconds. . . . The hand of the Almighty had indeed humbled our pride, and taught us the wholesome lesson that He alone is a sure defence." Without any delay every man in garrison was set to work and walls of clay and earth were run up around the city.

The enemy, who rode up to see the ruins, galloped back with the report that the white man's magic had prevailed even against an earthquake! In all this trouble the sepoys had behaved nobly, and when provisions ran short they stinted themselves to feed their white friends in our army. Great numbers of the British soldiers had friends amongst the sepoys, and some, when on the point to die, would send for their sepoy friend to be with them in their last moments.

Thus, when Jellalabad had been saved and the brave garrison had marched to Ferozepur, being received at every station by Lord Ellenborough's order with presented arms, the native officers came to Seaton and said, "Sir, we shall soon be separated from our white brothers, the 13th Light Infantry, and the whole regiment wish to give them a dinner." When Seaton approved of this, one said, "We will buy everything for our brothers but pig's flesh."

Hindoos and Mahommedans abhor swine's flesh; the Hindoo holds the cow sacred, but for all that there was plenty of beef on the tables. The dinner took place with éclat, aides-de-camp and staff officers looking in to see the fun: and soon after, the 13th gave a dinner to the native regiment, the 35th, and showed they were indeed brothers in arms. It is good to think of these things; even though the dark brothers, under the influence of religious frenzy, were soon to lose our respect and behave like cruel demons.

At last Seaton was free to rejoin his wife at Simla, where he spent thirty days of peace in a lovely cottage girt about with whispering deodars. He was then appointed Major of Brigade and was sent to Agra; where, one day, as he sat at his desk writing, a sudden darkness came on, and a strange sound was heard, and the silent native orderlies, who were just outside, began to talk excitedly. Seaton called out:

"What is it?"

"Tiddee, sahib" (locusts, sir).

He went out and saw the air and sky teaming with millions of locusts and the only sound heard was the rustling of their wings. Some settled on big branches and broke them down; every vestige of foliage was devoured in a few minutes, and then they took to wing again.

In 1851, Seaton again went to England to escape ague, on a sick furlough of three years. He landed in Calcutta in December in 1854 in good health and joined his regiment at Sealkote in the Punjab as colonel. The station faced the north, and the Cashmere Mountains rose directly in front, covered with snow, peak after peak, stretching right and left for 200 miles.

Seaton had not seen the regiment for ten years, but fully half the men were old friends and had shared with him the perils of Jellalabad. However, his first week showed very plainly a marked change for the worse in the bearing and feeling of the sepoys towards their officers. The other officers, being used to it, did not notice the growing independence of the native soldiers: the power of the officer to keep strict order had been impaired, and the sepoy swaggered about as if he were the master and could court-martial any captain among them.

In April 1857, Seaton had a return of his old malady and went to Simla: a strange disinclination to start had troubled him and nearly kept him at Sealkote, but he thought it the result of his ailment and set off, reaching Simla on the 8th of May.

On the 11th, news came to Simla of a revolt of the troops at Meerut on the day before, and all officers of the Meerut division were ordered to return at once to their stations. In the afternoon the adjutant-general, Colonel Chester, told Seaton it was the desire of the commander-in-chief that he should proceed to Umballa and take command of the 60th N.I., which had shown strong symptoms of disaffection. Seaton reached Umballa on the 15th of May, and discussed affairs with Lieutenant Shebbeare: they spoke of the previous acts of insubordination, the burning of the

MUNGUL PANDY

Mungul Pandy fired at Lieutenant Baugh, the Adjutant, and wounded his horse. Baugh fired his pistol at him but missed, and the Sepoy, drawing his sword, cut him down. Pandy was one of the first of the Sepoys to fire on the British, and from this circumstance the mutineers were known as "Pandies."

telegraph office at Barrackpur on the 24th of January, the refusal of the sepoys to take the cartridges on the 25th of February, the nightly meetings of the 2nd and 34th N.I. at Barrackpur. H.M.'s 84th regiment had been sent for from Rangoon and had encamped a few miles above Barrackpur, but the sepoys of the 34th N.I. were reported to be highly excited. On the 29th, one of them, Mungul Pandy, had stalked through the lines with a loaded musket, shouting, "Rise, boys, rise, and shoot the white men." Lieutenant Baugh, the adjutant, galloped off to the parade to restore order; but Mungul Pandy aimed at him and fired, wounding his horse in the flank and bringing down the rider. Baugh, however, jumped up, fired his pistol at Pandy but missed him.

Then the sepoy, drawing his sword, cut the lieutenant down: as the sergeant-major ran out to help Baugh, he called out to the quarter-guard to come to his assistance.

The native officer commanding, upon this, ordered his men not to move, and the sergeant was also cut down. Then the quarter-guard, with their native officer, ran in and began to beat the officers about the head with the butts of their muskets.

At this moment Lieutenant Baugh's Mahommedan orderly came running up and seized Pandy just as he had reloaded his musket.

Then appeared General Hearsy and his two sons, roused by the sound of firing, and with their help Baugh and the sergeant were rescued from the grip of the sepoys.

Then General Hearsy said to the orderly who had saved the lieutenant, "Shaikh Pultoo, I promote you to the higher grade of havildar for your prompt and courageous action."

Mungul Pandy was secured and lodged in the quarter-guard of the 70th N.I., and it was owing to this man's fanatical conduct so early in the Mutiny that the mutineers came to be known as "Pandies." General Hearsy had promoted this orderly on the spur of the moment for his brave conduct; but for doing this the general received a reprimand in a few days from Colonel Birch, Military Secretary to Government. It is the old story—not trusting the man on the spot: the clever man writing at his desk miles away from the occurrences thinks he knows better than the man who has all the facts at his finger-ends. Mungul Pandy was tried, convicted and hanged in front of the troops on the 8th of April.

Then the authorities at Calcutta began to congratulate themselves on having crushed the mutiny, and were hiring transports for sending back H.M.'s 84th regiment to Rangoon. But on the 4th of May they learnt by telegram of the mutiny of the 7th Irregular Cavalry at Lucknow, and the order for the 84th to return to Rangoon was luckily rescinded. It was then thought advisable to get rid of the 34th N.I. who had been present in the lines on the 29th of March when Lieutenant Baugh was attacked. So the regiment was paid up, marched across the river without arms and dismissed. The disbanded sepoys carried the seeds of mutiny to their homes or wherever they scattered in their fury and wild treason. It was probably owing to the too mild treatment of these regiments that the troops at Meerut began burning their officers' bungalows. General Hewitt, thinking there were plenty of Europeans in the station to prevent any riot, ordered a parade of the 3rd Light Cavalry on the 5th of May; but 85 men refused to touch the cartridges. They were tried and condemned to six or ten years' imprisonment.

This fired the smouldering passion: they rose *en masse*, burnt the buildings and made off to Delhi.

All this and more Seaton must have been discussing when the news came that the commander-in-chief had ordered all troops to assemble at Umballa, to prepare for an advance on Delhi.

The commander-in-chief arrived on the 15th of May, and on the 16th a council of war was held to discuss the question of disarming the two native regiments in the station, the 5th and 6th Native Infantry.

Seaton's advice was to disarm at once, and as he knew more about the native mind than most, his opinion carried weight, and he left the council table with the order in his pocket to disarm at 4 p.m. But when Seaton was going to the parade appointed, he found there the Persian interpreter and Military Secretary, who told him that the chief had changed his mind: the men were to be trusted!

However, disgusted as he was at this vacillation, Seaton had to make the best of it: so he addressed the men, saying it had been resolved they should have an opportunity of being faithful. They received his speech well and swore fidelity to their colours.

After parade, Seaton chatted with the native officers, amongst whom was a soubahdar-major whom he had known before. A little talk with him and a few inquiries after old friends pleased the man, for he was a genial, intelligent old fellow, "and from that moment he seemed to bear me goodwill," says Seaton.

Thus, then, the troops began their march on Delhi, and reached Kurnal on the 24th: but the European soldiers, having heard of the atrocities committed at Meerut, and having seen the mutinous conduct of the 60th N.I., began to say loudly that they would not remain in camp with the 60th. The only thing the staff could think of now was to order Seaton to march with the 60th to Rohtuck, which was forty-five miles from Delhi: he was to intercept troops which had mutinied at Hansi and Hissar and had massacred their officers: and he was to do all this with a regiment ripe for mutiny!

There was a good road from Rohtuck to Delhi, and the most probable consequence of this move would be that the sepoys would massacre all their officers and join the mutineers at Delhi with their arms, camp equipage and service ammunition.

SIR THOMAS SEATON, K.C.B.

When Colonel Chester, the Adjutant-General, gave Seaton his orders, so thoroughly ashamed was he of this cruel, half-hearted measure that he could not lift his eyes from the paper before him. And when Seaton and his officers bade their friends good-bye, there was a wistful look in their eyes, as though they knew their friends were going to certain death.

However, the doomed men put a good face on the matter and spoke cheerily to all. The first day's march showed the mutinous spirit of the 60th: for as they crossed a canal, Colonel Seaton halted his men to let them drink. There was a grove of young mango trees in full bearing close at hand; this the sepoys tried to pillage of its fruit, but the officers hurried up to stop them. One young sepoy was very insolent to his captain and answered roughly when ordered to fall in. Captain S—— collared him to force him back to the ranks: the sepoy resisted and the men began to look angry.

Seaton felt that instant interference was necessary; so, stepping slowly up to the man and looking him sternly in the face, he said, "Do you know what you are about? go and fall in instantly; you are all mad."

The sepoy at once put up his hands in submission, and obeyed his colonel. The calm, determined tone of the officer and the habit of obedience had their full weight for the moment.

At the halting-place, Seaton sent for that sepoy, a fine, handsome young fellow, looking rather troubled.

"What had become of your senses this morning?" asked the colonel in a serious tone.

"Sahib," the man replied respectfully, "I did great wrong: I have repented, and will never do so again: forgive me."

"The commander-in-chief has been very good to this regiment: instead of punishing you all for your mutiny at Umballa, he freely pardoned you. He took me from my own regiment and sent me to this, that I might be kind to you and warn you against further error. Is this the return you make?"

"Colonel Sahib, I have repented; forgive me."

"Very well; your soubahdar says you are sorry, and your captain says you are generally a well-behaved man, so I forgive you."

We see in this and similar cases that the Indian temper was susceptible even at the beginning of the Mutiny of gentle influences: this man expected to be met by a burst of anger and to be tried and punished. His colonel's calm and kindly feeling disarmed all resentment, and, as events proved, this sepoy became a faithful friend in the hour of danger. The heat became intense, the dust choked them as they marched on through the night: Seaton nodded sleepily on horseback and often had to get off and walk to save himself a fall.

They had halted at a walled village at 2 a.m. and the men were clustered round a well and were drawing water eagerly.

When an hour had passed, Seaton rose from his horse-cloth on which with his officers he had been lying, and ordered the call to be sounded. As the men did not leave the well readily, Seaton went up and called out, "Now, men, don't delay: let us get this march over in the cool of the morning."

No one spoke, but one man came up and saluting, said abruptly, "My lotah has fallen into the well: I want leave to stay behind to get it out."

A lotah is a brass pot which every sepoy carries strapped on his knapsack. Seaton knew this was an excuse, but something prompted him to say kindly, "What is the value of your lotah?"

"A rupee and a half, sahib."

"Well, don't be so foolish as to risk being killed by staying behind amongst these wild people. Come on into camp and I will give you a new one. A lotah is nothing to me, but a sepoy's life is a great deal."

The man's face brightened, he snapped his fingers and called out, "Come along, brothers, you hear what the Colonel Sahib says."

So the march was resumed, and the colonel thought no more of it. But some days later, after Seaton had escaped to the camp at Delhi, a Sikh servant said to him, "I heard about you, sahib, from a sepoy who helped me to escape from the mutineers."

"Indeed! What was it you heard?"

"Do you know what the men were about, sahib, at the village well? You remember, when we halted there was a lot of talking."

"Oh yes, I remember; a sepoy's lotah had fallen into the well."

"No, sahib, that was all pretence: the men were all of the grenadier company, and when you came up they were debating whether they should shoot you and the officers: and if you had been angry with the sepoy who spoke to you and had answered him roughly, he would have shot you at once: for his musket was loaded."

Gentle words and kind deeds prevailed for a time in keeping the 60th true to their salt; but the colonel, conversing cheerfully with the men whenever he passed through the lines, and visiting the hospital daily, could see under their respectful demeanour that some deep fire of discord was smouldering in their hearts.

For three days after his arrival at Rohtuck, Seaton saw no change: but on the 4th of June, about 5 p.m., as he was writing in the mess-tent, the adjutant came in and said, "Colonel, I wish to speak to you."

"Well, Shebbeare, what is it?" said the colonel.

"I have just heard from two of our drummers (Eurasians) that the regiment is to mutiny to-night, murder the officers, and be off to Delhi."

Seaton thought it out for a bit and replied, "Very well: in half an hour the men will assemble in front of their tents for evening roll-call. I will go on parade and tax them with their intended outbreak: tell the officers to look out."

Accordingly the colonel at sunset went on parade, called the native officers in front, away from their respective companies, and taxed them with their intended treachery.

The sepoy officers were confounded when they knew that their secret plot was discovered: they one and all denied the charge and swore to be faithful. The men who had been listening quietly made no movement, and Seaton went to each company and said a few warning words.

When Seaton rejoined the European officers who stood at a distance, "What is it, colonel—is it all right?" they asked anxiously.

"Oh yes," Seaton replied cheerfully, "I think our throats are safe for to-night, and you may turn in without fear."

The next few days were spent in anxious expectation of a revolt. On the 8th of June, as Seaton was going in the evening to visit the hospital, and as he was about to cross a deep ditch, the young sepoy who had been rude to the captain by the well came out of his tent and gave the colonel a hand. As he stooped, he whispered, "Colonel Sahib, when your Highness's people shall have regained the Empire, I will make my petition to your Highness."

These words, so full of mystery, made Seaton think the moment for rising had come. He says, "I had no other course to pursue than to do my duty as firmly, as honestly and as wisely as I could, and trust to God's mercy and goodness for a favourable result."

Seaton had been forgotten by his superiors: they had been too busy to send him the news of victories won on the 30th of May. The news of these successes would have served to keep the 60th quiet, he thought. No wonder his officers felt a little embittered: "the men in power sent us off to Rohtuck to be out of the way: they seem mighty indifferent as to what our fate shall be."

Next day, as all seemed going on as usual, five of the young officers arranged to go out shooting. At 4 p.m., as the colonel sat writing letters in short, cotton drawers and shoes, a great explosion startled him. With his pen in his hand he ran out to see what was the matter, but could find no noise or tumult: most of the sepoys were lying down asleep, and a few were cooking.

As he gained the centre of the camp, the havildar-major, or native sergeant-major, rushed up and caught him by the arm and said hurriedly, "Colonel Sahib, don't go to the front."

"Why not?"

"The grenadiers are accoutring themselves."

"By whose order, havildar?"

"Biggur-geea our kya" (They have mutinied).

At once the colonel called out for the native officers: it was in vain: not one answered his appeal. So, seeing the game was up, Seaton returned to his tent, put on a pair of corduroy trousers and called for his syce to bring his horse. Just then the grenadiers burst out of their tents and fired at the white officers, while the other sepoys, who were not in the secret, started up and stared stupidly about them. The shouts and the shots, the rush of mutineers and camp-followers, the cries of terror from the camp-followers and the galloping of horses formed a confused medley of sights and sounds.

Seaton snatched up his watch and keys and, without his sword, jumped on his horse when the mutineers were only ten paces from him. Luckily they had discharged their muskets, and so he got off unwounded. They rode through the night to Delhi, and Seaton dismounted at Sir H. Barnard's tent about 9 a.m.

The general was at breakfast with his staff. They all turned in surprise. "Good God! why, we have just been told the 60th had mutinied and killed all their officers except five that were out shooting!"

After having some breakfast, Colonel Seaton went round

the British camp like a beggar, securing a coat, a sword, a pair of boots, etc.

His friend Hodson invited him to share his tent and got him a good charpoy (bedstead). The Assistant Adjutant-General Ewart provided him with a sword and belt and posted him to the first brigade as a field officer.

"My first night's rest was heavenly. I heard distinctly all the firing, but it did not disturb me. For three nights before the 60th mutinied I had had little rest, and I had been on horseback from 4 p.m. the day before until 9 a.m. this day. . . . No wonder, then, that my sleep was profound."

We will not follow Colonel Seaton through his adventures during the siege of Delhi, as that part of the Mutiny war can come in later. On the 23rd July, however, as Seaton was helping two men to carry Captain Law, he was himself struck by a bullet on the left breast. Finding that no air issued from the wound, he concluded his lungs were unhurt. Dismounting, he felt faint, and was placed in a charpoy: soon he met his friend Hodson, who at once galloped off to camp and called a surgeon. The ball had struck on a rib, fractured it and driven it forcibly on the lung, passing out finally at the back. Seaton says:—

"Hodson's care for me I shall never forget. He watched and tended me with the affection of a brother: he anticipated all my wants, prevented me from speaking (according to the doctor's orders) and carefully excluded every one from the tent."

This is high praise for Hodson, who has been so unmercifully condemned for one act of swift vengeance committed in a moment of excitement. On the 20th of September, Seaton went to Simla to regain his strength; he had latterly been acting as prize agent, but the foul air of Delhi interfered with his recovery.

He soon was able to ride about, and in November received this telegram:—

SIR THOMAS SEATON, K.C.B.

"If you wish to command the 1st Fusiliers, come to Delhi as soon as you can. Colonel Gerrard has been killed in action."

Seaton accepted, and on arrival at Delhi found he was ordered to escort a convoy of grain and stores through the Doab, land between the Ganges and the Jumna, to the commander-in-chief's camp. With a force of 2300 men, Colonel Seaton was to guard 4500 bullock-carts, 8000 camels, 1500 camp-followers and 16,000 bullocks: the whole might cover some eighteen miles of road. Before starting, Seaton asked General Penney if, instead of taking the squadron of dragoons detailed for him, he might have Major Hodson with his regiment of horse.

"But Hodson's corps is not so strong as the others, nor so well mounted," said the general.

"I know that, sir, but as the safety of the convoy will depend mainly on getting accurate information of the enemy, I wish to have Hodson; for I know well that if any man can get it, he is the man. He is indefatigable—a soldier of the highest class. I have unbounded confidence in him, and would rather have him than 500 more men."

General Penney, on hearing this, assented to his request.

Just before starting the news came in that a large body of rebels was on the road, and threatening Colonel Farquhar and his small force. So a message was sent to Farquhar that help was coming. When Seaton and his convoy were well on their way, Hodson was sent on scout to discover the position and numbers of the enemy: he took with him Major Light of the Artillery.

Camp was marked out and the men began to pitch their tents, but to make things safe against a surprise, the horses were kept close to the guns, and the cavalry were ordered to keep their horses saddled.

Presently Major Light was seen to be returning at full gallop. "Captain Hodson desires me to say, sir, that the enemy's cavalry are advancing in force on both flanks."

Seaton, wondering if the enemy thought they had only Farquhar to tackle, sang out, "Bugler, the alarm! Mount, and turn out the artillery." Captain Trench turned out the dragoons, who drew their girths and were in saddle in three minutes.

At the sound of the alarm the 1st Fusiliers dropped their tents, and slung on their accoutrements.

In front of Seaton's camp was a village about 400 yards off, and beyond this was a slight rise in the ground, so that any view of the enemy was cut off by a sort of ridge crowned by hillocks and tufts of grass. Hodson had retired slowly and now came at a smart trot round the village and made his report of the enemy having artillery. Meanwhile two large bodies of cavalry appeared on the crest of the hill and their artillery began to open on the British troops.

"They are getting our range! Captain Bishop—your battery to the front."

Instantly Bishop dashed out and carried with him vast clouds of dust, driven by a strong wind into the faces of the enemy.

The dust prevented the enemy from seeing how many they had to fight, but the terrible accuracy of our guns startled them not a little.

"Look out, sir," cried the bugler, and as he spoke a cannon-ball came bounding along the plain, and fortunately leapt over the colonel's head, while a second ball just skimmed over his croupe.

The infantry under Colonel Farquhar advanced rapidly, and Hodson on the left moved forward with the whole of his regiment against the rebel cavalry, who were trying to take our guns in flank. Captain Wardlaw and his dragoons then charged and captured the guns of the enemy. Upon this the rebels, utterly routed and astonished, abandoned their last gun and two ammunition waggons: the infantry threw away their arms and hid themselves in the cotton crops, but a vigorous pursuit was kept up by our guns and cavalry. Captain Wardlaw, a good and gallant soldier, was unfortunately killed in this pursuit by desperate men darting out suddenly from the tall pulse. Our loss was 48 killed and wounded, but the enemy lost ten times that number, and bitterly regretted the trap into which they had flung themselves. It follows that the Hindoo villagers had not given the rebels any hint of our reinforced numbers; for they did not actively sympathise with the cause of revolt: a gentle, indolent race—they do not seem to care who rules them, so long as they are treated with justice. Next morning, after leaving Khasgunge and on entering Suhawir, they found a man hanging by the heels to the branch of a tree—quite dead. He had been one of Seaton's scouts, had been caught and slowly shot to death as he hung.

As Seaton was congratulating himself on having cleared the country of rebels and of having made it safe to bring on the treasure and stores, Mr. Cocks, the able commissioner of the district, rode up to say that a notorious traitor, Jowahir Khan, a pensioned rissaldar who with his sons had fought against us, had just returned to his home at Khasgunge.

"Hodson, take a troop and apprehend him," said the colonel.

In a few hours Hodson returned, saying, "I've got him, colonel: we rode in at a gallop, surrounded the house, burst open the door, killed the son and seized the traitor."

This man had been honoured and richly rewarded by the Company: he was sentenced to be blown away from a gun—a painless death, but one which makes a great impression on the native spectators.

We must remember that the feelings of our soldiers were excited to a pitch of fury by the sepoys' cruelties to English women and children. Some of us can remember how the tale of Cawnpur roused every town and village in Great Britain to call meetings for revenge: we cannot wonder, then, that men like Hodson threw away all thought of mercy. Early in January, 1858, Colonel Seaton met

Sir Colin Campbell and his Highlanders, and was warmly congratulated for his vigorous opening of the country.

In the course of a few days, Seaton was made a brigadier, but his hopes of sharing in the relief of Lucknow were dashed by his being appointed to command the Futtygurh district, because he was the only brigadier who could speak the language and manage the natives.

The country along the Jumna was a network of ravines, a perfect hiding-place for all the ruffians and outlaws of the district, while at Alagunge there was a body of 15,000 rebels with cavalry and artillery. The day before Sir Colin marched, he said to Seaton: "You'll be mobbed, my dear friend, as soon as I leave, but you must hold out till I come back. Push on the repairs of the fort and indent on Agra for ammunition for your guns."

Sir Colin took with him all Seaton's movable column and Hodson. Of the latter Seaton writes: "All through the siege of Delhi we had shared the same tent. When I was wounded, he had tended me with anxious care and kindness;—he was the very perfection of a commander of irregular cavalry—one of those men who, from sound judgment, high courage, skill in the use of weapons and intuitive knowledge of human nature, are fitted to be the eyes and ears of an army, or to plan and carry out a bold and dashing enterprise. His untimely death was a calamity to our country, and I mourned for him as for a brother."

Seaton at once set about repairing the fort of Futtygurh, had all the boats within twelve miles moored under the fort, and instructed the 82nd in gun-drill; for the enemy threatened to bombard the fort from the farther bank of the river, which was at that point 1700 yards wide. Across the river was a small village. Seaton turned the people out for a couple of hours while he fired a few shots and took the range.

Next day a native walked up to the brigadier's quarters with a 32-pound shot on his head, which he dropped at

Seaton's feet, saying, "Huzzoor, your Highness, cherisher of the poor, your slave was working in his fields yesterday, two miles away, and while the guns were firing, your slave heard something rushing through the grass, and at once this big ball jumped over his head and lodged in a bank. I am a faithful ryot of the Sircar Angrez, and I have brought the ball to your Highness."

"Very well," said the brigadier, "you shall have a present; but, tell me, do you think the rebels at Alagunge heard the sound of our guns?"

"Your Highness, yes! their livers melted with fear, and half of their army ran away last night."

Though the rebels did not dare to attack Futtygurh and Seaton's fort, yet they raided about and burnt many villages; and at last they formed three strong posts along the river bank.

Seaton felt it necessary to attack one of these, or the rebels might cross the Ganges and raise the whole country up to the Jumna, and when Sir Colin arrived at Futtygurh he would give the brigadier "a bit of his mind."

Therefore Seaton resolved to attack Kunkur, the central post. Absolute secrecy was kept, and the amazed soldiers assembled at the bridge-head at 11 p.m. without sound of bugle.

The hot and dusty road concealed the files; at dawn they reached a walled grove of trees with low swampy ground on the right, and an old river-bed in front. A shot was fired, and then came shouts, hubbub, confusion.

In a few minutes two splendid bodies of cavalry, well mounted, rode right and left to take Seaton in flank as he moved forward on the grove.

"Major Smith, cover our advance, please, and bestow some favours on the cavalry to our right."

The enemy's cavalry to the left had entered the dry river-bed, and, thinking themselves unseen, were riding leisurely to wait till the English flank was exposed. Riding up to Colonel Hall, Seaton desired him to draw out two companies of his best shots and try to disturb this little manœuvre.

This was done: the musketry instructor gave the number of yards and before three calm and deliberate rounds had been completed, there was a terrible shaking amongst the spears in the river-bed; the enemy's cavalry turned and bolted and were pursued by our horsemen, while the whole infantry line burst out into cheers and laughter.

"This|was the first time I had seen the Enfield rifle used in the field," says Seaton, "and I thought it the king of weapons."

Major Smith meanwhile had persuaded the cavalry on the right to turn and escape: our troops charged the grove and the rebels fled in all directions, leaving their guns, stores, tents and baggage.

As our men were eating a well-earned breakfast in the enemy's camp, 200 native horsemen rode up from Alagunge to see if their friends needed anything, for they had heard firing.

Three or four well-planted shots from Major Smith's guns gave them all the information they required, and off they galloped, helter-skelter, for their fort.

This day, the 7th of April, was Seaton's lucky day; it was on this day sixteen years before that he had shared in the honour of defeating Akbar Khan and saving Jellalabad.

Out and home had been 44 miles, done in twenty-two hours, fighting thrown in, and not a single straggler left behind; the captured guns and stores were also brought safely in, and the rebels were so cowed that the two other forts were deserted, as well as Kunkur.

When the brigade-major came in to Seaton's tent next day he was laughing.

"What's the joke, major?"

"Do you know, sir, what the soldiers are calling you?"

"No, I don't; but I hope it is nothing very outrageous."

"Oh no; they are only calling you the Kunkuring hero!"

Seaton's still weak health needed the tonic of a laugh; this and the feeling that success brings helped to restore his wearied frame.

Fourteen days after the Kunkur affair Sir Colin Campbell (Lord Clyde) arrived with his force, *en route* for his Rohilcund campaign.

There was a kindly smile on his weather-beaten face as he shook his fist at Seaton and said, "So you must have your little flourish, sir."

But the chief was glad enough to find his communications safe and the rebels driven off. Seaton and his chief had a few days' quiet conference, and the former writes: "I felt very much at home with Lord Clyde—there was something in his features, in the squareness of the lower jaw, in his occasional abruptness, that reminded me of my old commander, Sir Robert Sale. He was a thoroughly kind and warm-hearted man, rather peppery at times, like Sale, and in all cases of neglect of duty, very stern."

General Penney came on the 24th of April to consult with his chief, and joining his force next day rode into a rebel battery and was killed by a discharge of grape. He had been misled by the civil officer, who had assured him that the enemy were miles away.

General Penney had been a friend of Seaton's, a kind-hearted, generous and clever soldier; he was sincerely lamented by his numerous friends.

In May, as the brigadier sat alone in his tent, after Lord Clyde had left and taken away many of his friends, and when he was tired with copying telegrams for the chief of the staff, and wondering if it were not time for him to resign and rest his worn-out frame, a note was brought him addressed to Brigadier Sir Thomas Seaton, K.C.B., and congratulating him on the honour conferred.

A rather cruel joke he felt it to be just then, and wrote back to the sender: "None of your nonsense; if you boys chaff your brigadier, he'll have to pitch into you."

The reply came again with a copy of the Gazette and

hearty congratulations. He was amazed to see his name —and the honour conferred.

"My first thought was, God save the Queen! she has not forgotten me! the next, what will my wife and family think of it?"

Then he went back in thought to the day when he landed at Calcutta a thoughtless boy of sixteen, without a friend to take him by the hand, and he loved to trace a kind Providence in all his Indian career. In June 1859 his resignation was accepted after a service of more than thirty-six years.

Though he left India disgusted at the treachery of the sepoys, yet "time is a kindly god," as the Greek tragedian puts it; and Sir Thomas lived to make allowances for their temptations.

"Kind words," he says, "patience, good humour and courtesy are never thrown away upon them: if the English in India would make themselves sufficiently acquainted with the language of the natives so as to converse fluently and express themselves with elegance, and not in the barbarous jargon so commonly used; if they would exercise more patience, forbearance and good temper; if they would drop their proud superciliousness and haughty conduct—then their own manliness of character, their truthfulness and honesty of purpose would rapidly make way with the people, and they would soon be as much liked and respected as they are now hated and feared."

Years have passed since this wise and generous hero penned these words, and the highest in our land has more than once visited his Indian subjects and friends. Let us hope that such proof of sympathy has not been in vain.

From *Cadet to Colonel.* By kind permission of Messrs. Routledge.

CHAPTER III

SIR HERBERT B. EDWARDES, K.C.B., K.C.S.I.: THE CHRISTIAN KNIGHT

HOW many of England's heroes would be missing if we had maintained the celibacy of the clergy! When human wisdom begins to improve upon Divine forethought, as the Roman Catholic Church has done in the matter of enforced celibacy, the result is not surprising. From Sir Herbert Edwardes to Cecil Rhodes there have been many men of heroic mould whose lives began in an English Rectory.

Herbert Benjamin Edwardes was the second son of the Rector of Frodesley, a pretty village in Shropshire not far from the Caradoc hills and Shrewsbury. His grandfather was Sir John Cholmondeley Edwardes, eighth baronet of Shrewsbury. They were of Welsh descent, and connected with the ancient kings of Powysland. In the time of Henry VII., John-ap-David-ap-Madoc assumed the name of Edwardes: like so many other Welsh families they foolishly discarded their own poetic names for such names as Edwards and Jones. Herbert, born in 1819, lost his father at the age of four, and was sent to school at Richmond in Surrey, where he soon showed the grit in him by becoming the champion of all that were bullied or too weak to defend themselves.

As a boy he was fond of a joke, quick in wit and ready in repartee, a writer of poetry and romance: he had been adopted by relatives, Mr. and Mrs. John Hope of Netley in Shropshire, where he used to pass his summer holidays. Here he was left much to solitude and his own thoughts and to reading, an education from within which serves to strengthen the will for the great conflict of life.

In 1837 he was attending classes at King's College. His friend Cowley Powles writes: "Edwardes' principal *forte* lay in what would now be called the 'Modern Side.' In classics he did not distinguish himself, nor in mathematics: his taste was more for modern literature. At that he worked hard: he was then amongst the leaders of the college, and in the Debating Society was one of the very foremost speakers."

In those days he excelled in drawing caricatures, but in later life, as he grew more tolerant and tender, he gave up that habit; because, he said, it led to dwelling on the weaknesses or bad points of another, while he preferred to dwell on the good qualities of his neighbour.

Amongst his friends at college were Charles Kingsley, Fitz-James Stephens, Nassau Senior and Benjamin Shaw, with whom he used to carry on wordy duels in their dusty lodgings.

When some one advised him to take more sleep for the sake of his constitution, he replied, "Constitution indeed! Life is nothing, time is nothing, but the things for which we live are all that is to be regarded."

Edwardes wished to go to Oxford and study for the Bar, but his guardians did not approve of this, so he went at once to Sir Richard Jenkins, a member of the old Court of Directors of the East India Company and a friend of his father, and asked for a direct appointment to India.

Sir Richard consented, and years after, when the fame of Herbert Edwardes in Bunnu came to England, Sir Richard wrote to a kinsman in Salop, "I congratulate you upon the high name young Edwardes has gained for himself by exploits so brilliant and so advantageous to his country. I feel much elated with the thought that I have been the means of placing such a man in the Company's service."

In October 1840, Edwardes set sail for Calcutta, feeling all the sorrow of an exile, for he did not relish a mere soldier's life. A fellow-passenger thus describes him: "His figure was slim and his general appearance gave the impression of delicate rather than robust health. He did not often join in the active games and amusements in which young men on board ship generally engage . . . the expression of his face was bright and intelligent . . . in amateur theatricals he was the leading spirit and was editor of a witty weekly newspaper."

On arriving at Calcutta, Edwardes was appointed to the 1st Bengal Fusiliers (since the Royal Munsters) and went by boat to Dinapur. An amusing letter to his friend Cowley thus describes the daily routine: "On the Ganges, March 1841. . . . Well, a black rascal makes an oration by my bed every morning about half an hour before daylight. I wake and see him salaaming with a cup of hot coffee in his hand. I sit in a chair and wash the teaspoon till the spoon is hot and the fluid cold, while he introduces me gradually into an ambush of pantaloons and wellingtons. I am shut up in a red coat, and a glazed lid set upon my head, and thus carefully packed ride a couple of hundred yards to the parade. Here two or three hundred very cold people are assembled and we all agree to keep ourselves warm with a game of soldiers, and we wheel and turn about till the sun gets up to see what the row is about; then, like frightened children, we all scamper off for our home. If there be no parade, I take a gallop with my dogs: then comes breakfast, after which the intellectual day begins to dawn; for from this till 4 or 5 p.m. your occupation must be among your books, pen, pencil, etc."

Edwardes employed much of this leisure in learning Hindostani and Persian; in November 1845 he passed the "Interpreter's Examination."

At Kurnal he caught fever and had to get "leave" and go to Simla: whence he writes, after explaining his many theatrical triumphs to amuse the men, "I know how it will all end, so write you this last letter—I shall be going to pieces like barley-sugar in a teacup, and be swabbed up carefully and sent home to my afflicted relations in a pail."

Edwardes had plenty of friends, for he was the life and soul of every society in which he found himself. His chief pleasure was in showing kindness and sympathy to any who needed it, and many were the prayers that went up to bless him, even when he was only a subaltern.

In 1845 he began to write for the Delhi *Gazette* a series of letters, called "the Brahminee Bull letters," dealing critically with the mistakes and follies of the military events of the day.

He was inwardly amused to hear them discussed at mess, pronounced to be written by some general who had long experience in the field. These letters were the first step to promotion: for Henry Lawrence, then resident at Nepaul, was deeply interested in them: he sought out the author and persuaded Sir Henry Hardinge to appoint him as one of his assistants at the Sikh Court of Lahore.

But before he went to Lahore he saw, as aide-de-camp to Sir Hugh Gough, two victories won over the Sikhs, the battles of Moodkie and Sobraon.

Lahore was the capital of the Sikh kingdom of the late Runjeet Singh: his heir, Dhuleep Singh, was a child, and the Queen Mother as Regent pretended to govern through her corrupt sirdars.

Henry Lawrence, as Resident at this court, was surrounding himself with a band of earnest and vigorous young men who should help him in his endeavour to guide the government and protect the oppressed. Amongst these assistants were John Nicholson, James Abbott, Reynell Taylor, Hodson, George Lawrence and other worthy men who did great things for India's good in the years to come.

Out of these Henry Lawrence chose Edwardes as his private secretary: his opinion of his secretary was given after five months of close companionship: "Taking him all in all, bodily activity, mental cultivation and warmth of heart, I have not met his equal in India."

SIR HERBERT B. EDWARDES

Herbert Edwardes had now found the work which he loved: heart and soul he threw himself into his chief's chivalrous and philanthropic work—all in the highest interest of the natives. The Punjab had been misgoverned, and Lawrence was bent on steering the ship of State into less troubled waters.

When at last annexation was found to be necessary, Lawrence became the President of a Board of three members appointed by the Governor-General, who was sent out by the Court of Directors and was more autocratic than our modern viceroys.

So with Lawrence there was no "red tape," no acting according to law and rule; but he sent out his assistants into wild districts, leaving it to their wisdom and discretion to settle the country and make the people happy. That was the early history of our Punjab.

Thus, in February 1847, Edwardes was sent in command of a Sikh force to make an amicable settlement with the people of Bunnu, an Afghan valley west of the Indus, who had for twenty-five years failed to pay their annual tribute to Runjeet Singh, the "lion of the Punjab." How he succeeded in his bloodless conquest of these wild Mahommedan tribes Edwardes has described in *A Year on the Punjab Frontier*, and Ruskin has immortalised his deeds in *A Knight's Faith*: "I have asked you to hear this story, not that we may learn only how battles may be won, but that we may learn the happier lesson, how *man* may be won; what affection there is to be had for the asking; what truth for the trusting; what lifelong service for a word of love."

But we cannot follow Edwardes in this enterprise, nor in his services in saving Multan, for which he was made by the Queen a C.B. Little did England then know how important Edwardes' services had been: we may say that he and John Lawrence were the chief agents in rendering the Punjab loyal and true to us when the Mutiny broke out. His brave and generous nature made the natives love him; his confidence in them bred confidence in return; and when the storm of revolt surged about Peshawur, and Edwardes and Nicholson called for levies to fill the place of disarmed mutineers, readily the faithful wild men sprang up to answer to the call, and joyfully they marched to help us in the siege of Delhi.

Edwardes had gone through great exposure in the summer heat and had defeated the traitor Moolraj in two pitched battles; he had had many hairbreadth escapes in battle and from assassination; a price had been set on his head, and his servants had been bribed to poison him. An attack of fever made a change of climate necessary, so in the close of 1849 Edwardes left Lahore with John Nicholson and the two little girls of John Lawrence and dropped down the Indus in boats to Bombay, stopping every night to give the children a run on the sandy shore. In that long boat journey the two heroes cemented a friendship already begun, and from papers left it is clear they discussed the coming storm of revolt and the conspiracy that occurred in 1857. The Commander-in-Chief, Lord Gough, was going home in the same steamer to England, and as Edwardes stood on the paddle-box watching his countrymen cheer his Chief, he was surprised to hear, "Edwardes, come down; you are called for."

The people on the English shore were cheering the hero of Bunnoo!

His modesty comes out again a few weeks later, when he was being fêted at the Mansion House and was returning thanks in the presence of the Duke of Wellington and other distinguished officers. For, turning to his friend John Nicholson seated at his side, he said, "Here, gentlemen, here is the real author of half the exploits which the world has been so ready to attribute to me." The effect on the company was almost electrical; they felt that if Edwardes was extolling the bravery of his friend, he was unconsciously revealing his own moral greatness: they were all deeply moved. The Duke said it was impossible to speak too highly of that young officer Major Herbert Edwardes; and the Court of Directors had a special gold medal struck and presented to Edwardes in full Court.

In July 1850, Edwardes married Emma Sidney, the daughter of James Sidney, Esq. of Richmond Hill, and he finished his book on the Frontier in happy months of peace and quiet at Festiniog in North Wales.

In March 1851, Edwardes and his wife returned to India: he was soon appointed Deputy-Commissioner of Jalandur, a fertile and beautiful country, and here the people soon felt the power of his sympathy and justice. It was their first home together: fifteen months spent in a charming house with a large garden full of orange trees and flowers, with congenial work, protecting the weak and punishing the oppressor—these soon sped by; for they were startled at breakfast one morning by a letter from Lord Dalhousie ordering Edwardes to take charge of Hazâra, a wild hill country near the frontier of Cashmere.

In ten days they had to start, after selling house and furniture, and in their new abode there was no house and an Englishwoman had never been seen there before. The Commissioner much regretted his departure: "It is not his ability that I admire so much as his weight of character, high tone and principles. There is not a corner of the district where his impress has not been already felt—I grieve over his departure more than I can tell."

Rice fields four thousand feet above sea-level sounded healthy, while in the hedges grew wild roses, oleander, clematis and blackberries.

One Sikh regiment with four officers, two of whom were married, formed the whole society of the place; but sorrow and trouble came to them. The Sikhs on being ordered to build their own huts, refused; they were not coolies, they said. This looked like mutiny, and the Government called for a court-martial upon the commanding officer. He was only twenty-seven, and, fearing disgrace, shot himself, leaving a young wife and two little children.

Next, the medical officer, Dr. Keith, died of fever: his intended bride in Scotland was then preparing to join him, and the news of his death only just came in time to stop her.

The Sikhs were ashamed of what they had done, and began to build their huts before the new commander arrived.

In October 1853 the news came that Edwardes' commissioner, Colonel Mackeson, had been assassinated at Peshawur, as he was hearing appeals in the verandah of his house. For a very devout man, to all appearances, had spread his carpet near the commissioner's house, and had engaged in devotions through the day. Towards evening he went up and presented a petition: as Colonel Mackeson raised his arm to receive it, the fanatic stabbed him through the chest. As Peshawur was full of armed Afghans, the excitement was great; officers slept with their boots on, ready for an immediate call, and the Europeans felt as though they were living on the verge of a volcano.

In a few days Edwardes received a letter from Lord Dalhousie, offering him the commissionership of Peshawur. "In the whole range of Indian charges, I know none which at the present time is more arduous—holding it, you hold the outpost of Indian Empire . . . you have a fine career before you. God speed you in it; both for your own sake and for the sake of this Empire."

Edwardes began by putting down the spies formerly employed and trusted the chiefs of the wild tribes, warning them that swift punishment would be meted out to marauders and disturbers of the peace.

Whenever a plundering party raided the district, Edwardes barred the whole tribe from dealing at the Peshawur market until restitution was made: by this means he got the feeling of the tribe against all marauders, for plundering did not pay.

His next stroke of policy was to bring about a friendly feeling with Cabul, and to get a treaty signed with the Ameer.

He wrote to Lord Dalhousie on the subject, and received in his reply these words: "I give you *carte blanche*, and if you can only bring about such a result as you propose, it will be a feather even in your cap."

This treaty took a long time to negotiate, but with his wonted patience, wisdom and kindness, Edwardes won over Dost Mohamed and his chiefs to sending his son and heir to sign the treaty.

Sir John Lawrence, the chief commissioner at Lahore, wrote to Edwardes: "I so far agree with the Governor-General that I think all the merit of the affair, whatever it may be, is yours."

General Monro asserted: "Often have I been told by Khans and Afghans that we should never have kept Peshawur (and with it the Punjab) without Edwardes. They would say, 'Yes, yes, Nicholson was undoubtedly a great man, but *he* would not have kept us true to government. He was so stern; we feared him, but we did not love him. Edwardes compelled us to like him better than any other Feringhee.'"

This treaty was signed first in March 1855 and subsequently consolidated under Lord Canning on 26th January 1857.

To the honour of Dost Mohamed Khan we must record that all through the Sepoy war he remained true to the treaty, and abstained under great temptations from raising the green flag of Islam and marching with his wild legions into the Punjab.

Had he done so, it is doubtful if we could have kept India. Such power had the moral force of Edwardes to stay the great mutiny!

In February 1856, John Nicholson, who had been holding the post of deputy-commissioner at Bunnu, had had some differences with Sir John Lawrence, and, feeling himself aggrieved, had asked to be removed.

"I only knocked down the walls of the Bunnu forts," wrote Edwardes. "John Nicholson has since reduced the people to such a state of good order and respect for the laws that, in the last year of his charge, not only was there no murder or burglary, but not an attempt at any such crime."

So strongly did some of these wild men admire Nicholson's prowess that a brotherhood of fakirs in Hazâra established a worship of his genius. Often they fell at his feet as their guru, or religious teacher, and though Nicholson flogged them soundly for doing it they remained as devoted as ever, and at his death some of them pined away and died.

After having the charge of Cashmere for six months Nicholson was sent to Peshawur as deputy-commissioner, and the two friends once more were together, sympathising in each other's views and working in accord.

In March 1857, Edwardes had to take his sick wife to Calcutta for England: he took advantage of this to commend Nicholson to the notice of Lord Canning. "If your lordship ever has a thing of real difficulty to be done, I would answer for it, John Nicholson is the man to do it."

Whilst Edwardes was in Calcutta, conferring with the Governor-General on frontier questions, the first signs of the Mutiny appeared—the disbanding of the 19th N.I. at Barrackpur.

On his way back to the north-west Edwardes visited his spiritual father and friend, Sir Henry Lawrence, at Lucknow. He wrote home to his wife: "Sir Henry is happy in this new appointment: . . . he comes in as a peacemaker and is already winning golden opinions among the nobles and people by his kindness and sympathy: . . . this morning he read a chapter of the Bible to his nephew George and me: then he prayed with great earnestness. He laid great stress on, 'Enable us to live in love with many and charity to all.' I left Lucknow with regret."

The two friends never met again; for Sir Henry was sent to Oude too late to undo the mischief already made.

On 11th May the telegraph brought the news to Peshawur that sepoys had mutinied, killed European officers, and gone to Delhi. Edwardes advised Sir John Lawrence, by wire, to collect a movable column in order to march on any disaffected station and put down revolt with the bayonet. Sir John had not yet awoke to the danger of the revolt and did not wish any new troops to be raised! "We are amply strong enough in the Punjab," he writes, "to put down all mischief."

But General Reed, Brigadier Cotton, Herbert Edwardes and John Nicholson were alive and prompt to make ready; and orders were issued for the assembly of a field force of irregular troops to march anywhere: the Guide Corps too under Captain Daly made surprising efforts. Neville Chamberlain went down, at their request, to see Sir John, for already time was being lost; but Sir John summoned Edwardes down to Rawul Pindee, where he stayed two days. After this friendly meeting Lawrence opposed the raising of levies no more, and indeed became most eager to sanction any number.

We may be surprised to find that it was the gentle, peace-loving Edwardes who first rose to the height of daring resistance, while the iron-willed and colder chief commissioner needed spurring on. The time lost had operated in discouraging the chiefs in sending in levies of horse and foot for the purpose of overawing the disaffected Hindoos: for news soon came that the Delhi magazine had fallen into the hands of the mutineers, and that four guns had been captured and awful atrocities committed on all Europeans, male and female.

Edwardes and his friends in the Punjab were aghast at the failure of the Meerut division to strike a blow, and at the delay of the commander-in-chief at Umballa. "Lord Lake would have been at the gates of Delhi by this time, and the recreant mutineers swimming the Jumna for their lives."

Suddenly in the night came an express to Peshawur announcing that the 55th Native Infantry, on duty at Nowshera, thirty miles away, were in open mutiny, and all the women and children of the 27th Queen's Regiment were at the mercy of the sepoys.

But there was another Mutiny hero up and doing: Lieutenant Alexander Taylor of the Engineers cut away the bridge of boats, and thus prevented the 55th Native Infantry from joining the rest of the mutineers.

"We must disarm the whole of the native troops," said Edwardes.

The commanding officers were summoned and a painful scene followed: for they one and all protested their men were faithful.

But Nicholson and Edwardes had persuaded General Cotton over to their views, and he settled the question by saying, "Gentlemen, no more discussion. These are my orders, and I must have them obeyed."

The military council had lasted till 6 a.m., and at 7 a.m. the two regiments of European Infantry, the 70th and 87th, with guns, were ready on parade to enforce the command given to the sepoys, "Lay down your arms!"

They glanced at the guns and the stern white faces, and obeyed without a word. To their officers it was a most affecting sight to see their men putting their firelocks into the artillery waggons: some of the cavalry officers threw in their own swords with those of their men, and even tore off their spurs. But the good result was instantaneous. On the return from the disarming parade hundreds of Khans who had stood aloof the day before, watching which way the cat would jump, now offered their service: but their services were not wanted so much now, and they were treated rather coldly.

The sepoy regiments were in revolt, but the people of India—the patient, industrious millions—never stirred! and yet foreigners have asserted that the English rule in India was oppressive.

When we went to India we found the Hindoos being oppressed by the Mahommedans: we put down the oppressor and tolerated both. The Hindoo was deceived into believing that his religion was being menaced by us: but so soon as he saw a Mahommedan king set up in Delhi he knew that the hour of persecution would strike again.

Nicholson set off to bring the 55th Regiment, at Murdan, to order. When his column came in sight of the fort, all but a hundred and twenty men had mutinied and gone off towards Swat.

Colonel Spottiswood, their commander, had blown his brains out with a pistol: for he had known and loved his men many years.

The mutineers were pursued, after the fort had been secured; but only the cavalry could hope to catch them.

Nicholson on his big grey charger rode in front, was twenty hours in the saddle and rode seventy miles. Here and there the cavalry hunting the enemy in villages and ravines overtook desperate parties of mutineers, of whom a hundred were killed, a hundred and fifty taken prisoners, and about four hundred got clear away into the hills: the regimental colours were also recovered.

The news came to Peshawur on 19th June that General Anson was dead, and General Reid had succeeded to the command-in-chief. But he had only half as many men and guns as the enemy, and succour could not arrive from home for three months or more.

Fortunately Dost Mahomed Khan was true to his friendship and treaty of peace, and the chiefs of all the hill tribes were eager to send levies: if we had been on bad terms with Cabul, we must have lost all the Punjab, and in all probability India would have gone too.

And we must remember that it was Herbert Edwardes who won over the Ameer. One day while Edwardes sat in his study, busy with reports and orders and letters, one of his men ran in and cried, "O Sahib, armed hill men are coming into the cantonment and calling out for your house."

And Edwardes looked and saw nearly three hundred Afreedees, laden with arms of all sorts and sizes, and asking to be enlisted as regular soldiers. They were mostly outlaws who had done evil deeds and had taken to the hills to escape English justice: they doubtless thought that now was the time to clear off old scores, and get reward instead of punishment. Edwardes made them sit down on the lawn and seated himself in their midst: then he ordered his moonshea to bring out the records. Each man who had done a wrong or injury was adjudged to pay a fine to the injured party before he was allowed to put his name down as a recruit.

"What a scene it was!" says Edwardes: "it might have been an ambush as easily as anything else. They might have cut me in pieces and dispersed themselves immediately . . . but the great secret of association with these utter barbarians is to take them as they come, like wild beasts, and show no fear of them. Habit has taught me this: so I went among them and picked out their young men and enrolled them as recruits: then I brought the older men into our willow-walk in the garden, set them down in the shade, and after a good talk dismissed them to their hills again with a rupee each, quite satisfied that they had been honourably treated."

In June, Nicholson started for Delhi, and on his way visited Sir John Lawrence and urged upon him the advisability of holding the frontier of Peshawur. Edwardes himself had told the chief commissioner that if the order to retreat came from Lahore he should resign his post at once, and inform Lord Canning of his reasons: so strongly did he feel that disaster must follow the abandonment of Peshawur. Meanwhile 700 Multanee horse and foot, voluntary levies, were being fitted out to reinforce Nicholson. These men had fought against us in the war of 1848, and had been liberally treated after their defeat: that liberality now brought in its reward—in the alacrity with which they rushed to our assistance. On 6th August, Sir John Lawrence telegraphed to Edwardes: "My brother Henry was wounded on 2nd July, and died two days afterwards." In his letter to his wife Edwardes writes:—

"We have really lost our dearest friend, and India her greatest public servant. What a blow it is! it is like a good king dying. What a number of hearts loved him, at home and here, black as well as white. He was our master, friend, example, all in one; a father to us in the great earnest public life to which he led us forth . . . for him, dear fellow, we happily have no grief. Trials and mercies, storm and sun, had ripened him for a better world, and poured that drop of the love of Christ into his heart which hallows the love of our neighbour."

And in a letter to Nicholson, commenting on the fine spirit in which Sir Henry Lawrence bore his dismissal from Lahore in favour of his younger brother, Edwardes writes:—

"Cruelly was he removed from the Punjab, which was his public life's stage. But he was equal to the trial: his last act at Lahore was to kneel down, with his dear wife, and pray for the success of John's work . . . nothing but Christian feeling could have given them the victory of that prayer."

And in reply Nicholson wrote: "If it please Providence that I live through this business, you must get me alongside of you again, and be my guide and help in endeavouring to follow dear Sir Henry's example; for I am so weak and unstable that I shall never do any good of myself." So wrote the "Tower of Strength," John Nicholson, the leader of the wildest men in Asia, the hope of all the British forces round Delhi! He clung to Herbert Edwardes spiritually, as a child to his mother!

It was very trying to Edwardes to have to stay at Peshawur collecting levies, disarming traitors, and arming the faithful for the conflict, while his greatest friends were risking their lives in the struggle. But no less was he working for the crushing of the Mutiny, almost exhausting the Punjab of troops in order to strengthen the Delhi force.

Nicholson wrote to Edwardes: "Delhi, 12th August 1857.—I came into Wilson's camp ahead of my own column by mail-cart from Umballa and spent three days there, looking over our position." Of the camp at Delhi he says: "Our position is a perfectly providential one . . . the Ridge with the strong buildings on it in front, and the river and canal protecting our flanks and rear, has saved us."

Nicholson with his movable column had fought on his way to Delhi, and crushed whatever force he attacked; he had destroyed the Sealkote mutineers and taken their guns; then, arrived at Delhi, he had gone round quietly and unbeknown to examine daily every battery, breastwork, and post: often at night he would ride round the outer line of sentries, to see if the men were on the alert. He did not forget his wounded friends, but visited them, or escorted them when convalescent. "No woman could have shown more consideration," wrote Sir Neville Chamberlain.

In October, Edwardes heard that Agra had been relieved. For after the capture of Delhi, General Wilson dispatched a corps of 2800 men, under the command of Colonel Edward Greathed of the 5th Foot, to open the country between Delhi and Agra.

Greathed started on the 24th of September in a south-east direction and punished where he found the natives had committed atrocities.

He took Bulanshahr and Málagarh. In the latter he had the misfortune to lose, by an accident, Lieutenant Home of the Engineers, one of the survivors of the gallant officers who had blown up the Kashmir gate at Delhi. On reaching the next town, Khurjá, the fury of the troops was roused by the sight of a skeleton stuck up on the roadside for all to see—the medical officers pronounced it to be the skeleton of a European female. There was a cry for instant vengeance, but the civil officer accompanying the force contrived to calm the troops and spare the city.

When forty-eight miles from Agra, Greathed received a letter from the authorities at Agra imploring help. He therefore sent off that night of the 9th October, the cavalry and horse artillery, and four hours later followed with the infantry, mounting his men on elephants, carts, and camels.

Pushing on rapidly, he crossed the bridge of boats under the walls of the fort at sunrise on the 10th and encamped on the parade-ground. It was a spacious grassy plain having some high crops about 300 yards distant. The camp was pitched, the horses picketed, and the men threw off their accoutrements and betook themselves to breakfast.

Greathed had been informed that the rebels were ten miles away, so few precautions were taken. He did not know they were lying hidden in the tall crops close at hand.

Presently four of them, dressed as conjurers, came strolling up to the advanced guard of the 9th Lancers. They were ordered off by the sergeant in charge of the post, whereupon one of them drew his tulwar and cut him down; the others gave a signal to their men in the crops, and while the troopers were running to dispatch them, round shot came pouring in. Our soldiers needed no further alarm: they turned out at once, but the rebel cavalry now started up as if by magic and charged the guns, sabring the gunners of one gun, when a squadron of the 9th Lancers dashed on them and drove them back in disorder. But French, who led the Lancers, was killed, and Jones, his subaltern, was dangerously wounded.

Still, this gave Greathed time to deploy his line, covered by a battery of Eurasian soldiers under Pearson, which rendered excellent service. The sudden transformation of a sleeping mass of men into an organised army scared the rebels, and they fled to their camp seven miles away. They were pursued by horse and guns to the river; thirteen guns and vast quantities of waggons full of ammunition were brought back. The weary victors had done over sixty miles in thirty-six hours before this battle; so splendidly was Agra saved and law and order once more established.

Edwardes at Peshawur heard the news with a feeling of relief. "By God's mercy," he writes in his diary, "Delhi, Agra, and Lucknow are recovered, and it only remains to settle the country."

We have chosen this Christian knight as a hero of

the Mutiny, because it was primarily owing to him that the Mutiny was crushed. Edwardes made the Afghans our friends, and so rendered the Punjab secure and able to send all its troops down to Delhi.

Men in India understood this, but away in England his services were for a long time overlooked.

Lumsden wrote from Candahar in January 1859:—

"The honours have begun to come out, but where is So-and-so? . . . Will England never learn to recognise the right men? Taylor took Delhi; and some people we know saved the Punjab."

Edwardes was one of those men who cannot push themselves to the front, and who out of modesty keep silent about their own merits. Such men are apt to be overlooked by the distributors of honours.

It was not until 1860 that Edwardes received the honour of knighthood, K.C.B., for his services. In January 1862, Sir Herbert and his wife again set sail for India to take up his new appointment of Commissioner of Umballa, whence he returned in 1865. They were both worn out with work and anxiety, and when Lady Edwardes told the doctors she was strong enough to stay on in India for his sake, they replied: "If you wish Sir Herbert not to go home on your account, you must go with him *on his own*, for he needs rest as much as you do."

Sir Herbert passed away on 23rd December 1868, towards midnight. Among his last words were: "I am quite happy. I love God: I trust entirely to Jesus: I put full confidence in Jesus, and I couldn't do more if I lived a thousand years."

A monument was placed in Westminster Abbey to his memory by the Indian Secretary of State and Council: it is close to that of Warren Hastings, and all that was mortal of him was laid in the Highgate Cemetery.

The "Edwardes Gateway" at Peshawur and the well-fountain at Bunnu, now called Edwardes-a-bad, commemorate his services in India.

By kind permission of Messrs. Kegan Paul, Trench, & Co.

CHAPTER IV

HODSON OF HODSON'S HORSE—THE PRINCE OF SCOUTS

OF all the heroes of the Indian Mutiny, Hodson won for himself the brightest and the most short-lived fame. In the midst of a brilliant career of soldierly daring he committed one act which has been regarded from different points of view: as necessary severity, or cold-blooded retribution.

We shall see later what was the ambiguous deed which Hodson committed: but lest this preface should prejudice any reader against our hero, let us hasten to assert that few men had warmer and nobler friends and stouter admirers than Brevet-Major William S. R. Hodson. Like Sir Herbert Edwardes, he was the son of a country rector, who lived at Maisemore Court, near the Severn, to the north of Gloucester. William Hodson's father, a Canon of Lichfield, had been seventh Wrangler and second Chancellor's Medallist: his mother, May Stephen, belonged to a family of lawyers, intimate with Wilberforce and Macaulay.

Born in 1821, he grew up a shapely, slim lad with frank blue eyes and yellow hair: being troubled with headaches, he pursued his early studies at home under his father, and learnt by long country walks and runs to observe keenly and love wild nature.

At fifteen he was sent to Rugby, being older than most boys at entrance: his good teaching secured him a place in the middle fifth, so that he escaped fagging, and in two years was placed in the sixth form under Arnold.

Though an athlete Hodson never cared for cricket, but he was the best long-distance runner in the school, and excelled in the gymnasium.

He was a good hand at keeping order, and when Cotton's house was growing unruly from lack of præposters, Arnold transferred Hodson from Price's house to Cotton's —in a week all disorder ceased!

Thomas Arnold writes: "His expansive and impulsive temper won him many friends, and for my own part I always liked him greatly. His faults were arrogance, rashness, and a domineering temper; if one bears this in mind, it is easy to understand the errors into which he fell in India."

In October 1840, William Hodson entered Trinity College, Cambridge, and took up boating, rowing in the 2nd Trinity boat, while he did not neglect his studies. By the time Hodson took his degree he was too old to get an Indian cadetship: but obtained a commission in the Guernsey Militia from General Sir William Napier, then Lieutenant-Governor of Guernsey and the historian of the Peninsular War. On leaving Guernsey, Sir William wrote him a flattering testimonial, in which he remarked: "I think you will be an acquisition to any service." By passing thus through the militia, Hodson was enabled to obtain a cadetship, offered by Sir Robert Inglis, on the Bengal Establishment. On the voyage to Calcutta Hodson was deeply grieved at losing his dog: the poor little creature had been shut up during a gale, and on again seeing his master was so overjoyed that he fell into convulsions and died. Hodson was a great lover of animals; dogs and cats instinctively clung to him for love and protection.

After staying three weeks with the Chief Justice of Bengal at Garden Reach, a pretty suburb by the river-side, Hodson went by river towards Agra, to join a native regiment, 2nd Bengal Grenadiers, which was to form part of Sir Henry Hardinge's escort from Agra to Ferozepur.

At Agra he was the guest of the Lieutenant-Governor, James Thomason, a friend of his father, who from that time treated Hodson as a son.

Thomason gave Hodson a horse, which carried him many a march, from 4 a.m. to sunset, with a rest in the hot hours. During the Mutiny he grieved over the wounds of his charger as of his dearest friend.

The officers used to ride before the band, and frequently Hodson would dismount in the cold dawn and run seven or eight miles to keep himself warm.

At Umballa he saw 12,000 of the finest troops drawn up in one line: the Sikh army of the Khalsa, or chosen, were encamped round Lahore, clamouring for their pay and threatening to cross the river Sutlej and plunder Hindostan. Sir Hugh Gough, the commander-in-chief, was preparing to meet these warriors.

Hodson's first battle, Mudki, was fought after a fasting march of twenty-five miles: he was grazed in the cheek by a ball fired by one of his own sepoys, who stood behind him. In the battles fought against the Sikhs the sepoys often refused to face the grape, and only the British regiments stood firm. After four days' fighting, and nights spent on the ground in great cold, they got a rest and some real food, and water flavoured with gunpowder!

Infantry attacking guns—that was his first ordeal of war, and the enemy were the proudest and bravest fighting race in the East. In sixty days the Sikh army was overthrown. "I had the pleasure," Hodson writes to his sister, "of spiking two guns; and once more I have escaped, I am thankful to say, unhurt, except that a bullet took a fancy to my little finger and cut the skin off the top, and spoilt a buckskin glove."

The Sikh loss at Sobraon, the decisive victory, was some 8000 killed and wounded, while our loss was some 2500 killed and wounded.

When England was ringing joy-bells to welcome the glad tidings of great victories, Hodson was writing letters in criticism of his superior officers. He says: "Will it be believed that a large proportion of our losses was caused by our own regiments being so badly handled that they fired upon one another incessantly! My own regiment received a volley from behind as we advanced! The 1st Europeans fell before our eyes in numbers by a volley from our own 45th Sepoys."

His opinion of the native regiments was given to his friend Thomason at Agra: he found the discipline bad, and the native officers were more troublesome than the men. In disgust he asked to be transferred to a European regiment, the 1st Fusiliers; war had decimated them, but they had covered themselves with glory.

In August 1846, Hodson went to Simla to spend a week with Sir Henry Lawrence. He stayed a month and enjoyed a friendship with that good and great man which lasted all his life. Sir Henry wrote: "I have seldom met so promising a young fellow: I get a good deal of help from him; he works willingly and sensibly."

In October, Sir Henry invited Hodson to come with him to Cashmere. A motley army went with them, composed of stalwart Sikhs in small blue turbans and giant Afghans with voluminous headgear, Brahmins and Gurkhas—all bent on frightening the men of Cashmere into submission to Gulâb Singh, whom we had placed over them for a large concession! This maharaja, with all his engaging personality and gentlemanly manner, had a habit of skinning his personal enemies alive!

When accused of having flayed 12,000 men, he replied indignantly: "It is no such thing: I have only skinned three—what! well, it might have been three hundred, if you count every little rascal."

Resistance melted before the approaching army, and Hodson had an opportunity of admiring the lovely glens and woods and rocks. The women of Cashmere, Hodson describes as a wretched set, only good for beasts of burden, dirty, and atrociously ugly.

HODSON OF HODSON'S HORSE

In the spring of 1847 Hodson was superintending the building of an asylum founded by Sir H. Lawrence for the children of our soldiers among the pines of Himalaya. He had to learn how to cut down trees and make planks, doors, and windows; how to quarry rocks and make bricks—and then teach all this to his 600 native workmen.

He liked the work, because it was to rescue the soldier's child from an infancy of contamination and ignorance, and perhaps from an early death. And yet this was the young Englishman whom some moralists pronounced more unfeeling than the dissolute princes of Delhi!

Sir Henry had lately formed a new and splendid corps —the Guides—he now asked Hodson to accept the adjutancy of this regiment. As first raised it consisted of one troop of horse and two companies of foot, and was placed under Lieutenant H. Lumsden, afterwards Sir Harry Lumsden. Amongst the men enlisted were old Sikh soldiers, Pathans, and Hindostanee soldiers who had served with the Sikhs.

The object of this corps was to train men in peace to be efficient in war: to know all roads, rivers, hills, ferries, and passes, and to give accurate information of what their neighbours were thinking of doing. In addition to all this work, Hodson was still kept on the staff at Lahore, and worked in Sir Henry Lawrence's office. "He has been a brother to me ever since I knew him," writes Hodson.

But in November 1847 Henry Lawrence had to go to England on sick leave for two years, and the friends were parted.

Among those who rejoiced at Hodson's appointment to the Guides was Herbert Edwardes, who wrote home: "I think Hodson will do it justice: he is one of the finest young fellows I know, and a thorough soldier in his heart."

One of Hodson's functions was to stop plundering and detect the plunderers: many cases of robbery did he unravel by sending out clever natives, disguised as fakirs, or religious beggars, to talk to the people in their villages. It was astonishing how he picked up cases of cruelty and violence; the Sikhs seemed quite indifferent to murder, but were horrified at the idea of shutting up a sacred ox who had gored his thirteenth man in two days! So venerable a beast, they said, should have fair play.

In 1848 the second Sikh War and the siege of Multan occupied Edwardes, and the Guides distinguished themselves by courage and Hodson by strategy: the latter received the special thanks of General Wheeler, not only for his services in the field, but for the information which he collected for him.

In a letter home Hodson describes one of his little affairs—one bold hill-man had beaten off four sowars (troopers) one after another. He then rushed at Hodson like a tiger, and closed with him, yelling, "Wah guru-ke-jai," and wielding his tulwar fiercely. "I guarded the three or four first blows, but he pressed so closely to my horse's rein that I could not get a fair cut in return. At length I pressed in my turn so sharply upon him that he missed his blow, and I caught his tulwar with my bridle-hand, wrenched it from him and cut him down with the right, having received no further injury than a severe cut across the fingers."

From the time that Hodson got promotion in the Guides jealousy began to whisper tales of evil against him. Hodson's plain speaking offended the older officers—for he inveighed against promotion by seniority (or senility); all elasticity, he said, was gone when men became colonels; all energy and enterprise was worn out. One cavalry commander at Chilianwala could not mount his horse unaided. A brigadier of infantry was so blind he could not see his regiment until his horse's nose touched the bayonets, and even then he asked plaintively, "Pray, which way are the men facing, Mr. Hodson?"

Three days Hodson spent on civil duty in Sir Charles Napier's camp; a man of iron, but most kind and cordial to the young adjutant. "I only trust he will remain with us as long as his health lasts, and endeavour to rouse the army from its present state of slack discipline," writes Hodson.

At the close of 1851 Hodson went down to Calcutta to meet the lady he was to marry, the widow of John Mitford. The wedding took place privately in the cathedral, and, after a visit to Mr. Thomason at Agra, Hodson had to leave his bride at Umballa. For he was obliged to make his way to Ludhiana, "to try a lot of gentlemen who had devoted their youthful energies to strangling their neighbours by the simple art of Thuggi."

In September, Lumsden went to England, and the Governor-General gave Hodson the command of the Guides—the most honourable and arduous command on the frontier, one that Hodson had long coveted. An expedition among the wild tribes of the Hazâra gave him an opportunity of showing how he could handle his men in mountain warfare.

In February 1853, Sir Henry Lawrence was removed from the Punjab, and Hodson lost a good, sincere friend.

In 1853 it was bruited about that Hodson was very unpopular with his regiment and with military men generally; but Sir Richard Temple said he had marvellously attached the Guides to himself by the ties of mutual honour, daring, and devotion. But there is no doubt that this young soldier, who took war so seriously and scientifically, began to be disliked by the slow-moving men of the old school.

One of his bitterest enemies was his own adjutant, Turner, who was transferred in 1854 from the Guides to a regiment of Punjab Cavalry.

Hodson's chief commissioner, John Lawrence, must have heard stories to his discredit; for he wrote to Hodson and stated that neither the European nor the native officers were contented under his command.

Hodson had taken great pains to discover the men who had plotted the murder of Mackeson; he had seized and imprisoned a border chief named Khadar Khan, for it was one of his servants who dealt the blow. This prisoner was acquitted, but Hodson still believed him guilty. Major Edwardes reported the case to Lord Dalhousie as one of wrongful imprisonment. Soon after, the Court of Directors decreed that Hodson should never again be employed in any civil capacity.

Fools may make mistakes, but if a genius trips every dullard is eager to hound him down and impute low motives.

Turner had been going about saying that Hodson had falsified the regimental accounts; in December 1854 a court of inquiry sat at Peshawur, and Hodson was ordered to give up his command during the sitting.

A most extraordinary order was published, calling upon all who had claims upon Hodson to bring them forward without delay. Such an order among Orientals was grossly unfair; of course all the scoundrels in the regiment came forward with false claims.

Lord Napier did what he could for Hodson, and urged him to have all the Persian accounts translated into English. By working night and day Hodson managed to get the translation finished.

He asked for a full and public examination of the whole case, and said he did not fear the result, if only they would hear him on his defence. The Court decided that Hodson's accounts were most unsatisfactory. Then Hodson demanded a court-martial, but John Lawrence asked Major Reynell Taylor to examine and report upon Hodson's alleged misdealings. For three months the Major worked at the accounts; he did not like doing it, but as he proceeded he found that all had been quite satisfactory, though unbalanced and undetailed—but Hodson had taken the accounts over from Lumsden in considerable confusion. "I believe it to be an honest and correct record from beginning to end," was the Major's verdict.

Colonel (Lord) Napier was delighted; he was a good soldier and rejoiced that Hodson had been found honourable and upright. But there it ended! No public acquittal was made known, though the Government gave Hodson his papers and closed the case. Taylor's report to Simla was filed and put away and forgotten. Hodson quietly made his way to the hill-station of Dagshai and resumed his place as regimental subaltern in the 1st Fusiliers.

So the Prince of Scouts might have remained unnoticed; but when real warfare begins we cannot afford to throw away such talent. Of course Hodson felt the reverse very keenly: his wife felt it, and they had just lost their only child! Sorrows have a habit of coming in jolly troops; the best way is to fight against despair, and not put down every disagreeable *contretemps* to an overruling Providence. Hodson had also come down from an income of £1200 a year to £250! But he says: "I trust I am too much of a soldier to permit myself to be subdued by reverses, or to sit down and fret over the past."

His colonel soon made him quartermaster, and later made an appeal to the adjutant-general of the army for his promotion. Subsequently Hodson had an interview with General Anson, the commander-in-chief, who had never heard of Major Taylor's good report! General Anson was most kind and cordial, and promised to write to Lord Canning about the case.

Meanwhile the Mutiny broke out, and no letters could pass between Simla and Calcutta; but General Anson gave Hodson a staff appointment on his own responsibility.

As soon as the telegraph wires flashed to Simla the news of the bloody revolt at Meerut on 10th May, and of the atrocities at Delhi, where English men, women, and children were butchered in street and square and palace, within sight and hearing of the king and his sons, General Anson at once ordered the dispatch of the white troops that garrisoned the hill-stations of Kussowlie, Dagshai, and Sabathu. So Hodson marched with his regiment to Umballa, and met his chief on the 15th May. This was no time for snubbing young heroes because they were arrogant and masterful.

Anson made Hodson assistant quartermaster-general to

his new force *en route* for Delhi: But he did more: he empowered Hodson to raise one thousand Irregular Horse, set him at the head of the Intelligence Department, and sent him to Kurnal in order to restore communication between that place and Meerut.

Hodson started from Kurnal for Meerut on 20th May with a troop of Sikh horse—at dawn the next day he galloped through the pickets, having ridden seventy-six miles. He interviewed General Wilson, took a bath and some breakfast, had two hours' sleep, and then rode back, having had to fight his way some thirty miles of the distance.

How men talked of this daring and successful ride! All old libellous tales were forgotten when the presence of danger called for a real man. The officers at Kurnal sat watching him in awestruck silence as, after a wash, the tired rider tackled his plate with ravenous appetite. "I will answer no questions till I have had a square meal." Suddenly he put down his knife and fork and said, "Now I'm ready." Whereupon he began his awful recital of all that had befallen at Meerut, a story told with flashing eye and fierce tone. When he had finished, someone wishing for more, said "Well?"

"Well," rejoined Hodson, changing from tragedy to cheery mirth, "here we are! the wires cut, north, south, east, and west: not a soul can interfere with us: we have the cracking of the nut in our own way: and here we are, as jolly as a bug in a rug."

It was the spirit of Baden-Powell at Mafeking, heartening the desponding with such a merry laugh as Robin Hood might have sent forth in the glades of Sherwood Forest.

For Hodson was the life and soul of the whole force marching down to Delhi. Pathan and Sikh listened to his merry voice, and the spirit of worship grew in their brave and generous souls. Here was a white man who knew not fear: him they could reverence. Meanwhile Hodson began to raise recruits for his Irregular Horse—2000 if he could get them.

His friend Montgomery helped him, and called upon the sirdars to send men, many of whom knew Hodson by repute.

In batches they kept on coming to Delhi, where Hodson and two or three subalterns set to and drilled them into form.

General Anson had died of cholera, and Sir Henry Barnard, his successor, took at once to Hodson.

Seaton had just ridden to the Ridge, escaping from his mutineers, and Hodson shared his tent with him: but he was ever riding away to get information, and thought nothing of eighty miles, for he could sleep on horseback without falling off, a feat not for every one to perform.

General Thomason gives a lively account of one of Hodson's single-combat fights near Delhi. "He had ridden a very short distance from us when he found himself confronted by one of the enemy with shield and tulwar. I shall never forget Hodson's face as he met this man. It was smiles all over. He went round and round the man, who in the centre of the circle was dancing *more Indico*, and doing his best to cut Hodson's reins. This went on for a short time, when a neat point from Hodson put an end to the performance!"

Next morning the Guides under Captain Daly arrived in Barnard's camp, having done a hot march of 580 miles in twenty-two days.

When the men of the Guides saw their old commander, they shouted "Hodson sahib!" till they were hoarse; they cheered, shouted, and wept and sung like frantic creatures: they kissed his bridle, dress, hands, and feet, and salaamed to the ground before his horse.

Officers hearing the hubbub and seeing the crowding round the tall, yellow-haired Englishman, ran out of their tents, crying, "What is it? Are they mobbing him?" Then, when they saw how matters stood, they murmured, "Good God! and they said this fellow was unpopular with his corps!"

The news spread and produced a great sensation in camp: it had a good effect on our native troops, for they were more willing to follow their European officers when they saw the enthusiasm of the Guides—their own countrymen. Almost every day there were fights and alarms, sorties to be repelled, houses to be cleared and blown up. Sometimes Hodson would ride and take a look round. Some officers grumbled and said the way he exposed himself to fire was sheer madness; but Hodson, like Nicholson, preferred to see things for himself. When he caught a severe cold, General Barnard insisted on having him in his own tent. "I woke in the night and found the kind old man by my bedside, covering me carefully up from the draught."

In one fight Captain Daly was hit through the shoulder, which gave Hodson more work; for the General requested him as a personal favour to take command of the Guides until Daly had recovered. He could not help feeling proud at being earnestly requested to resume a command of which his enemies had deprived him out of jealousy.

On 23rd June, the centenary of Plassey, the rebels came out with all their available men and guns: for a prophecy had long been quoted that on this day they were destined to overthrow the Faranghi rule.

All day long the fight went on under a burning sun which knocked over many officers and men; Hodson was in the saddle most of the day and bears testimony to the conduct of his old Guides and his new Sikhs and Gurkhas. We might have suffered more than we did from this fierce sortie, but Hodson's native spies had warned him of the coming danger.

These spies, says Seaton, came in at all hours and in all disguises, carrying mysterious little scrolls about their person: those who brought verbal messages Hodson cross-examined severely—such a mastery had he of the native languages. The English soldiers soon got to know and appreciate the great scout.

"There goes that 'ere Hodson," said a drunken private, as Hodson cantered down the lines: "he's bound to be in every mortal scrap—he'll get shot, I know he will: and—I'd a deal rather be shot myself: we can't do without that 'ere Hodson; blame me if we can!"

On 4th July, a large body of rebels, Hodson was informed, had marched past our right flank along the Alipur road. Major Coke with a force of all arms and the Guides set out to intercept the rebels and had to struggle through swamp and marsh; both men and horses were terribly knocked up, and could hardly crawl back to camp. "I was mercifully preserved," writes Hodson, "though I am sorry to say my gallant Feroza was badly wounded twice with sabre-cuts, part of his bridle was cut through and a piece of my glove shaved off."

On 5th July, General Barnard died of cholera brought on by exposure.

One day the laugh was raised against the wily scout: for a body of sowars was seen riding leisurely after our men who were returning from pursuit. "Who are those?" asked Hope Grant, who sent his aide-de-camp to find out their identity. "Our own cavalry, sir," said young Anson. But Captain Hodson too must needs ride up to them; he accosted them, and a friendly and even merry conversation ensued—"A party of the 9th Irregulars, are you? Then we're all irregular!"

When Hodson turned his back, they put spur to their horses and galloped off to Delhi like wild-fire. They were rebel cavalry in retreat!

How they laughed at mess that night when the story was told how the cunning intelligence officer had chummed with the enemy, and had seen at a glance that they were friendly sepoys! To catch that weasel napping was a comedy worth laughing at. A distinguished officer writes: "Affairs at times looked very queer from the frightful expenditure of life. Hodson's face was then like sunshine breaking through the dark clouds of despondency and gloom that would settle down on all but a few brave hearts."

Recruits for Hodson's Horse now came in faster: M'Dowell was the second in command, and Hugh Gough of the 3rd Cavalry, Chalmers and Ellis and Shebbeare and others were always well to the front.

It was strange how many hairbreadth escapes Hodson had: so that the natives thought he possessed a charmed life.

General Reed was ill; Chamberlain was wounded, because his men hesitated and he jumped his horse over a wall into the throng of rebels to give them a lead; Wilson of the Bengal Artillery took the chief command, but he was unequal to the strain, and had little force of will.

On the 19th of July, the news of the Cawnpur massacre came in: spirits went down, and cholera burst out in mad fury.

General Wilson met this by ordering a regimental band to play cheerful tunes every morning: and the remedy seemed to do good.

On July 23rd, Colonel Seaton was wounded and carefully tended by Hodson. "Then I saw," wrote Seaton, "that the brave and stern soldier had also the tenderness of a woman in his noble heart."

By the end of July—what with disease and wounds, our Delhi force could muster only 2200 Europeans and 1500 Native Infantry.

On 4th August, the news came that Havelock had fought his way into Cawnpur, but was too late to save the women and children. Hodson's mouth closed with a grim determination. "Such fiends as these our arms have never met before. May our vengeance be as speedy as it will unquestionably be sure." Hodson never forgot those women and children, and the thought made him forget mercy.

On 5th August, Nicholson rode into camp, and men took heart again as the Punjab column, 3000 strong, marched into camp with bands playing and followed by cheering soldiers.

The many rides and adventures of Hodson's Horse are too numerous to detail: when the rebels saw the khaki tunic, scarlet turban, and scarlet sash worn over the shoulder they knew the Flamingoes were coming and 'twere best to beat a safe retreat.

An officer who served before Delhi thus describes Hodson's manner: "In a fight he was glorious: if there was only a good hard scrimmage he was as happy as a king. A beautiful swordsman, he never failed to kill his man; and the way he used to play with the most brave and furious of these rebels was perfect. I fancy I see him now, smiling, laughing, parrying most fearful blows as calmly as if he were brushing off flies, and calling out all the time, 'Why, try again now!' 'What do you call that stroke?' 'Do you call yourself a swordsman?'"

But on 3rd September all seemed lost! There were 2500 men sick in hospital, and General Wilson had lost all nerve.

But on 4th September came the heavy siege guns and mortars drawn by elephants, and miles of bullock-carts laden with shot and shell. All through the first week in September the troops were busy making ready for the assault soon to be made upon the city. On the morning of the 12th some fifty heavy guns and mortars were playing upon the crumbling walls and giving the rebels little rest from their constant hail. It was arranged, at Nicholson's request, that Hodson should accompany the column which Nicholson would lead in pursuit of the mutineers after the capture of Delhi.

But Nicholson was to lead one of the storming columns on the 14th, and this "gambler's throw," as the sick General Wilson called it, might prove fatal. For the rebel gunners were every whit as skilful as the British, since it had been the practice of the English in India to train the sepoys to serve the guns. The besieged had seen what was impending, and had mounted heavy guns all along the northern face: they had even made in one night an advanced trench

BLOWING UP THE KASHMIR GATE

The bags of powder were laid and the men were turning back when the rebels opened fire. Horne leaped into the ditch unhurt. Salkeld, who was shot through the arms and leg, handed the port-fire to Burgess, who fell dead before he could take it. Then Sergeant Carmichael lit the train, and with a deafening crash the gate was blown open.

parallel to the left attack, covering their entire front. This trench they lined with infantry and sharpshooters.

On the afternoon of the 13th, Wilson directed that the breaches should be examined. Medley and Lang inspected the Kashmir bastion, Greathed and Home the Water bastion; both reported the breach practicable. Then Baird-Smith advised Wilson to assault on the morrow.

Thus at 3 a.m. the five columns of assault were drawn up: they waited while an explosion party, Lieutenants Home and Salkeld and others, covered by 100 men of the 60th Rifles, hurried on to attach kegs of powder and blow up the Kashmir gate: a bugle was to give the signal of success.

The bags were laid and the men were turning back when the rebels opened fire. Home jumped into the ditch unhurt; Salkeld was shot through the arms and leg, and fell back on the bridge.

"Light the fusee, Burgess" he murmured, and handed the corporal his port-fire. But Burgess fell dead. Then Sergeant Carmichael sprang forward and lit the fusee: he too fell mortally wounded.

The next moment a fearful explosion shattered the massive gate. Home then told the bugler, Hawthorne, to sound the advance.

The bugle-call, three times repeated, was never heard in the din and tumult. But Campbell, the commander of the third column, had noticed the explosion and ordered the advance. They entered the city just as the first and second columns had won the breaches.

For two hours, whilst these assaults were being made, Hodson and his men had to sit on horseback under heavy fire, waiting to prevent the enemy from coming out.

"Hodson sat like a man carved in stone," writes an officer, . . . "and only by his eyes and his ready hand could you have told that he was in deadly peril." Six hundred horsemen, of whom only 200 were British, had to sit unmoved all that time under a hurricane of lead

—it was a feat of great endurance, and a proof of high discipline.

That afternoon Wilson removed his headquarters into that part of Delhi which the columns led by Nicholson, Jones, and Campbell had won at the cost of so many brave lives: and Nicholson lay in a tent dying.

The death of Major Jacob made Hodson a captain: Hodson assisted at his burial, and said, "I would far rather have served on as a subaltern than gain promotion thus." Hodson gained later his brevet-majority as a reward for his services in the Punjab campaign: he had little time, however, to think of such things, for his business now was to ride round and ascertain the rebels' line of retreat.

General Wilson was sadly discouraged by the day's work. He had been told that Delhi would fall, but his columns had been stopped and one had been driven back: his troops only held a short line of rampart. "Ought we not to withdraw to the ridge?" he asked Baird-Smith. "Can we hold what we have taken?"

Baird-Smith looked at the invalid and replied, "We *must* hold it."

Sixty-six officers killed or wounded and 1104 men! Wilson shook his head! But the fact that the British had beaten the sepoys in hand-to-hand fight and were firmly lodged on the rampart cowed all,—from the old king in his palace to the meanest sowar.

On the 16th the British stormed the great magazine and captured guns and ammunition. Bit by bit the city was being wrested from the rebels. Alexander Taylor did splendid work on the 19th in effecting the capture of the Burn bastion, and Brigadier Jones seized the Lahore gate. There were still many thousand armed rebels in the city and its surroundings, and we had only 3000 left fit for service.

On the morning of the 20th, Hope Grant took his cavalry, including Hodson and his Irregulars, on a reconnaisance to the west of the city. From a hill they could see the native camp under the king's general, Bakht Khan, formerly a lieutenant of artillery.

Hodson was looking through his glass. "Did you hear that, sir?" They all heard a loud explosion.

"They are going to abandon their camp," cried Hodson, and at once detached two troopers to ride down and see. On their confirming his guess, Hodson got leave to carry the news to Wilson.

After seeing the General, Hodson took M'Dowell and 75 men and rode right round the city to the Delhi gate on the extreme right, which they found open. By evening they had ridden some miles beyond Delhi and executed many a straggler, brought away three guns and many camels and the mess plate of the 60th Native Infantry with their standards and drums.

Delhi had been evacuated during the night, and India was saved. But the old king, Bahadur Shah, was still alive and might become a focus for fresh rebellion. Hodson pleaded with Wilson for leave to fetch him back a prisoner: and the dying Nicholson added his voice for the king's arrest. So Hodson with only 50 horsemen rode through miles of ruinous tombs and palaces over the site of old Delhi for the king's hiding-place nearly seven miles off. As they reached the tomb of Humayun, the second great Emperor of the Tartar line, Hodson drew rein at the noble gateway of the wide court, in which rose the dome-capped glory of the marble tomb, glistening white. Concealing his men in a building near, Hodson sent his faithful Rajah Ali inside to negotiate the terms of surrender, and himself awaited the result not far off the gateway.

For two hours he waited, and his cold blue eyes sparkled angrily at the long delay. Why! the life of the king had been promised, that of his favourite wife and her son, Jamma Bakht.

At last his messenger reappeared, saying:

"Sahib, the king will accept if Hodson Bahadur will

enter and repeat with his own lips the promise made by the Government."

So Hodson went in and repeated the pledge aloud, but added, "If there be any attempt at rescue, I shall at once kill the king." And the King of Delhi accepted his terms.

So at length there issued out of the gate a train of palkis conveying the royal prisoners, but closely guarded on either side by Hodson's sowars.

The march back to Delhi by a circuitous road, to avoid the seething crowd of angry Mahommedans, was the longest seven miles, Hodson says, which he ever rode. For his eyes had to turn on every side, watching the throng of fanatics, who were eager to strike a blow on behalf of their captive king: but they dared not lift a hand; for Hodson, the yellow-haired devil, rode close by the king, ready to shoot the old man if any rescue were attempted.

Passing slowly along the street of Silversmiths, the little band of troopers approached the red sandstone walls, loopholed and crenelated, which enclosed the Dewan Khas: they halted at the palace gate, and doubtless a feeling of relief took the place of that long tension of nerve all along the crowded roads.

For there was imminent danger at every step, though some writers who wish to belittle Hodson assert that the natives were too cowed to offer any resistance to these 50 horsemen!

So Hodson saluted the new commissioner, Charles Saunders, and made over his royal charge for safe lodgment in the royal palace. Saunders stood agape, admiring the brilliant audacity of the man.

"By Jove! Hodson," he exclaimed, "they ought to make you commander-in-chief for this." Then Hodson rode on to General Wilson's quarters to report his success, and to deliver up the royal arms.

The General greeted him gruffly, saying, "Well, I am glad you have got him, but I never expected to see either him or you again."

That remark goes to prove what soldiers at the time thought of the peril incurred by Hodson and his sowars. What they thought, when all the facts were staring them in the face, far outweighs any peaceful opinions written down in the seclusion of the study long afterwards.

So now Delhi had fallen, and the Bahadur Shah, the figurehead of the rebellion against English rule, was safe in British hands.

Hodson was not yet satisfied: he wanted to go again to the tomb and fetch the villain princes, the young men who had stirred up the city on 11th May to hack and butcher all the white men, women, and children in Delhi. General Wilson at first refused his consent: then grumbled forth, "Go then, but don't let me be bothered with them."

So, early on the morning of the 22nd, Hodson, taking his subaltern M'Dowell and 100 picked horsemen, started again for Humayun's tomb. He posted his men so that none could enter or come forth, and then sent in one of the lower members of the royal family and his one-eyed maulvi, Rajah Ali, to bid the shahzadas come forth.

Two hours again were spent in arguing and protesting, and then there came forth Mirza Moghul, Mirza Aboo Bukr, and Mirza Kisz Sooltan, the last being the grandson of the king.

They asked Hodson if the Government had promised them their lives. "Most certainly not," replied Hodson, and before they could step back they found themselves being hustled to a native carriage and driven off under escort towards Delhi.

Hodson then formed his troopers across the archway and slowly drove back into the courtyard the armed mob of retainers who were following the princes. Then riding in with M'Dowell, he ordered all to lay down their arms. The natives looked from one to another, but a second loud command had its effect. They threw down tulwar and gun and dagger, and Hodson made them collect horses, bullocks, and covered carts, or "ruths," which were used by the women and eunuchs of the palace.

Five hundred swords and guns were piled up in carts, and left in charge of a small guard, then Hodson galloped away to overtake the princes. This he did near Delhi. We will now give his own words as to what befell. "I came up just in time, as a large mob had collected and were turning on the guard. I rode in among them at a gallop, and in a few words I appealed to the crowd, saying that these were the butchers who had murdered and brutally used helpless women and children, and that the Government had now sent their punishment." Sir T. Seaton shall now say what he heard: "There was an immense crowd surging round them which was increasing every moment, closing in and pressing on his men. Hodson stopped the carriage and made the three prisoners descend. The wretches, seeing that something was about to happen, put up their hands and fell at his feet, begging that their lives might be spared, and that an investigation might be made into their conduct. All that Hodson said was, 'Choop ruho (be silent); take off your upper garments,' and they did so. 'Get into the ruth!' They obeyed. Hodson, then putting out his hand and taking a carbine from one of his men, shot Mirza Moghul, and immediately after, the two others. Hodson's men shouted, 'Now justice has been done'; and the crowd dispersed."

The bodies were then taken into the main street, the Chandnee Chouk, were dragged out of the ruth by sweepers, and exposed on the raised platform at the cut-wallee (head police-station) on the very spot where, on the 11th of May, the bodies of our unfortunate countrywomen, their husbands and children, had been exposed.

Hodson adds: "I deliberately shot them one after another. 'God is great!' was the cry that broke from a multitude of lips, and slowly but quietly the crowds of awestruck Mussulmans melted away. I am not cruel, but I confess I did rejoice at the opportunity of ridding the earth of these wretches. I intended to have had them hanged, but when it came to a question of they or us, I had no time for deliberation."

And in a letter to his wife Hodson wrote: "It was they or we! and I recommend those who might cavil at my choice to go and catch the next rebels themselves. I must be prepared to have all kinds of bad motives attributed to me."

Hodson had done a deed which startled and wounded many consciences. Critics jumped to the conclusion that if he could bring in the King of Delhi safely, he could have brought in the princes also.

His act has been branded as "a stupid, cold-blooded, threefold murder."

The second in command on that occasion, M'Dowell, says: "The increasing crowd pressed close on the horses of the sowars, and assumed every moment a more hostile appearance.

"'What shall we do with them?' said Hodson to me. 'I think we had better shoot them here; we shall never get them in.'

"So ended the career of the chiefs of the revolt, and of the greatest villains that ever shamed humanity. Before they were shot, Hodson addressed our men, explaining who they were, and why they were to suffer death. The effect was marvellous: the Mussulmans seemed struck with a wholesome idea of retribution, and the Sikhs shouted with delight."

Unless these two English officers were lying, it seems to have been necessary to shoot the princes or they would have been rescued.

The native officers, too, averred that it was a "touch and go" affair, that some of Hodson's own men were wavering, and only prompt and decisive action could have saved them from the menacing crowd.

It is clear that a critic safe at his desk, writing in security years after, is not a fit umpire to decide whether the threats of the crowd made such drastic treatment necessary.

At the same time this impulsive, indignant officer, thinking of the shame of English women, and seeing before him the disgusting authors of that hideous outrage, might have been tempted to make himself "judge, jury and executioner" all in one. If it were so, every sane person would deeply regret that a brave man should have been tempted to take the law into his own hands to his own discredit.

But of what sort of human beings were these shahzadas?

An officer who knew the princes thus describes them:

"On the countenance of these three princes there was not a trace of nobility, either of birth or of mind; but, on the contrary, they were stamped with everything vile, gross, ignoble and sensual; as their education and pursuits had been, so were their features . . . these wretches, with the cold, calm hand of death on them, showed nothing of kingly descent or nobility of heart, their countenances being as forbidding as the despicable passions in which they had indulged could make them."

M'Dowell, who was there, has said, "Our own lives were not worth a moment's purchase"; and Dr. Anderson, surgeon to Hodson's Horse, when asked if he thought the escort were really in any danger, replied, "All I can say is that I dressed the wounds of my own orderly, who came back with his ear half cut off."

Sir Robert Montgomery wrote this note:—

"My dear Hodson,—All honour to you (and to your Horse) for catching the king and slaying his sons. I hope you will bag many more!"

General Wilson in his dispatch of 22nd September writes: "Three of the shahzadas, who are known to have taken a prominent part in the atrocities attending the insurrection, have been this day captured by Captain Hodson and shot on the spot"; and he speaks further of Hodson's good and gallant service.

We must remember, too, that General Wilson had said

to Hodson, "Go at once and take them if possible: but for God's sake do not bring them in, if you can help it; for I should not know what to do with them." General Thomason says: "The only time I ever saw Hodson otherwise than cheery was one day when I dropped in on him and found him 'writing his defence,' as he called it. . . . Poor fellow! he could not understand being called to account for a feat which must ever stand out in history as unbeaten by any Englishman, which is saying a good deal."

We must confess that most officers would have shrunk from the duty of shooting the princes—but they would probably have been butchered themselves, and the princes might have escaped, like the Nana, to do more mischief.

Let us also confess that some of Wilson's officers disapproved of the shooting: Sir Hugh Gough, for instance, regrets that Hodson should have placed himself in a position unworthy of so brave a man. "The wretched princes, cowards and miscreants as they were, deserved their fate, and I have always held that Hodson was right in all he did, only excepting that one false step."

Sir Hugh apparently thought Hodson might have risked the hostility of the crowd: but this—the main point—is incapable of proof either way. It was not Hodson's duty to expose himself and his 50 or 60 sowars—a guard had been left at the tomb—to be overpowered by the fanatic throng and torn to pieces. He may have erred: but a man who had served his country so well, deserves a merciful verdict. Let us end this episode by a quotation from Lord Roberts' *Forty-one Years in India.* He says:—

"I went with many others to see the king; the old man looked most wretched, and as he evidently disliked intensely being stared at by Europeans, I quickly took my departure. On my way back I was rather startled to see the three lifeless bodies of the king's two sons and grandson lying exposed on the stone platform in front of the kotwali. . . . Hodson had shot them with his own hand—an act which, whether necessary or not, has undoubtedly cast a blot on his reputation. . . . My own feeling is one of sorrow that such a brilliant soldier should have laid himself open to so much adverse criticism: moreover, I do not think that, under any circumstances, he should have done the deed himself . . . unless there had been evident signs of an attempt at a rescue."

That is a fair judgment; poor Hodson had suffered in reputation before the siege of Delhi, as we have seen, and suffered unjustly. There is no doubt he was too hasty in temper, and his severe critics have been too hasty in judgment, possibly from the highest motives.

Jealousy still haunted the steps of Hodson: stories of his looting were bruited about and refuted when he had time to get off his horse and explain things. It may be enough for us to remember that when he died Hodson had not enough money left to pay his widow's passage back to England.

We have related in the chapter on Seaton how, after the capture of Delhi, Hodson helped his friend in guarding the convoy and clearing the country of rebels. He then joined Sir Colin Campbell in his march from Cawnpur to Lucknow: and while before the latter place he received notice from home that he had been promoted to major! Some one wondered why Hodson had not been given a V.C. "Why, you fool, he wins it every day of his life," was the reply. But there is a better reason: for the V.C. was not given to the Company's officers until early in 1859.

When Hodson rode seventy miles from Brigadier Seaton to Sir Colin's camp with dispatches, the news went round the 93rd Highlanders like wildfire: for they were all eager to see the man of whom they had heard so much. Mr. Forbes-Mitchell in his interesting *Reminiscences* (Macmillan & Co.) writes: "During the afternoon of the 30th December a man of my company rushed into the tent, calling, 'Come, boys, and see Hodson! He and Sir Colin are in front of the camp: Sir Colin is showing him round, and the smile on the old chief's face shows how he appreciates his companion.'

"I hastened to the front and had a good look at Hodson,

and I could see that he had made a favourable impression on the chief. Little did I then think that in less than three short months I should see Hodson receive his death-wound, and that thirty-five years after I should be one of the few spared to give evidence to save his fair name from undeserved slander."

We will now pass on to the assault on the Begum's Palace before Lucknow on 11th March. Forbes-Mitchell had sent two men back to the breach in the outer wall for some bags of gunpowder to pitch into a dark room which was full of the enemy.

Instead of finding Colonel Napier and his engineers they saw Hodson, who had come with Napier as a volunteer for the storming of the palace. Hodson told the men where to find the powder and came running up, sabre in hand, crying, "Where are the rebels hiding?"

Forbes-Mitchell pointed to the door of the room, and Hodson, shouting, "Come on!" was about to rush in.

The Scot implored him not to do so, saying, "It's certain death; wait for the powder, sir."

Hodson made a step forward, and Forbes-Mitchell put out his hand to seize him by the shoulder, when the major fell back, shot through the chest. Hodson gasped out a few broken words—"Oh! my wife!" but was immediately choked by blood: a dhoolie was near and the wounded man was lifted into it.

"It will thus be seen," the 93rd Highlander writes, "that the assertion made that Major Hodson was looting when he was killed is untrue. That the major was killed through his own rashness cannot be denied."

When Dr. Anderson came, he found the ball had gone through the liver and just avoided the lungs: Hodson's feet and hands were cold, for there was much internal bleeding, and he suffered great pain. At midnight he fell asleep: next morning, after a short rally, the bleeding began again, and when Napier came to see him he spoke and breathed with difficulty.

"I feel that I am dying, Napier. I should like to have seen the end of the campaign, and—to have returned to England to see my friends, but—it has not been permitted. I trust—I trust I have done my duty."

He asked Colonel Napier to give his love to his wife and say his last thoughts were of her: at a quarter past one he whispered, "Oh, God! Oh, what pain!" and in a few minutes died quietly, without a struggle.

On the evening of 12th March his body was buried in the garden of the Martinière at the foot of a clump of bamboos.

Sir Colin Campbell, who attended his funeral in order to show his respect for "one of the most brilliant officers under my command," burst into tears as his remains were being lowered into the grave.

Lord Napier of Magdala, one of Hodson's friends, set a wall round the tomb: and in a letter to Hodson's brother he says, "I am now, as I have always been, fully convinced of his honour and integrity."

In Parliament, Lord Derby and Lord Stanley spoke his praise: but Hodson had not received any reward in his life-time, except the feeling in his mind and conscience that, like his great friend, Sir Henry Lawrence, he had tried to do his duty. Of all the heroes of the Indian Mutiny this soldier's fate is most pathetic, because somehow he made enemies as well as friends: the cruel breath of scandal had poisoned his reputation, and it has been many years before it could be fully proved that the bravest of the brave was not also an unscrupulous thief. Had Hodson been the wicked man some have painted him, he would never have won such noble friends as Seaton and Napier, Gough and Lord Clyde and Sir Henry Lawrence.

By kind permission of Messrs. Blackwood.

CHAPTER V

GENERAL SIR HENRY D. DALY, G.C.B., C.I.E.: THE LEADER OF THE GUIDES

HENRY DERMOT DALY was born near Poona, in the Bombay Presidency, in 1823: his mother was the only child of Captain Hugh M'Intosh of the 16th Light Dragoons, who served in Spain. His father, whose family possessed estates in West Meath and Connaught, joined Wellington's army in the Peninsula, and afterwards served in America and India, and was at the siege of Ghazni.

Henry Daly was sent home to be taken care of by his grandmother, Mrs. M'Intosh, at Newport, Isle of Wight.

In 1840, Daly was given a nomination to the East India Company's service, and was posted to the 1st Bombay Fusiliers (now 1st Dublin Fusiliers), but he did not go round by the Cape as most travellers did in those days. The passengers landed in Gibraltar and saw the mixed races of the East for the first time: the Turk and Christian, Jew and Arab and Moor all jostling in the narrow streets; the Rock, the galleries, the numberless steps, the strange tongues and little monkeys of the Rock and stranger vegetation—all made a clear and distinct impression on the mind of the seventeen-year-old cadet.

At Alexandria they found one British man-of-war riding at anchor at the mouth of the harbour; to prevent the egress of the whole Turkish fleet! Mahomet Ali kindly permitted them to pass through Egypt.

There was but one steamer then on the Nile, "of three

donkey power!" But they reached Cairo at last, and wished to cross the desert to Suez at once. No horses! no camels! But each man was given two donkeys and a boy; at his shouts and shrieks the donkey trotted forward, taking no notice of any vagaries of the rider expressed by whip or rein.

They accomplished the 80 miles under twenty-four hours, and found at Suez a sea-going steamer. Thus they left on the 23rd September and reached Bombay on the 10th October.

Daly's regiment was at Aden, but his father got him attached to a corps at Poona that he might learn Hindustani for the Presidential Examination. So, on landing, Daly started for his father's house at Kirkee, 100 miles from Bombay, where he stayed some months. In May 1841 he returned to Bombay to be examined in colloquial Hindustani, and came out first as Qualified Interpreter.

We may note how men who rose early to distinction in India were often helped to the first steps by knowing how to speak to the natives: those who studied languages while others played games, or shot animals, reaped a rich reward in promotion when their services were really in request.

In his leisure Daly learnt a second language, Mahratti, and in May 1842 passed his examination well. Lady M'Mahon, wife of the commander-in-chief, had laughingly promised that if he passed she would obtain from her husband two months' leave for him to go to the hills.

Next day Daly was sent for by Sir Thomas, who said, "Daly, I have a reward for your industry—you are to be adjutant of an irregular infantry regiment." As he was only an ensign, this appointment changed his pay from 200 to 500 rupees a month.

The Guzerat battalion to which Daly was appointed was stationed at Kaira, where Daly's mother had been buried: thus for months he passed his mother's grave every day.

"My poor mother! I was a child when she died, but

so often had I read her beautiful letters that her memory was a living feeling."

All round Kaira the country was luxuriantly beautiful; trees planted by the conquering Mahommedans rose to a magnificent height, and verdure and culture met the eye on every side. Here began a friendship with a fellow-officer named Anderson which only ended with his death at Multan.

They were in the same regiment and had the same tastes; they used to sit in the cool nights talking of the days to come, of hopes and fears and successes: then Anderson joined Sir Charles Napier's staff in Sind, caught fever and went to England. About this time Daly also was seized with fever and had to sail for England in December 1843, losing a good appointment worth £700 a year.

If he had gone no farther than the Cape or Egypt, he could by the rule of the service have kept his staff appointment: but he preferred to risk that.

Daly travelled with a friend through Sicily, Naples, Leghorn, to France; there he again met Anderson and with him visited his friend's family in Scotland, and thus his days passed joyously. But he began to realise mentally the prophecies of those who had warned him against going home. If he spent his full three years of leave, what would he not miss?

However, in March 1846, during the Sutlej campaign, came an order: "Rejoin your regiment; ordered on service."

In fifteen days he was off and joined his regiment: just then the adjutancy was vacant, and it was offered to him! A few days' delay, and he would have lost a favourable opportunity.

Daly's friend, Anderson, after travelling through Persia, joined him at Karachi, and there they lived in the same house for many months, until Anderson went to Multan.

At Karachi, Anderson introduced Daly to Sir Charles Napier, who was to become a kind friend in the years following.

As Sir Charles left for England in 1847, his soldiers near the pier preserved a sad silence—they all felt his going so much: as he passed down the line of troops where with dropped sword Daly sat on horseback at the end of the formation, Sir Charles recognised the young officer and said: "Ah, Daly, is that you?" then turned his horse and shook him by the hand, with "Good-bye! good luck to you, my boy."

Daly felt that kind words from so great a soldier were to be remembered with pride.

In 1848 the Punjab seemed to be profoundly peaceful: Sir Henry Lawrence had gone to England, leaving his charge to his brother John until Sir Frederick Currie should come to Lahore.

The dewan, or ruler, of the Province of Multan, to the south of the Punjab, was Mulraj; he had succeeded his father, who had amassed great riches and constructed strong fortifications at Multan, a city more than two miles in circumference, having walls of sunburnt bricks forty feet high.

Now this Mulraj came to Lahore and told John Lawrence he wished to resign. No arguments could dissuade him; so the Sikh Durbar, at Currie's request, decided to send two British officers to accept the Dewan's resignation and instal his successor. Vans Agnew and Anderson were chosen to accompany the new governor designate, Sirdar Khan Singh.

The escort consisted of 1400 Sikh infantry, a Gurkha regiment, 700 cavalry and 100 artillerymen with 6 guns.

Anderson, writing to Daly from a boat on the Ravi, says: "The Sirdar is a fine fellow and has lots of pluck . . . to say that I am a lucky fellow, Daly, is less than the truth. I could not in all India have a better appointment given me—I am indebted to John Lawrence and Outram for it."

The poor fellow little thought he was going to his death!

They reached Multan on the 18th April 1848; on the 19th, as they rode back from the fort of which they had taken formal charge, the British officers were attacked in the street and both wounded, Anderson seriously. Mulraj was actually riding by their side at the time and made no effort to protect them. They were brought back to the quarters of their escort, a Mahommedan walled temple outside the walls of Multan.

Next morning their escort deserted them and joined the rioters.

Sirdar Khan Singh and a dozen faithful horsemen alone stood by them; and in the evening Agnew and Anderson were murdered by a fanatical mob. But Agnew had had time to pencil a note to Sir Herbert Edwardes, 90 miles away, and call for help. Edwardes crossed the Indus and besieged Multan and fought and won three battles, until General Whish, with Daly coming later as volunteer, arrived in August 1848 to besiege the fort. Here Daly was under fire from heavy guns for the first time: he tells us the Sikh gunners in Multan were beautiful shots and we lost many men.

"The other day I made a most ludicrous blunder; I have never yet seen the general. I was suggesting some change in our position, when an old gent in a white jacket came up; Major Napier turned to him while I was speaking, and the old gent addressed some question to me, which, deeming irrelevant, or of no importance, compared with Napier's attention, I answered curtly and abruptly.

"Gordon, who was behind, listening, said to me:

"'Daly, you treat the general rather coolly!'

"'Lord! Lord! I thought he was an old sapper sergeant! The general!'"

The siege of Multan cost us in its first stage 17 British officers and many men; General Whish had to raise the siege and ask for reinforcements from Bombay.

Daly served in the final siege as Adjutant of the 1st

Bombay Fusiliers under General Dundas, and was thanked by the Chief Engineer, Major R. Napier, for his zeal and ability.

The Bombay Column reached Multan on Christmas Eve, 1848, and began operations on 27th December by attacking the suburbs, driving the enemy at the point of the bayonet from their strong positions in nullahs, or ravines, orchards and walled gardens.

General Whish had placed his batteries in the first siege nearly 3 miles from the city; now they were 500 yards from the walls.

On 30th December a shell struck the Jumma Musjid, or Great Mosque, and another blew up a powder magazine in the city, killing 1000 men.

On the 1st of January 1849, at 4 p.m., the signal to storm was given, the Fusiliers in advance led by Captain Leith; twice were the besiegers repulsed with heavy loss; Leith and his subaltern Grey were dangerously wounded.

A third time the Fusiliers, furious at the loss of their officers, and raising an Irish yell that dismayed their foes, rushed up to the steep breach, shouting, "Remember Anderson," and won the summit, where Colour-Sergeant Bennett, amid a shower of bullets, planted the British colours, and by sunset the city of Multan was captured. However, there still remained the clearing of many narrow streets, no easy task, and many casualties occurred.

Then our men lay down in square or gateway, food was brought them and chains of double sentries guarded them from surprise.

As they slept, worn out with their exertions, suddenly a terrific explosion at midnight set the houses rocking and falling.

Was it a mine? None knew the cause; but as the men started up from the ground, officers were heard calling to their men: "Be steady, boys, and stand to your arms."

Heart-piercing cries and groans of men buried alive unnerved their comrades in the dark; lanterns showed here and there the glimpse of a ghastly hand or leg protruding from the dusty débris.

In one regiment 10 were killed and 30 injured by falling stones.

Next day a hospital for the wounded and sick of the enemy was organised; there were no outrages and but little looting.

The citadel was on the point of being stormed when Mulraj with 3000 men surrendered. The bodies of Agnew and Anderson were carried with military honours through the sloping breach and buried side by side on the summit of Mulraj's citadel.

After the capture of Multan a garrison of Bombay troops was left there, and the remainder of the force hurried away to join Lord Gough's army of the Punjab which had fought two battles at great cost against the Sikhs (Ramnuggur and Chilianwala) and was in a very critical position.

When the Multan reinforcements arrived, the General was able to fight the battle of Gujerat on 21st February 1849; in this engagement 60,000 men with an immense number of guns were signally defeated; 14,000 laid down their arms, and the Punjab was annexed. We may then conclude that the battle of Gujerat saved India to us in the time of the Mutiny. For the Punjab, under the masterly administration of the Lawrences, Edwardes and Nicholson, became a loyal province of brave and faithful Sikhs, who marched down to Delhi and fought side by side with their British brothers on the Ridge. Lord Gough had led his men well and bravely, but his great losses made the people at home cry for a change of commander; and Sir Charles Napier was appointed, to Daly's great content; yet he felt for the grief and shame which this change would entail upon the old General. At the end of May, Daly received a letter from Sir Henry Lawrence:—

"My dear Sir,—You are nominated to the command of the 1st Cavalry Regiment to be raised at Peshawur.—Simla."

After an expedition through the Kohat Pass under Sir Charles Napier, Daly's regiment now complete, and consisting mostly of Pathans and sons of great chiefs, was stationed at Pashawur, where Daly made friends with Sir Colin Campbell and Colonel Mansfield. Of the latter, Daly says: "He is versatile and accomplished: he will travesty Hamlet, or write you an essay on Military Defence, discuss Montaigne, or play an active part in a joke. There is a wondrous fund of life and humour about him."

In 1852, Daly was again down with fever, and went home by Aden and Trieste. After visiting the Isle of Wight he crossed over to Ireland, where his father was living in a big house dropped down on the edge of a marsh: he found him surrounded by colts and horses, well and merry. No doubt father and son told many a tale of war and peace, comparing experiences of many lands.

When Daly returned to the Isle of Wight he married a girl he had known from boyhood, Susan Kirkpatrick; they settled down at Shanklin. In March 1854 he saw the British fleet sail for the Baltic, Queen Victoria receiving the admiral and his captain on board the *Fairy* before they sailed. By Christmas, 1854, he was again at Bombay, hoping to be sent to the Crimea. But Colonel Mansfield wrote, advising him to stay in India. After some months' service at Karachi as Brigade-Major, Daly received two telegrams from the Viceroy's private secretary—"Go to Agra"; "You are to command Oudh cavalry." So, leaving his wife at Karachi, Daly went by sea to Calcutta; Oudh had been just incorporated in British India; Outram had become Chief Commissioner and had got Lord Dalhousie to send him Daly to command an irregular force of cavalry.

Daly's wife followed with her new baby and met her husband at Cawnpur: hence by dâk ghari (or wooden carriage with venetian blinds) they went to Lucknow; passing many mosques and temples with tall minarets, they went through the Dilkusha Park, full of magnificent mango trees, acacia and banian till they arrived at the flat-roofed house near the river Goomti, which was to be their home.

There, every morning, men and horses from all parts of India came to be selected for the new regiment; the horses, wilder than the men, covered with all sorts of bright saddle-cloths and scarves from nose to saddle-girth.

At the end of January 1857, Mr. Jackson, the chief commissioner, brought two pretty nieces to Lucknow, and the ladies got up a ball for them. Alas! in a few months these pretty girls were seized by mutineers, and no one knows what fate pursued the elder sister, Georgina: Madeline, a bright sunny girl, was held captive in Lucknow city, half-starved, but rescued at last. On Daly's return from chasing an outlaw, he found a telegram from Sir John Lawrence, offering him the command of the Guides in Lumsden's absence. Meanwhile Sir Henry Lawrence had been made chief commissioner at Lucknow and wrote asking Daly to visit him at the Residency.

Mrs. Daly writes: "24th March.—We came in here last night. . . . Sir Henry is a most charming person; his manner so kind, cheerful and affable; it sets every one at his ease . . . but he looks sadly weary . . . he hates state and does not care for driving out with four horses . . . he gives one the feeling of living for another world, he believes that the real life is to come."

Daly had accepted the Guides by Sir Henry's advice, and on 14th April they left Lucknow and proceeded by Cawnpur to Agra.

They reached Delhi on the 18th April, talked to officers about the disaffection of the sepoys, and so on by Umballa to Lahore: Mrs. Daly and her child went to Simla and saw the Lawrence Asylum for children of white soldiers, to which Sir Henry Lawrence had given £10,000 in the last four years.

How nearly they had missed destruction—Lucknow, Cawnpur, Delhi! and only one month more, when the floods of mutiny would rise and swell. Daly had done his

212 miles in twenty-one hours by mail-cart. He says: "Grand doing, wondrous whipping, desperate driving in the dash across narrow bridges of boats—10.30 a.m., found Sir John in his office, no coat on—shirt sleeves tucked up—amidst a heap of papers—we had many familiar chats—he is prompter and harder than Sir Henry . . . has not that generous delicacy of his brother, is energetic, bold and vigilant."

Daly went on to Attock, where the morning air was cool and fresh, and to Mardan, where the Guides were stationed. There he found Battye second in command; Kennedy, commandant of cavalry; Hawes, adjutant; and Stewart, assistant-surgeon.

It was a bare fortnight after he joined the corps that Daly heard the first news of the mutiny at Meerut: an hour afterwards came an order from Colonel Edwardes, for Daly to move with his corps to Noushera. At midnight he arrived, and two hours later received an "urgent" to proceed at once to Attock. Into Attoch galloped Chamberlain, a resolute, thoughtful soldier, with whom Daly had a grave talk.

In his diary Daly writes: "Swam the Indus last night and again to-night; the current was strong, and I found I had no spare strength on my return."

Marching by night they escaped the great heat and dust storms. On the 18th they were overtaken within 4 miles of Pindi by Edwardes, riding in a buggy to visit Sir John Lawrence. Daly jumped in, and they found at 5 a.m. Chamberlain in bed at the door: Sir John, in bed within, called them inside and conversed frankly and cordially.

Telegrams were read and discussed: Meerut with 1600 English troops making no effort to crush the mutineers was the worst item.

The young soldiers resolved on a course of action, without delay or hesitation. Edwardes and Nicholson, Cotton and Chamberlain stoutly told the old and somewhat bewildered General Anson what to do, and he did it!

Chamberlain was to command the movable column—high-minded he, and bold as a lion, knowing what to do. The Guides were to press forward for the scene of action. Daly and other officers could hardly keep awake as they rode;. the men were cheerful and willing. They reached Lahore on the 26th and set about recruiting: many Sikh sirdars offered help: not one noble had joined the rebels. On 1st June they reached Ludhiana and enjoyed splendid quarters at the grand house of Mr. Ricketts, with iced water and cold sheets to lie on!

At Kurnal, on the 6th June, cholera broke out in Daly's corps and attacked three Gurkhas and others; one cook died and five sick men were left behind. Edwardes writes: "We are all delighted at the march the Guides have been making. It is the talk of the border. I hope the men will fill their pockets in the sack of Delhi."

On the 9th of June the Guides joined the Delhi force: a great excitement was caused as they appeared on the Ridge; for their stately height and martial bearing struck all beholders, and they came in as fresh and light as if they had marched but a few miles. Yet the march from Mardan to Delhi, a distance of 580 miles in twenty-two days, at the hottest time of the year, has been considered one of the finest achievements of the war.

They had just completed their last thirty miles to Delhi when a staff officer galloped up. "How soon can you be ready to go into action?" "In half an hour." That was rather sharp work; but some of them had seen hotter work at Multan. Three hours after their arrival they were engaged hand-to-hand with the rebels, and every British officer of the Guides was wounded.

Battye was mortally wounded; Khan Singh Rosa hard hit; Hawes cut across the face with a tulwar; Daly had his horse killed under him and was hit in the leg by a spent bullet; Kennedy was slightly hurt.

Edwardes writes to Daly: "Amidst all our joy at the march and brave deeds of the Guides, we are greatly grieved to hear of poor young Battye's death. He was full of hope and promise, and is indeed a flower fallen from the chaplet of our Indian Army."

Quintin Battye was shot by a sepoy within a couple of yards of him, right through the lower part of the stomach: he had fought gallantly and died a hero's death: he had two other wounds.

Of the commanders-in-chief, General Anson had died on the 27th May; General Sir H. Barnard died on the 5th July; General Reed was invalided on the 17th July; Brigadier-General Archdale Wilson was the fourth to take up the command. Hodson had said in his trenchant way, "We shall never do anything till all these old gentlemen pass away"; and this was the hard truth. War is certainly not a profession for old age: there are only a few elderly men, like Lord Roberts, who maintain the vigour and decision of youth. Within the city were 40,000 sepoys trained to shoot and charge by English officers; on the Ridge there were a little over 6000 on the 8th July. It was no wonder if the besiegers sometimes felt more like being besieged. The Guides were posted on the right of the Ridge, and during the siege had to repel twenty-six separate attacks on this side of our line.

Sir John Lawrence wrote to Daly his congratulations and said he was sending every man they could muster; but Peshawur gave anxiety, and three European regiments had to be held back in the Punjab, for none of the Hindoo corps could be trusted. And in censuring a certain general who had allowed all the Jullundhur rebels to escape, though they had a river to cross, Sir John bitterly remarks: "When I see some of the men we entrust with our troops, I almost think that a curse from the Almighty is on us."

On the 19th July, Daly was very severely wounded; for the enemy, taking advantage of the British being engaged in the front, moved round to our right and rear under cover of thick foliage. It was a surprise; for we had only a portion of the 9th Lancers, the Guides cavalry, and four guns with which to meet the attack.

Sir Hope Grant, who was in command, detached Daly to the left with two of Major Tombs' guns under Lieutenant Hills, a troop of lancers and the Guides cavalry. These quickly found themselves in the presence of a strong force with eight guns in position and a mass of infantry and cavalry. Daly directed Hills to get his guns into action, and with his Guides started off to clear the left flank already threatened by rebel cavalry. They were barely holding their own when Major Tombs came up with the remainder of his guns.

As the enemy began to close on Daly's men in great numbers, Tombs sent word to the Guides: "I must ask you to charge to save my guns." Thereat Daly led the Guides at a gallop, broke through the infantry and reached the enemy's guns.

But Daly got a bullet through his left shoulder which crippled his arm for life. As he lay on the ground in the dusk of evening his men searched for him in vain: until one of the enemy, who had served in the 1st Oudh Irregular Cavalry, came up and pointed to where he lay. Of this native Mrs. Daly had written a year before thus:—

"There is a young Shahzadah (prince) in this regiment, a grandson of Shuja-ul-Mulk. A handsome boy of eighteen, pale and delicate, with beautiful eyes; a very interesting lad. The grandson of a king, he is thankful to be a jemadar (cornet) with £40 a year. Henry has taken quite a fancy to him, has him into the house to talk to him, gives him quinine, etc."

This boy seems to have joined the rebels from compulsion: poor lad, when Delhi was taken, he was probably hanged. A poor return for having saved the life of his former colonel. Yule, who commanded the 9th Lancers, also fell wounded; he was not found, and the rebels prowled round the battlefield during the night and put him and others to death. "Poor Yule," wrote Daly, "he trotted by me as I lay on the ground: it was quite dusk: he ought not to have been killed." For it was pitch dark when our men retired, otherwise we might have taken all their guns; one gun and two carriages were taken the following morning when, at Daly's suggestion, a party was sent out to search the ground.

Major Tombs said the enemy got so close to his guns that they could pick off his gunners as they worked the guns, and rendered it almost impossible to serve them. Daly's charge saved the battery; but it was a desperate charge right up to the enemy's guns. It was then that Hodson took the command of the Guides for five weeks, and was subsequently succeeded by Shebbeare.

On the 23rd of June, the Sikh corps arrived from the Punjab, and soon gave the rebels a specimen of their fighting powers.

On the 24th, the sepoys came out in great force, sniping and occupying gardens: their loss was so immense that they did not fire a shot next day. We found out what was going on in the city by Hodson's spies; there were also native officers who got in for three or four days at a time, and reported how there was dissension amongst the rebels, quarrelling over loot, robbing and fighting and much disease.

John Lawrence sent down in July 200 picked Punjabis, well mounted, under Lieutenant Bailey—a good reinforcement for the Guides.

The new arrivals of mutineers, it was said, were not allowed to enter Delhi until they had shown their prowess outside; thus many of them got cut up by our men and never saw the inside of the city.

On the 6th of July, Daly writes: "Poor General Barnard died yesterday of cholera: no doubt in him, like General Anson, worry and anxiety laid the seeds of the destroyer. He was the gamest, kindest, and kindliest gentleman I ever met. But he had no mind, no resolution save what he got from others. We have lots of good men and true, though heaps of muffs and old women."

When General Reed became commander-in-chief, Chamberlain became the real head: he was for waiting a little and would make no assault until more troops and guns came up: but Daly and Hodson were for immediate assault. Even as early as the 12th June, Wilberforce, Greathed, Maunsell, and Chesney had prepared a plan of assault: but an accident enforced its postponement. Men's spirits rose when they heard that Phillour, Agra, and Allahabad had been saved to the British. Phillour saved by an hour and a half! from this place most of the supplies for the siege were brought. Agra saved by stratagem: Allahabad by the fearlessness and prompt action of Lieutenant Brasyer, a young man who had been promoted from the ranks for his splendid conduct during the Sutlej campaign of 1846. Brasyer with his Sikhs, some invalid Europeans and Eurasians, disarmed just in time the 6th Native Infantry and expelled them from the fort.

These arsenals were of prime importance to the army before Delhi; but they were not saved by the foresight of the Indian Government.

On 15th July, Chamberlain had his arm broken: his tent was next to Daly's, and they were great friends. Daly says of him:

"Chamberlain is of heroic mould, gallant and forward to a fault: tall, with a soldierly gait, fine principles, and an honest heart."

As to the price of provisions in camp, a buggy (covered dog-cart) was sold by auction for a pot of jam. Tins of bacon fetched four rupees a mouthful: grain was cheap, but fowls were unknown.

On the 29th July, Daly reports that a victory at Fattehpur, below Cawnpur, had cheered the men vastly. Havelock had given the perpetrators of the Cawnpur Massacre a lesson in retaliation: Captain Maude, R.A., had shown them what eight guns could do, and if they had had cavalry to follow up the victory, it would have been complete.

The dark days of the Delhi siege were now passing: the men played merry games when they were not fighting; provisions were brought in by willing natives, who no longer thought that the British rule was doomed. Sheep began to be common now, poultry abundant; troops from China were expected.

Then Sir John Lawrence wrote, 25th July, to say he was sending down upwards of 4000 good and reliable troops, of whom 1200 might be Europeans: he dare not send more from the Punjab.

Edwardes writes 27th July: ". . . Our fancy man, Nicholson, has gone down from this side with his shirt sleeves up; so I hope this is the beginning of the end and Delhi will be assailed and squashed . . . Your native soldiers never write to their fathers, mothers, or sweethearts—and a precious row I hear at my house about it. If you would only send up some captured trophy, you would do good."

On the 4th August a letter from Havelock told how he, with the 78th Highlanders, 1st Madras Fusiliers, and Sikh corps, had beaten the rebels in three battles and taken all their guns: the Nana's residence had been destroyed, and Havelock was now on his way to relieve Lucknow. The Cawnpur tragedy, however, and the death of Sir Henry Lawrence sadly dashed the growing feeling of optimism among the men.

There were many deserters from Delhi, but the wretches were plundered by the villagers: there remained now in the city only about 15,000 effectives.

On the 14th August the Punjab column came in with Nicholson, and the men began to talk about the assault being near.

On the 26th of August the camp heard that the siege train of heavy guns was not far off: the rebels, too, in Delhi heard this, and sent out 6000 men and eighteen guns to intercept it.

This rebel force was attacked by Nicholson, who took

twelve guns and thoroughly routed the enemy. But Major Lumsden's brother was killed, a fine gallant young soldier. Daly says:

"Nicholson accomplished what I believe no other man here would have done, and this is the impression of every man here—he is able, vigorous, and brave as a lion: so many guns were not taken even on the 8th June."

On the 4th September the siege train came safely in.

Two batteries were erected on the night of the 7th, 600 yards from the walls: the enemy were simply astonished when the firing began, and cavalry came out to take the guns, but a shower of grape quelled them.

By the 9th, ten heavy guns were at work tearing down the defences. Baird-Smith and Alexander Taylor had worked hard to reconnoitre and choose the ground and get the batteries erected. On the 11th September, Taylor called on Daly, saying all his work was over: one battery was to open 160 yards from the wall, and it was fully expected that Pandy would get a surprise packet.

On the 12th, there was a meeting at the General's to hear the plan of assault: three columns, led by Nicholson, Campbell, and Jones, were to assail the walls and bastions. Great regret was felt this day at Fagan being shot as he sat on the trail of his gun watching the effect of the shot for which he had just laid. He was an officer respected by all, cheerful, hardy, heroic: if all the heroes of this war were mentioned in any detail, many volumes could be filled. In fact it was no ordinary war: the supreme danger put every one on his mettle, and brought out unsuspected heroism.

Up to now Daly's wound had prevented him from taking active duty; he was able neither to ride nor run, but he watched the assault from the top of Hindu Rao's house.

From this coign of vantage he could not see the breach, but on the 15th could see our mortars shelling the palace, and a long train of fugitives leaving the city, and of animals laden with spoil: the mortal wound of General Nicholson and the broken arm of Greathed gave him great sorrow.

The Guides during the assault were in action on the right: in this young Murray fell, shot through the chest.

On the 22nd, Daly reports: "The old king is in our hands . . . some Sikh sowars of Hodson's came on the sons, not knowing who they were: they plundered them and took no heed of their capture. We shall get them yet, I hope; that Mirza Moghul must be hanged as high as possible."

On the 27th, Daly was staying with Major Coke in a palace in Delhi, being unable yet to ride. He saw the vision of a looted city: doors and windows broken; no life, save it were that of a derelict cat furtively peeping round the corner of some old bedding or furniture; the citizens either fled or roaming about with hungry eyes—no beggars these, you see, but haply nobles of yesterday and Indian ladies delicately bred, carrying their jewels about their person, sorely famished for want of food and clothing.

The rebels had made a stiff resistance in places up to a certain point: but you could still see sand-bags piled up across some narrow street, guns loaded and placed in position, but not fired: for there were none to lead them. In October, Daly was granted a few weeks' leave to Simla: thence he wrote letters criticising Lord Canning for his delay in helping Lucknow, Lord Palmerston for babbling in debate instead of acting at once; for even 500 men sent to Bombay might have done real good. "Sir John is most kind, most cordial . . . nevertheless he is not to me what Sir Henry was. I had a *love* for him exceeding even the admiration and reverence in which I held his lofty character and great attainments; as Lumsden said, "It is much, Daly, to have known one such man."

The Guides left Delhi on the 18th December 1857: at Peshawur they were given a great reception; the troops of the Peshawur cantonment were paraded under General Sir Sydney Cotton to welcome them; and a royal salute was fired on their approaching the parade-ground. Of the 19 officers who had been attached to the Guides during the siege, 3 were killed, 1 died, and 8 were wounded; of the last, 1 was wounded six times, 1 four times, and 2 twice. Amongst the men there were 313 casualties out of 550. Twenty-five native officers and men of the Guides received the order of merit; 54 were specially mentioned and promoted on the spot for gallantry in the field. The Court of Directors addressed the Government of India in August 1858 and dwelt on their wonderful march to Delhi, their services before the rebels, and their singular fidelity, as shown by the fact that out of 800 men not one deserted to the enemy.

Daly then spent his few weeks' leave at Simla with his wife, who had been left there in May, when the station was entirely without defence. Mrs. Daly and children started for England in January 1858; being accompanied by her husband as far as the Indus, where they took boat. Then Daly returned by mail-cart to Lahore, wishing he could join Sir Colin Campbell in clearing the rebels from Oudh.

He thought how that General, strong in artillery, cavalry, and prestige, would sweep the cowed sepoys before him into their forests and deserts: while he remembered how the rebels fought in the beginning of the Mutiny, sure of victory with their thousands against our poor hundreds, buoyed up by prophecies and elate with the first massacres of helpless women and children, they fought then for our extermination, now they knew the tables were turned.

Daly's old friend Mansfield was now chief of the staff to Sir Colin, and while Daly was visiting Edwardes at Peshawur, a telegram came: "The chief of the staff inquires where is Captain Daly?" The reply was, "At Peshawur, waiting for orders."

On the 23rd of February, Daly underwent a painful operation in order to recover the use of his left shoulder. Two days later came another telegram: "Ask Daly to come to Lucknow and live here with me—he may be in time for the struggle, if he makes haste." With Sir John Lawrence's permission Daly set off at once.

He found his friend and Sir Colin at the Martinière, a

college founded by General Martino, a French officer in the King of Oudh's service. Daly met with a hearty reception; Sir Colin being markedly cordial.

On the 12th of March, Daly reports: "The cordon is closing in on every side. Poor Hodson was badly wounded in the city, whither he had gone to speak to Colonel Napier. Mansfield wishes me to assume command of his corps, which is stronger than any here."

It chanced that Daly was at Bank's house when Hodson was brought in on a dhoolie: he fetched a doctor and helped to attend on him.

"Hodson was a wondrous compound," writes Daly; "ability high and strong; power and energy, physical and mental. His ability had received more culture than fell to the most of us. For he did not quit England till twenty-three years of age, when he was a B.A. and somewhat distinguished at Cambridge."

Hodson's Horse numbered just then 750 sabres with 7 officers: many of the men had never bestrode a pony before leaving the Punjab. Mr. Montgomery and the Rajah of Jhind had raised some troops at first: the men, bumping through the camp at Delhi on the big obstinate horses, were nick-named "The Plungers": they quickly learned to ride, however.

Soon after taking this command Daly had to ride out with the 7th Hussars and attack a mass of rebels collected at Nawabgunge: there was much single-combat fighting: some of the Irregular Horse, who had been attracted to the corps by hopes of plunder there, were found unfit for the service.

Daly discovered a good deal of loot gathered by his men and tried to equalise profits: for while some looted, others were busy fighting and got nothing: all had had much rough work to do; long patrols, hard gallops, difficult reconnaissances. They were a strange medley of men from the plough, robbers from the hills and border, nobles' sons and small land proprietors. They all needed to be managed with tact and genial talks rather than scoldings and severity.

After the relief of the Lucknow garrison, the city looked like Delhi after its capture: camp followers filled courts and houses, plundering and searching: dead bodies of sepoys, carcases of animals clogged the narrow passages and rendered the air nauseous and unhealthy. Most of the inhabitants had fled, but they had left behind the tokens of their skill in preparing for resistance in loop-holed walls and timber-built barricades; batteries and trenches in many places intersected each other. The Residency was a heap of ruins, pillars were broken, rooms were choked with the débris of fallen ceilings and roofs: the church was levelled to its foundations. Much of this damage was done during the rebel tenure of the place, after Sir Colin relieved and withdrew the garrison in November 1857.

It is said that one officer of the 13th Native Infantry, Sergeant Macpherson, had been accidentally left behind in the Residency: he had fallen asleep in a dark corner, and had not heard the warning cries of those about to leave. When he awoke, several hours after the garrison and all had gone, he was amazed by the strange silence, and jumped up to find he was alone in the fort and buildings. Quickly he ran in the dark down the lonely streets, through deserted palaces and courtyards, meeting none; till he reached the Secundra Bagh, where, to his delight, he came upon the rear-guard of the Highlanders: he was known afterwards as "Sleepy Sandy." Captain Waterman was also left asleep in the Residency: he too contrived to join the rear-guard in safety; but the fright so affected his nerves that he was never the same man afterwards.

Daly reports on the 25th March having led a pursuit of rebels through the long grass, which was still full of armed men who started up like hares, but fired ere they bolted.

All round Lucknow for miles the country was covered with dead carcases — men, horses, camels, bullocks, and donkeys lay about everywhere, and swarms of flies pestered the soldiers, settled on their plates of rice in black masses, and were a veritable torment as well as danger.

When the men struck their tents at night, the flies were sleeping in the roofs; so when the tents were rolled up the flies got crushed and killed: on pitching the tents again, the sweepers of each company were called to collect the dead flies; and from one tent there were carried out five large basketfuls of dead flies.

As most of the rebels from Lucknow had retreated north-west towards Bareilly and Rohilkhand, Daly's force was sent to cut them off. The country soon became difficult with belts of trees and thick underwood, very unfitted for movements of cavalry: also there were rivers and canals to cross, corn-fields and jungle full of desperadoes. At every minute men were being fired at and often wounded by these skulking sepoys. Outram had been attacking Moosabagh at the end of March, and one morning Daly received a note from the brigadier:—

"Come up as quick as you can and order a squadron of your regiment to follow: the rebels are streaming out of the fort."

The 1st Sikh Cavalry helped in the pursuit, but the officer in command, Wale, a gallant, cheery officer, was shot dead after cutting up a large number of the rebels.

One thing which Daly noticed was the small attention given to the war by the husbandmen: only for an hour or two were the sheaves of corn deserted; the bullocks were seen to be yoked to the well, ready to turn the wheel for irrigating the soil; the cucumber seed was sown, and all was carried on as if war were like a passing shower that need not interfere with the more important operations of life and nature.

It was reported that a large force, chiefly consisting of Lucknow rebels, was collected in Bareilly under Khan Bahadur Khan, who had issued orders to his men for their guidance in these words:—

"Do not attempt to meet the regular columns of the infidels, because they are superior to you in discipline and have more guns: but watch their movements; guard all the ghâts on the rivers; stop their supplies; cut up their piquets; keep constantly hanging about their camps; give them no rest." Wise words no doubt! the old Mahratta tactics!

The Indian who had organised the Mutiny from the first, the Moulvi, the man who had proclaimed the restoration of the King of Delhi, was going about Rohilkhand with a large force of cavalry. He and the Nana were together at Mohumdee, and John Jones of the 60th had attacked them with great spirit: but the British forces were not numerous enough to meet the enemy at so many scattered points.

In June 1858, Daly was ordered to accompany General Hope Grant in an attack on rebel rajahs, etc., at Nawabgunge, whose forces numbered some 12,000 men with ten guns, for many rajahs who wished to help the British were being compelled to join the rebels, or have their estates plundered. In one fight Daly made three charges and captured nearly all the enemy's guns.

Some men were beginning to blame Sir Colin for not clearing the country more successfully; but Daly always spoke well of the old General: "To my mind, knowing how terribly he is enveloped in ancient prejudices, it is wonderful to contemplate what he has done: . . . Sir Colin would have been happier in command of a brigade: . . . all in all, he has done well. The peerage will bring him no satisfaction: he said to me one day very mournfully, I am wifeless and childless—a lone man. The rank and wealth and honours which would have gladdened those dear to me, come to me when all who loved me in my youth are gone. Ah! Daly, I have suffered poverty and hardship. For years, for the want of a few hundred pounds, I was compelled to live in the West Indies, unable to purchase the promotion I craved for, and which younger men about me were getting as they wished: those were bitter days."

GENERAL SIR HENRY D. DALY

The richest men in high command, and old generals not superseded! One wonders how victory ever came to grace our arms!

Forbes-Mitchell of the 93rd Highlanders describes vividly the charge made by 360 Rohilla Ghâzis or religious fanatics at the battle of Bareilly.

Sir Colin saw them coming and called out, "Ghâzis, Ghâzis! close up the ranks! beyonet them as they come on."

The Ghâzis charged in blind fury, with their round shields on their left arms, their bodies bent low, waving their tulwars over their heads, throwing themselves under the bayonets and cutting at the men's legs. Colonel Cameron of the 42nd was pulled from his horse by a Ghâzi; but his life was saved by Colour-Sergeant Gardener, who got hold of a tulwar and cut off the Ghâzi's head. The struggle was short: every one of these brave Ghâzis was killed; 133 lay in one circle in front of the colours of the 42nd.

Sir Colin caught the glint of the eye of one Ghâzi as he lay on the ground, shamming dead. "Bayonet that man!" he cried. But the Ghâzi was enveloped in a thick quilted tunic of green silk, and the blunt Enfield bayonet could not pierce it: the Highlander would have been cut down, had not a sikh Sirdar rushed to his aid and cut off the Ghâzi's head with one sweep of his keen tulwar. These fanatics made no bones of killing non-combatants. Mr. Ross, chaplain of the 42nd, all unarmed, was seen to be running for his life, dodging round camels and bullocks, with a rebel sowar after him: at last, seeing some Highlanders, he rushed to them breathless for protection, stammering out, "Ninety-third! shoot that impertinent fellow!" The sowar was shot down and his Reverence escaped with his life. In these fights with the rebels we often hear of the marvellous keen blade of the tulwar. There were three brothers named Ready in the 93rd, two of whom were cloven in twain by tulwars in the assault on the Begum's palace at Lucknow. David, the remaining brother, dropped his bayonet, seized a tulwar and in a kind of frenzy swung it round with terrible effect, cutting off men's heads as if they had been mere heads of cabbage. The curve of this tulwar was about a quarter circle, and it was sharper than most razors. The wonder is how such tempered steel could be wrought with such simple appliances.

Some of the rajahs were faithful to us in heart, and some also in deed. The Rajah of Bulrampur was most steadfast—one wonders if his loyalty was ever repaid! His elephants were sent to Sekrova for the transport of the ladies and children to Lucknow, and with him took refuge all the officers and civilians who were saved. In 1858 his position became difficult, when the sepoys from Delhi and Lucknow were thronging the towns and hiding in the fields. Nevertheless the Rajah held his ground, though his chief town had been plundered in December. The English General had congratulated him on his staunchness, and all the small rajahs were then seeking his influence, which he was proud to use in their behalf. An amnesty had been proclaimed, but the sepoys did not know about it, and kept skulking in the forests, spiritless and hopeless, but armed. So the Oudh rebellion was slowly dying out: but in Central India, Tantia Topee was still giving much trouble.

In April 1859, Daly handed over his command to Hughes and sailed for England. Thus ends the story of Daly as far as the Mutiny is concerned. But he returned to India and did good service in Central India as political agent: in his political career he showed great sympathy with the native princes. To commemorate his work the chiefs of Central India subscribed towards a handsome building named "The Daly College"; and Lord Dufferin in opening the hall spoke of Sir Henry Daly as one of the most accomplished and high-minded public servants in India—the champion and friend of the Native Princes and the Native States.

He died at Ryde in July 1895, having lived a life of action throughout: a grand horseman, a lover of dogs and horses, he had also a rich fund of Irish humour and delighted in telling and hearing anecdotes. He was well read in history and biography and was deeply religious at heart.

"To my mind," he says, "there is no religion so holy as that of helping and comforting our fellow-creatures."

Sir Neville Chamberlain wrote: "The natives were at once led to trust him; they accepted him as a just judge and as a friend who would do his best to see that their rights were respected by the State."

Thus the dashing cavalry officer developed into a healer of discord and a saviour of his Indian brethren.

Life of Sir H. Daly, by kind permission of Colonel Daly and Mr. Murray.

CHAPTER VI

FIELD-MARSHAL LORD ROBERTS OF KANDAHAR, V.C., THE YOUNG GUNNER

FREDERICK SLEIGH ROBERTS was born at Cawnpur in September 1832. His father was General Sir Abraham Roberts, G.C.B., and his mother Isabella, daughter of Major Abraham Bunbury, 62nd Foot.

Lord Roberts was educated at Eton, Sandhurst, and Addiscombe, and began his army career as 2nd Lieutenant in the Bengal Artillery.

On the 20th February 1852 he set sail from Southampton for Calcutta. On landing at Alexandria they were hurried on board a large mastless canal boat, and towed up the Mah'moudieh canal for ten hours. At Atfieh on the Nile they changed into a steamer and reached Cairo in sixteen hours.

After two days' stay at Shepperd's Hotel they set out across the desert in a sort of bathing-machine, holding six persons and drawn by four mules. Roberts' companions were five cadets, who made the journey of eighteen hours fairly tolerable; the baggage was carried on camels together with the mails and the coal for the Red Sea steamers.

At Madras young Roberts went ashore to see Addiscombe friends, who were excited at the prospect of a war in Burma: the transports being actually then in the Madras roads, ready to start for Rangoon.

As an artilleryman Roberts made his way to Dum-Dum, and found only one other subaltern at mess, as the rest had embarked for Burma. The life here was extremely dull and the sanitary arrangements defective: the adjutant-bird, highly protected, was their most efficient scavenger.

Calcutta, lighted at night by smoky oil-lamps, had no great attractions. The senior officers took little notice of the juniors, and Roberts began to wish he had never come, especially when he heard that nearly every officer in the Bengal Artillery had served over fifteen years as a subaltern. In those days a subaltern could not return home under ten years, and there was no going to the hills: Roberts felt home-sick, and wrote to his father, asking him to get him sent to Burma. His father replied that when he got command of the Peshawur division he would send for him. That gave him some hope at last: and in August he got his marching orders to proceed to the north-west of India.

From Calcutta to Benares, Roberts travelled in a barge towed by a steamer, taking nearly a month to accomplish it, owing to sandbanks.

From Benares to Allahabad he rode on a horse-dâk; and on arrival was most kindly and hospitably received by Mr. Lowther, the commissioner.

His next halt was Cawnpur, his birthplace. Here he stayed a few days, and then proceeded to Meerut, where he first saw the far-famed Bengal Horse Artillery, and said to himself, "I, too, will be a horse-gunner some day." For the men were the pick of the Company's service, their physique magnificent and their uniform handsome.

From Meerut to Peshawur, 600 miles, Roberts had to ride in a palanquin, for there were no more metalled roads. Eight men divided into reliefs of four carried the traveller through the night hours; chattering coolies bore the baggage, and a torch-bearer lighted the path in front with stinking oil.

Three miles an hour was a good pace, and dâk-bungalows, or rest-houses, were erected by Government at intervals. Here you could get a bath and shake off some of the dust;

the khansameh, or host, would chase a thin chicken round the yard and serve it up to you in twenty minutes.

In November, Roberts reached Peshawur, his journey having occupied nearly three months, whereas now it only takes three days.

Sir Abraham Roberts, then in his sixty-ninth year, had just been appointed to command the division with temporary rank of major-general. He was considered a young and active officer for this responsible post.

Father and son had met very seldom before, but they soon made great friends, and the younger man learnt much about the Afghans which came in very usefully when, twenty-five years later, he commanded in Afghanistan.

The Peshawur station included Attock, Rawal Pindi, and Jhelum, as well as the hill-station of Murree. As the frontier was so near, piquets were posted on all the roads leading to the hills, and every house was guarded by a well-paid watchman belonging to a robber tribe; it was dangerous to ride beyond the line of sentries, and officers with ladies had been attacked.

Here Roberts first began to enjoy life in India: there was plenty of adventure, and he made good friends. The two senior officers on Sir Abraham's staff were Lieutenant Norman and Lieutenant Lumsden; both destined to carve out distinguished careers. Like Seaton, Roberts was horrified by having to attend a flogging parade: fifty lashes were given to two fine young men in the Horse Artillery for selling their kits. After the flogging they were sent to prison.

No sooner were they released than they repeated the offence, probably as a way of showing their resentment at their ignominious treatment. A second time they were tried by court-martial and sentenced to be flogged. A parade was ordered. One man was stripped to the waist and tied to the wheel of a gun. The sentence was read out, a trumpeter stood ready with a whip, when the officer in command, instead of ordering him to begin, addressed the prisoners kindly, and said if they would promise not to commit the same offence again he would remit the flogging. They did promise, and they kept their word. Not only that, but they both became good, steady, and loyal soldiers.

In 1853, Sir Abraham, being sick, was advised to retire and go to England.

In 1854, Roberts got six months' leave and travelled in Cashmere—that hilly country of gardens and woods. So productive is the soil that if you cut a stick and put it in the ground, it will strike root and bear blossom or fruit in a short time: and yet Britain sold this country for three-quarters of a million pounds! As Lord Roberts remarks, it would have made the most perfect sanatorium for our troops, and from its height would have proved invaluable as a colony for cultivation. As it was, the people were poor and miserable; for the Mahommedan peasants were ground down by Hindu rulers who seized all their earnings.

In November, Roberts, to his great delight, was given "his jacket," and was to remain at Peshawur, the young officer's paradise. Nearly all the men in his troop were big Irishmen, fine riders, as they needed to be when the horses were half wild and full of spirit.

In 1855, when at Simla, Roberts lunched with Colonel Becher, the quartermaster-general, who was so taken by the young artilleryman that he said, "Roberts, I should like to have you some day in my department." This meant a staff appointment, and Roberts felt supremely happy.

In the winter he sometimes rode over to Mardan, where Harry Lumsden and his Guides were stationed. There he had many a gallop after the hawks, hunting the aubara; it was here he became so fine a rider.

The brigadier at Peshawur, Sydney Cotton, who did not believe in mere drill, kept them alive with field days, preparing for real war. And yet this able officer had not yet got the command of a battalion, though he had been forty-three years in the army and was over sixty.

That indeed was the age of elderly generals and irresolution, and of discontented subalterns. But Roberts was vastly surprised to hear in 1856 that he had been selected with Lumsden to assist in the survey of Cashmere. It was just what he wished; but soon his hopes were dashed by the Governor-General refusing to confirm his appointment, because he had not passed the prescribed examination in Hindustani.

It was then May, and the half-yearly examination was to be in July. Roberts set to work, engaged a good munshi, or instructor, and studied Indian literature from morning to night. Roberts passed the examination and won the appointment.

A year later, 1857, Roberts went with General Reed on a tour of inspection as staff officer. Jhelum was first visited; the sepoys seemed contented and respectful, and were praised highly by their British officers.

They went on to Rawal Pindi, where Sir John Lawrence offered Roberts a post in the Public Works Department. Roberts, not wishing to leave the army, respectfully declined the offer.

One day in April, Roberts was surveying in the hills at Cherat and found to his surprise a camp pitched close to his tent: Lieutenant-Colonel John Nicholson was on his tour of inspection. Roberts had heard this officer spoken of with admiration, and even awe, in the Punjab: he had just left Bunnu, a wild district which he had ruled as a semi-divine hero.

"I have never seen anyone like him," says Lord Roberts. "He was the beau-ideal of a soldier and a gentleman. His appearance was distinguished and commanding, with a sense of power about him which to my mind was the result of his having passed so much of his life amongst wild and lawless tribesmen."

During March and April rumours came to Peshawur of mysterious chupatties or unleavened cakes being sent about as a token of some change coming. Then they heard of the outbreak at Berhampur and of Mangal Pandy at Barrackpur; of the disbanding of two regiments and the refusal of the cartridges. Yet these warnings passed unheeded: it seemed a partial trouble; no one believed the whole Bengal army could mutiny; the officers were positive that their own men were trustworthy.

At Peshawur the officers were sitting at mess on the evening of the 11th May, when the telegraph signaller rushed in, breathless with excitement, a telegram in his hand, which proved to be a message from Delhi "to all stations in the Punjab," stating that a serious outbreak had occurred at Meerut, and that the mutineers had reached Delhi, which was in revolt.

Instantly Colonel Davidson rose and said, "We must let the Commissioner and the General know at once: and, gentlemen, not a word to anyone!"

Davidson then hurried off to Sir Herbert Edwardes, who, with his deputy, Nicholson, lived close by: Edwardes, on hearing the news, drove to the General's house, while Nicholson came to the mess-room.

He too pointed out the importance of keeping the news from the native troops. There were at Peshawur 5000 native soldiers and 2000 European troops: in the city were 50,000 natives who might rise and help the native regiments.

Fortunately there were some good men and true at Peshawur, and not all elderly. Edwardes was thirty-seven, Nicholson thirty-five; Neville Chamberlain, the commandant of the Punjab Frontier Force, was thirty-seven.

At once Edwardes seized all native correspondence at the post office: letters and papers, when examined, showed that every native regiment was involved in the rebellion.

On Tuesday the 12th May, Roberts was summoned to a military council at General Reed's house, when important resolutions were passed.

Edwardes and Nicholson said, "The only chance of keeping the Punjab and frontier quiet is to trust the chiefs and people: get them to join us against the Hindustanis."

It sounded perilous; but the thing was done, because no one knew the frontier so well as these two men: and our trust was not misplaced: the men of the north-west responded loyally to our demand. General Reed was to join the chief commissioner at Pindi, leaving Cotton at Peshawur; a movable column was to be organised and the Hindu regiments were to be scattered as much as possible. Punjab infantry was to replace the sepoys in the fort of Attock, where there was a magazine: Attock also covered the passage of the Indus.

Chamberlain was nominated to the command of the movable column, and, to Roberts' delight and surprise, he offered to take him as his staff officer. This column was to move on every point in the Punjab where open mutiny required to be put down by force.

We will now relate in more detail the occurrences which happened at Meerut, and which startled every mess in India.

The Meerut division was commanded by General Hewitt, an officer of fifty-eight years' service; the station of Meerut by Brigadier Archdale Wilson, of the Bengal Artillery. The garrison consisted of the 6th Dragoon Guards, a troop of Horse Artillery, a battery of Field Artillery, the 1st battalion 60th Rifles, and three native corps, the 3rd Light Cavalry and the 11th and 20th Native Infantry. Towards the end of April 85 men of the 3rd refused to take their cartridges. A general court-martial was held on them: the court was composed of 6 Mahommedans and 9 Hindus.

On the 8th May they were tried, found guilty, and sentenced to imprisonment with hard labour for ten years.

Next morning there was a parade of the whole garrison, and the sentence of the court was read out to the men.

The 85 troopers were then stripped of their uniform, shackled, and marched down the line to the gaol: as each passed along, he called on his comrades to rescue him, but none stirred.

The commander-in-chief wrote his disapproval of the riveting of the fetters in the presence of the men. "This must have stung the brigade to the quick: the consigning the prisoners to gaol with no other than a native guard over them was folly that is inconceivable."

But General Hewitt at any other time would have been applauded for his attempt to make the punishment as marked and public as possible. In order to understand what followed, a few words on the plan of the cantonment will be necessary.

Meerut is placed between the rivers Ganges and Jumna, in a great plain stretching from the lower spurs of the Himalaya towards Central India. It is one of the oldest stations in India, and was at first a frontier post. The barracks of the English troops fronted north, to a fine parade-ground; on the right were the Bengal Artillery, the Rifles were in the centre, and the 6th Dragoon Guards on the left. Behind the men's lines came the hospital, gymnasium, canteens, etc., and then the officers' quarters.

To the rear of these was a wide road named the Mall, and behind this the ground was occupied by houses and bazaars.

The native lines, being about a mile to the rear, fronted west, and were built for seven battalions: the officers' bungalows, each surrounded by its compound, were only separated by a street from the great Suddur bazaar. Between these northern and western lines were hundreds of fine buildings, residences of civil and military functionaries, public gardens and colleges and squares, all shaded by well-grown trees.

The native walled city lay a little south of the whole: the English church was to the north of the British lines.

How sudden and unexpected the rising of the sepoys was we can see by the accounts given. For instance, the wife of Captain Muter of the 60th King's Royal Rifles had driven to church on Sunday evening—the day following the manacling of the sepoys; it was about 6.30 p.m. and near sunset. As this lady sat in her carriage, awaiting her husband and listening for the sound of the band, a gentleman approached and said:

"You need not be alarmed, but an outbreak has taken place requiring the presence of the troops: so there will be no service this evening." But the lady waited until 7 p.m., and as no congregation came Mrs. Muter ordered the syce to turn the carriage and go home.

Then she saw the native lines in a blaze and heard a dull sound of voices. Men were running in all directions, and when Mrs. Muter reached home the servants advised her to hide in the compound as her life was in danger. Fortunately a message came from Captain Muter, bidding her take refuge in the quarter-guard.

The chaplain of Meerut tells us he was about to start with his wife for evening service, when the ayah, or native nurse, besought her mistress to stay indoors—"Mem-sahib, there will be a fight with sepoys."

They took the two children in the carriage with them at the wife's request; but before the church was reached sounds of musketry were heard from the native lines. As the chaplain arrived at the church enclosure, the buglers of the 60th Rifles were sounding the "alarm" and the "assembly."

The men had been standing unarmed, as for church, in groups on the parade-ground, ready to "fall in"; when, on hearing the "alarm," they rushed tumultuously towards their barrack-rooms and armed themselves. This the rank and file did instantly without waiting for any order. Then Captain Muter, seeing no superior officer near, dispatched Lieutenant Austin and a company of riflemen to secure the treasury, which contained several lakhs of rupees to pay the troops withal. This was perhaps the best service done that day; but Captain Muter's prompt action escaped at first the notice of his superiors and of historians.[1]

The mutineers had made their plans craftily; they meant to begin their outbreak when the white soldiers were in church and unarmed. But they were not aware that, owing to the greater heat, the evening church parade had

[1] *My Recollections of the Sepoy Revolt*, by Mrs. Muter. John Long.

been altered to 7, instead of 6.30 p.m. In consequence of this, as the mutineers galloped down the 60th Rifle lines they came upon the men fully armed and falling in.

So they reined in, turned and galloped to the gaol, broke into the cells, and released the 85 prisoners, their comrades, and all the other prisoners, being about 1200.

Meanwhile the two native regiments were firing at random on their own parade-ground and burning their barracks. Their British officers hurried to the lines and tried to restore order, but in vain. The sepoys, whom they had believed to be as true as steel, warned them to be off, or they would be shot. These sepoys would not willingly kill their own officers. But when Colonel Finnis began to exhort the men of his own regiment, the 11th, to be true to their salt, some of the 20th came up and riddled his body with bullets: he fell from his horse and was slashed to pieces.

Besides Colonel Finnis, seven officers, three officers' wives, some children, and many European men, women, and children were massacred.

We must remember that it was dark almost directly after the first outbreak. General Hewitt at first drew up his men on the parade-ground, and sent a few rounds of grape into a humming mass which could be heard on his left: the hum ceased and all was still. Then the men were ordered to the Mall—the wide street behind their lines—and there they bivouacked, while a chain of sentries was thrown around the European lines.

But the bazaars and private houses were all night in the hands of thousands of Goojurs (plundering gipsies) and badmashes (rogues): terrible were the experiences of many during those hours of riot and massacre.

Next morning soldiers were sent round to collect the dead. Ladies, lying naked on the ground, hacked with sabres and almost unrecognisable, were picked up from smoking ruins or from streets and ditches.

In some houses a pile of dying and dead had been half covered with broken furniture. Everything had been rifled and stolen ; not by the sepoys, for they had ridden away to Delhi, but by the released gaol-birds and bad men from the lowest classes of the native city.

But the outrages and murders were not confined to Meerut: many villages around were looted, their inhabitants lay dead in the streets, and a few women and children only remained to weep over their loss and the absence of British justice and compassion. For this was really not an Indian revolt, but a sepoy mutiny.

We have mentioned the alacrity of Captain Muter in saving the treasury: there were other officers whom the suddenness of the shock had not paralysed. Colonel Custance, commanding the Carabineers, had ordered out his men and sent to ask for instructions at the first sound of firing. After a long delay, General Hewitt ordered him to proceed to a gaol some miles away: thus the services of this regiment were rendered useless to the rest of the troops. Fortunately the Carabineers lost their way in the dark and returned to the parade-ground, where they found the 60th Rifles and artillery waiting to be attacked.

Brigadier Wilson advised the General to return to the Mall, in case the mutineers had moved round to attack the European quarters. The General assented; and as the troops went south they saw lurid pillars of fire rising from many a bungalow. Search was made, but no sepoy could be found: for they had all gone off to Delhi. Captain Rosser of the Carabineers offered to lead a squadron of his regiment along the Delhi road, but his suggestion was not accepted. General Hewitt would hazard nothing, and do nothing on so dark a night. So the scum of the city were left to burn and rob and murder whom they would.

Even the commissioner, Mr. Greathed, knew nothing about the revolt until a howling mob surrounded his house; though an officer of the 3rd Native Cavalry had dropped hints, and an Afghan pensioner had given a warning of what might follow.

First he and the ladies sought refuge on the roof; but

when torches were applied, the roof was no longer safe. The servants, as so often elsewhere, were true, and helped to conceal them in the garden; while the rabble were led away on a false scent to an outhouse.

But many wives were slaughtered without mercy, chiefly by the butchers of the city: these ruffians went to Delhi next day, but had the audacity to return to Meerut, and were promptly hanged. One Mahommedan gentleman in the city sheltered two families at great danger to himself, and many families owed their lives to the devotion of their servants.

Thus, we see, the sepoys were permitted to get off clear, owing perhaps to the darkness falling so suddenly: but it is difficult to learn why no attempt was made next day to punish the marauders.

The commissioner in his report writes: "It is a marvellous thing that with the dreadful proof of the night's work in every direction, though groups of savages were actually seen gloating over the mangled and mutilated remains of the victims, the column did not take immediate vengeance on the Suddur bazaar, crowded as the whole place was with wretches hardly concealing their satisfaction." All that the authorities did was to collect and place in the theatre the bodies of the murdered men and women.

It must be recorded that the sepoys of the 11th Native Infantry behaved better than the others: some of them saw their own officers to a place of safety; and two sepoys escorted two ladies with their children to the Carabineer barracks. This regiment had joined the rebels unwillingly. It was reported afterwards that Lieutenant Gough had been told on the 9th May, the day before the outbreak, by a Hindoo native officer, that the men had determined to rescue their comrades.

Gough went at once to his commanding officer, Lieutenant-Colonel C. Smyth, and reported what he had heard. "Pooh! pooh! my boy, quite ridiculous! You must not believe anything so monstrous," said his colonel.

Later in the day Gough met Brigadier Wilson and told him about the warning: the brigadier smiled contemptuously, and naturally the young lieutenant said no more about it.

But next day, Sunday, the same native officer, attended by two troopers, galloped to Gough's house, crying, "The *hala* (row) has begun, and the sepoys are firing on their officers."

Gough mounted his horse and, accompanied by these three cavalry soldiers, rode to the native parade-ground, where he found the sepoys yelling and dancing as if possessed, while the glare from the burning huts shed a lurid light on faces working with the wildest frenzy. The three troopers persuaded Gough to ride off before he was shot; on his way to the European lines he came upon an enormous crowd of townsfolk, armed with swords and sticks, who tried to stop him. Through these the four men charged at a gallop, and his native friends did not leave him till he was near the artillery mess. Then they made him a respectful salaam and rode away to join the mutineers. Gough could never hear what became of these good friends.

Meanwhile the mutineers galloped along the flat road between Meerut and Delhi, 35 miles; and very glad they must have been when they saw the minarets of the Jami Masjid glittering in the rays of the morning sun. Once or twice they had drawn rein to listen for the sound of galloping; but, strange to say, no horses of the Carabineers were on their heels that night. So they reached the waters of the Jamnah, crossed noisily by the bridge of boats, cut down the toll-keeper on the farther side, set fire to the toll-house and slew the one Englishman whom they met.

They then made the best of their way to the great gate, Chandni Chouk, facing the principal street in Delhi, Silver Street, where the jewellery shops occupied one side, with gaily painted varandahs and Moslem arcades and porticoes, while handsome trees rose with shady foliage on the other.

Soon they came to an open square, in the centre of which was a tank where they stopped to water their horses. But the horses sniffed and turned up their lips in disgust; for already they smelt the blood of white men and women; though that tank was fated to receive many more bodies of butchered women and children in a few hours.

The buniahs, or shopkeepers, looked drowsily forth as the sepoy troopers trotted by on their way to the lofty walls enclosing the king's palace; soon bastions and embrasures and loop-holes met their gaze, and slabs of red sandstone that faced the walls made all seem stony and massive.

There were two Englishmen who held official positions of importance inside the palace walls—Mr. Fraser, the commissioner of Delhi, and Captain Douglas, the commandant of the Palace Guards.

The sepoys were making no little noise in the outer courtyard, demanding admittance: the aged king heard the noise and sent for Captain Douglas to ask why they were there. Captain Douglas said, "I know not, sir, but I will go and see." For he thought the sight of a British uniform would frighten these men away. The king timidly begged him not to expose himself to danger, for the sepoys looked wild and ferocious: the king's physician added his entreaties to those of his master.

Douglas, then, did not go down to the courtyard, but entered the balcony, and looking down, ordered the troopers to be off, as their presence there was an annoyance to the king. Thereat the sepoys laughed scornfully and spat towards him. They again demanded to be admitted: it happened that the sepoys on duty at the palace belonged to the 38th Native Infantry, and were disloyal to the core. When, therefore, the troopers of the 3rd Cavalry attempted to force an entrance into the palace, they admitted them as comrades. Once admitted, the mutineers made short work of all white men and women they found within.

They cut down Mr. Fraser, Captain Douglas, the chaplain, Mr. Jennings, his daughter, and Miss Clifford, a young lady staying with them. Mr. Hutchinson, the collector, was also found and killed. The orderlies of the king did not look on and wonder; they joined in the savage fray with fiendish delight.

The fury soon spread from the palace to the mercantile quarter: the Delhi bank was attacked first; though its manager, Mr. Beresford, defended it for some time most gallantly, he was slain and the bank was stormed and gutted: the English church and every house occupied by Christian or Eurasian were attacked and rifled: no quarter was given to age or sex.

About two miles from the city the cantonments for the native brigade were situated on the Ridge, commanded by Brigadier Graves.

The morning parade was over and the officers had just finished breakfast when the startling news came that the native troops at Meerut had mutinied and that the 3rd Cavalry had galloped across the bridge. The officers here, too, never dreamed of suspecting the loyalty of their men: there were quartered on the Ridge the 38th, the 54th, the 74th Native Infantry and a battery of native artillery. Thinking the Meerut affair a mere local disturbance, and that the Carabineers would soon be coming up, the officers of the 54th Native Infantry led their men towards the city gates.

Even as they went some men of the 38th, at the main-guard, when ordered to fire on the Meerut troopers who were seen approaching, refused with insulting expressions; while the 54th fired, some in the air, and some on their own officers. Colonel Ripley was wounded; Smith, Burrowes, Edwards and Waterfield were shot dead.

The colonel of the 74th then addressed his men, reminded them of their past good conduct and called upon volunteers to come with him to the Kashmir gate. The sepoys stepped forward and their officers trusted their loyalty until they came near the main-guard, when they met some men of the 54th Native Infantry who were returning from the city. These exchanged words with the 74th, but just then the din within the walls of the city became overwhelming: the sepoys evidently dreaded lest the English troops might have arrived from Meerut, and they thought it wise to await events.

So they halted all unbidden, silent and glum, at the main-guard. Then suddenly an awful explosion within the city shook the foundations of the main-guard. We must see what had caused this explosion. In the middle of Delhi, not far from the palace, stood the great magazine, full of powder, shells and cartridges.

On that morning the following officers were within: Lieutenant George Willoughby, in charge of it; Lieutenant Forrest and Lieutenant Raynor; Conductors Buckley, Shaw, Scully and Crow; Sergeants Edwards and Stewart.

About 8 a.m. Sir Theophilus Metcalfe, the magistrate of Delhi, came to the magazine to say that mutineers were crossing the river and to ask for two guns to defend the bridge.

When, later, Willoughby learnt that the mutineers had been admitted into the palace, he began to act. The magazine should be defended! All gates were closed and barred and barricaded, guns were set at salient points, charged with grape.

But all the under-workers in the magazine were natives! However, arms were served out to them under Willoughby's eye. He knew them well, they had been good comrades for some years; but he did not like the look in the men's faces as they took the weapons of offence.

However, there was no alternative to be taken; but in case things should call for desperate remedies, these few Englishmen had a train laid to the powder magazine.

They had scarcely finished this job when there was a great beating on the gate; sepoys had come to demand the surrender of the magazine in the name of the King of Delhi. No reply was returned to this. Then the sepoys sent down scaling ladders: no sooner were they fixed than all the native workers clambered up to the top of the wall and joined the rebels from Meerut amid loud cries of joy.

For some time a fire was kept up by the few defenders: Forrest and Buckley had been wounded, and death seemed to be certain when Willoughby gave the order to fire the train.

Scully, who fired the train, and four of his comrades vanished into space. Willoughby and Forrest succeeded in reaching the Kashmir gate; Raynor and Buckley somehow escaped with their lives; for no native was just then in a position to stop them, seeing that several hundreds of them had been blown to atoms or mutilated beyond recognition. The loud report, the concussion, the breaking of windows in the palace warned the king and his creatures that they had now to deal with a race who were most formidable when the odds were against them. It was about 4 p.m. when this explosion startled the sepoys near the main-guard; at first they were frightened, but on second thoughts it occurred to them that their friends were succeeding. The sepoys of the 38th Native Infantry raised their muskets and fired a volley into the group of officers near them. Gordon, the field-officer of the day, fell dead from his horse without a groan. Smith and Reveley of the 74th met the same fate.

The only way of escape for the rest was to dash through the embrasure in the bastion, cross the courtyard of the main-guard, then drop thirty feet into the ditch: after that they must climb the opposite scarp, gain the glacis and so plunge into the jungle beyond.

But as the unwounded officers ran, they heard the cries of women from the windows of the upper room and, staying their course, beckoned to them to come down.

Then hurrying all to the opposite embrasure, the officers fastened their belts together, and so helped the women and children to descend into the ditch. With difficulty they got the fugitives up the scarp; when this was done they pressed on into the jungle. But whither for safety?

Neither the cantonments nor the Metcalfe house were safe refuges. So away they ran, throwing away every ornament, crouching in lanes, fording rivulets, hiding in woods and hollows, carrying the little ones, falling and fainting from hunger and thirst and fatigue, racked by fever and sun-scorched, sometimes insulted by villagers, sometimes helped by kind Hindoos or loyal Mussulmans, until at length a small number of them reached Meerut, or Karnul, exhausted and half dead.

Meanwhile, in the city of Delhi some fifty Europeans and Eurasians had taken refuge in a strongly-built house and barricaded themselves in. But defence was impossible for long; the house was stormed and the defenders were dragged to the palace and thrust into an underground chamber, without windows. Here they stewed for five days; then they were led out into the courtyard and stabbed or shot. Their bodies were taken away in carts and pitched into the muddy-flowing Jamnah. After that 16th of May there were no more Christians left in Delhi.

The poor old king, Bahadur Shah, had been compelled to assume a power and responsibility for which he was unfitted by age; but his young queen was ambitious for her handsome son, and urged the old king to be brave. The cry was raised, "Restore the Mogul Empire": and the Hindoos believed that their patriotism would secure them happiness here and hereafter. But they had not reckoned on the feeling of the Mahommedans and the Maratha princes: as it was, the princes of Central India thought it wiser to remain safe under British suzerainty rather than help the Hindoo sepoys to restore a dynasty which they themselves had thrown in the dust.

As the sepoys of Meerut had risen in revolt half an hour too soon, to find our men arming instead of dozing in church; so the mutiny of all Bengal had exploded several days before the date fixed in their councils, namely, Sunday the 31st of May.

Though General Hewitt, the man of indecisive counsel, did not know it till long after, he had by his manacling of the 85 men put a match to the local explosion too soon, and robbed the sepoy mutiny of half its force.

If Lord Canning did not at first recognise the gravity of the crisis, surrounded as he was by men who trusted the sepoy, yet when he heard of the seizure of Delhi, he resolutely set to work to find means of defence. He telegraphed to Lord Elphinstone at Bombay to hasten the return of troops from Persia; he bade the commander-in-chief make short work of Delhi; he gave Sir John Lawrence full powers to act for the best; he sent for a regiment from Rangoon and two regiments from Madras.

We can now return to the doings of Roberts in the North-West, having given the reader more facts about the beginnings of the Mutiny than any officers in the Punjab had had time to discover and appreciate.

On the 15th May, Brigadier Chamberlain and Roberts arrived at Rawal Pindi where Sir John Lawrence then was. Edwardes was summoned from Peshawur and consulted about the wisdom of raising levies of frontier men, as Nicholson and he had advised. Roberts, during the six days' stay at Pindi, was occupied mainly in copying letters and telegrams, and thus learnt all that was going on in the Punjab. He was struck by Sir John's correct judgment and by his intimate knowledge of details: he was very anxious to collect all the wives and children of soldiers and civilians into fortified stations, and gave orders accordingly. Brigadier F. Brind, who commanded at Sealkot, objected to withdraw the families of his troops to Lahore on the ground that such a measure would show a want of confidence in the sepoys!

But John Lawrence insisted on the removal, and soon after this Brind's troops mutinied, and he was shot down by one of his own orderlies.

It was reported that at Peshawur disaffection was

spreading, English troops being few, now that the Guides and 27th Foot had been withdrawn. Nicholson felt this in the great reluctance of the frontier men to enlist.

Hence it was resolved to disarm the native regiments, as has been described. The native officers were loud in expressing their conviction that the disarming was wholly uncalled for, but Brigadier Cotton soothed their hurt feelings and excepted the 21st Native Infantry and two regiments of irregular cavalry. For in the cavalry both horses and arms were the property of the horsemen, and it was believed that the interest men had in the service would keep them loyal. The subahdar-major of the 51st had arranged for a revolt on the 22nd May; but this disarming spoilt his game, for when he deserted with 250 men to the Afridis and brought no muskets with him, the Afridis seized the deserters and made them over to the British authorities. What was the use of 250 hungry men who could not shoot? So the subahdar-major was hanged in front of the whole garrison.

On the 24th May, as Chamberlain and Roberts and Lieutenant Walker were riding in mail-carts to Wazirabad, the road being broken in parts, the drivers raced with one another and lashed their half-wild ponies in reckless rivalry.

One of the reins became unbuckled, and as long as the driver did not notice it, all went well; but at last he saw what had happened, lost his head and tugged at the one rein. The ponies went off the road, then came a crash, an upset and a scattering of bodies in collision.

It might have been of serious moment, but fortunately nobody was much hurt. At Wazirabad it was Roberts' duty to call upon the senior officer, Colonel Campbell, and inform him that Brigadier Chamberlain had come to take over the command of the movable column.

The colonel was lying on his bed and never moved when Roberts entered. "I am not aware," he said coldly, "that the title of brigadier carries with it any military rank. I understand that Chamberlain is only a lieutenant-colonel, whereas I hold the rank of colonel in Her Majesty's Army : I must therefore decline to acknowledge Brigadier Chamberlain as my senior officer." There was another reason for a soreness in the fact that Chamberlain was a servant of "John Company": for a certain jealousy always existed between the two services. However, things were smoothed down, and at last Campbell, who had only been a short time in India, consented to serve under the brigadier.

On the 31st May they reached Lahore and found it in a state of excitement: ladies and children had been hurried thither for security: in the city there were 100,000 people, mostly Sikhs and Mahommedans.

The headquarters of the Lahore division was Mian Mir, five miles away. Here there were four native regiments and very few European troops. Brigadier Corbett was in command, full of vigour, mentally and physically. The chief civil officer was Robert Montgomery, a man of a short and portly figure, gentle and benevolent, but able and of strong character. Montgomery, on hearing the Meerut news, got Corbett to call a parade, had guns loaded with grape, and then Corbett ordered, "Pile arms!"

Sullenly the men threw down their arms, for the guns faced them as they were ordered to change front to the rear.

So Lahore was saved by the decision of a soldier and a civilian, and when the movable column came in on the 2nd of June, it was hailed with delight by all the Europeans, for they had been living in great anxiety. But the 35th Native Infantry, which accompanied the column, seemed capable of mutiny. Chamberlain was employing spies to watch them, and one night—it was the 8th June—one of these spies awoke Roberts with the news that the 35th intended to revolt at daybreak, and that some of them had already loaded their muskets.

At once the men were ordered to fall in, their arms were

examined, and two muskets were found loaded. The two sepoys implicated were lodged promptly in the police station.

A drum-head court-martial was called, of native officers drawn from Coke's Rifles just arrived, composed chiefly of Sikhs and Pathans. The prisoners were found guilty of mutiny and sentenced to death. Chamberlain decided they should be blown away from guns in the presence of their comrades, in order to strike fear into the rest. A parade was at once ordered. Three sides of a square were made up of the troops; on the fourth side were two guns.

As the prisoners were being brought to the parade, one of them asked Roberts, "Are we to be blown from guns, sahib?" "Yes," was his reply.

As they were being bound to the guns, one requested that some rupees he had on his person might be saved for his relations.

"It is too late," answered the brigadier. The word of command was given, off went the guns, and two human beings were no more.

The sepoys in the ranks looked startled, but more crest-fallen than horrified. The scene they had witnessed did not deter them from escaping to Delhi. Coke's Pathans, however, in the 1st Punjab Infantry, were well known for loyalty and bravery, for they loved their leader, and he cared for them as a father.

During the operations in the Kohat Pass in 1850, several of the men were killed and wounded. Among the latter was a Pathan named Mahomed Gul. He was shot in two places through the body, and as Coke sat by him while he was dying, he said, with a smile on his face: "Sahib, I am happy; but promise me one thing—don't let my old mother want. I leave her to your care."

War mingles together in strange contrast the hideous and the beautiful, the savage and the gentle elements of human nature. The politician, sitting quietly at home, votes for war too often without realising all the horrors and sorrows which the soldier feels very keenly. The movable column remained some days at Lahore: many places claimed its presence, being more or less disturbed.

At Ferozepur the native regiments had broken out on the 13th May, and tried to seize the arsenal, which was the largest in Upper India.

Multan seemed very unsettled, but fortunately was in the hands of an able and experienced officer, Major Crauford Chamberlain. Multan was a very important post, as it commanded our communications with Southern India and the sea. Chamberlain found out that his irregular cavalry were loyal, the artillery doubtful, the infantry ready to mutiny at any time.

Night after night sepoys, disguised, tried to persuade the cavalry to join them. A plot was raised to murder Chamberlain and his family. This plot was frustrated by men of the cavalry, but it became clear that the only remedy was to disarm. But how? there were only a few European troops near, gunners.

At this juncture Sir John Lawrence sent the 2nd Punjab Infantry, and Major Hughes, on his own initiative, sent from Asia the 1st Punjab Cavalry. At 4 a.m. next morning the native regiments were marched out and halted at about a quarter of a mile away; then the Punjab troops moved quietly between them and their lines, thus cutting them off from their ammunition. A selected body of Sikhs was told off to cut down the native gunners if they refused to obey orders; then Major Chamberlain rode up to the Native Infantry regiments, and explained why he was going to disarm them.

"Pile arms!" the word of command rang out sharply.

But a sepoy of the 62nd shouted, "Don't give up your arms: fight for them." Then Lieutenant Thomson, the adjutant of the regiment, seized the rebel by the throat, and wrestling, threw him heavily to the ground.

The order was repeated, and this time it was obeyed.

The Punjab troops remained on the parade-ground until the arms had been collected and carted off to the fort.

Lord Roberts says: "It was a most critical time, and enough credit has never been given to Major Crauford Chamberlain. He was very insufficiently rewarded for this timely act of heroism."

Umritsar, being a very important place and on the road to Jullundur, where the authorities had taken no steps to disarm the sepoys, was the next point on which the column moved. It was reached on the 11th June.

There a telegram came to Neville Chamberlain, offering him the adjutant-generalship of the army, since Colonel Chester had been killed before Delhi. He accepted the offer, and Roberts was eager to go with him, but he was told he must remain with the column. Roberts' first disappointment was tempered by content when he heard that Chamberlain's successor was to be his friend, John Nicholson.

Then the column moved on Jullundur, which was reached on 20th June. The place was in great confusion, the sepoys having been allowed to break into the treasury, plunder right and left, and then get safely over the wide Sutlej in a ferry: all this for fear of hurting the feelings of the sepoy! The commissioner, Major Edward Lake, who had repeatedly urged Brigadier Johnstone to deprive the sepoys of their arms, now accepted the offer of the Rajah of Kapurthala to garrison Jullundur with his own troops. And all through the Mutiny the Rajah loyally stood by us and kept the road open, though his general took the opportunity at this moment to show his scorn of our feebleness. But how he was reproved and humiliated by John Nicholson we may defer to another chapter.

On taking over command, Nicholson organised a part of his force into a small flying column ready to go anywhere at a moment's notice. Though Nicholson had spent most of his time as a civilian of the frontier, yet Lord Roberts says,

"He was a born commander, and this was felt by every officer and man with the column before he had been amongst them many days." The column left Jullundur on the 24th June, and next morning it was thought necessary to disarm the 35th, as the native troops were too numerous. It was a great surprise to both British officers and men when the 35th were suddenly brought to face the unlimbered guns, and the order to "pile arms" was given.

However, the commandant, Major Younghusband, looked relieved and was heard to murmur, "Thank God!" He had been with this regiment thirty-three years, through the first Afghan War and at Sale's defence of Jallalabad: but perhaps he was now glad they were to be saved from disgracing the regiment. The sepoys threw down muskets and belts without a murmur. Then came the turn of the 33rd regiment: but the British officers in this case protested, for they believed in the loyalty of their men. Colonel Sandeman had been with them thirty-two years, and had commanded them through the Sutlej campaign. They were all his pride! On hearing the general's order, he exclaimed: "What! disarm my regiment! I will answer with my life for the loyalty of every man!"

"On my repeating the order," says Lord Roberts, "the poor old fellow burst into tears."

Shortly after this, when Roberts was in the Philour fort with Nicholson, the telegraph-signaller gave him a copy of a message from Sir Henry Barnard, the new commander-in-chief, asking that all artillery officers not doing regimental duty might be sent to Delhi.

Roberts realised that his hopes might now be fulfilled, though he did not like the idea of leaving Nicholson. Nicholson, too, did not wish to lose Roberts; but as soon as his deputy could be found, Roberts started for Delhi.

In a mail-cart he rattled across the bridge of boats for Ludhiana, and while he rested there in the hospitable bungalow of the deputy commissioner, George Ricketts, he heard the tale of what the mutineers had done after breaking away from Jullundur. Ricketts, it appears, had gallantly opposed the rebels with a few men of the 4th Sikhs and two guns: he could have stopped their crossing the Sutlej if the Jullundur force had given any help.

It was ever the same tale—heroic deeds done by many; foolish, ignorant or lazy counsels followed by a few, and mostly by elderly men, who ought to have retired and gone home before they were worn out.

On the 27th June, Roberts reached Umballa: on driving to the dâk-bungalow he found it crowded with officers, all eager to get on to Delhi. When Roberts, the young gunner, expressed his intention of going on at once, they laughed heartily, "Not a seat to be had, my boy."

But Roberts had a little talk with the postmaster; and he said, "Make friends with Mr. Douglas Forsyth, the deputy commissioner."

The result was that Roberts got a seat on an extra cart laden with small-arm ammunition. He was allowed to take two other men with him. These were Captain Law, who was killed on the 23rd July, after having greatly distinguished himself, and Lieutenant Packe, lamed for life before he had been forty-eight hours in Delhi.

Through Kurnal they drove and Panipat, where there was a strong force of Patiala and Jhind troops: but at Alipur, twelve miles from Delhi, the driver pulled up, shook his head and vowed he dared go no farther.

So they took the mail-cart ponies, for a consideration, and rode on; they heard the boom of guns and saw several dead bodies, already as dry as mummies. They had not the vaguest notion where the Ridge was, but luckily hit on the right road, got safely through the piquets and lay down for a long sleep.

In part, from Lord Roberts' *Forty-one Years in India*, by kind permission of the author.

CHAPTER VII

LORD ROBERTS AND DELHI: IN THE GREAT SIEGE

BEFORE recounting what befell Roberts at Delhi, we must give a short account of the events which preceded his arrival.

Sir Henry Barnard had succeeded General Anson on the 26th May, but he was an utter stranger to India and had only been in the country a few weeks. He had been chief of the staff in the Crimea and was an energetic officer. He knew how the critics had blamed Anson for not attacking Delhi off-hand without guns or soldiers, and he recognised the difficulties of his position. Not waiting for his siege-train, he set out from Kurnal on the 27th May and reached Alipur on the 6th of June.

Meanwhile, the Meerut force had been ordered to take the field, and when they came to a village close to the Hindun River on 30th May, a vedette reported that the enemy were coming in strength. The Rifles crossed the Hindun suspension-bridge and attacked, while the Carabineers forded the stream and turned the enemy's left. Seven hundred British soldiers attacked and defeated seven times their number, captured 5 guns and only lost 1 officer and 10 men.

The intense heat prevented them from following up the victory: so it was that next day the sepoys returned to the battleground.

They took up position on a ridge to the right of the Hindun, and opened fire from their guns on Wilson's force: for two hours there was an artillery duel, then Wilson ordered a general advance. The sepoys retreated with their guns to Delhi, our men being too prostrated by the heat to follow.

Among our wounded was an ensign of the 60th Rifles, a boy named Napier, full of gallantry and vigour and much liked by his men. He had been hit in the leg, and when he was brought into camp, it was amputated. When the operation was over, the poor boy murmured to himself, "I shall never lead the Rifles again—never lead the Rifles again." He felt his career was so soon over and he must leave the regiment he loved.

There was some satisfaction felt in camp that the Meerut Brigade had, after all, been the first to retaliate on the sepoys.

The next day, 1st June, Wilson's force was strengthened by the arrival of the 2nd Gurkhas, 500 strong, commanded by Major Charles Reid.

On the 7th of June this force joined Barnard's at Alipur, and the Meerut men were loudly cheered as they marched into camp with the captured guns.

On the 8th, Hodson reported that the rebels were in force half-way between Alipur and Delhi, at Badli-ki-Serai, where many large houses and walled gardens supplied good means of defence. The rebels' guns were of heavier calibre than ours, and it became necessary to charge them. When Hope Grant with cavalry and horse artillery appeared on their rear, they fell back. The Lancers kept charging the retreating sepoys till they abandoned their guns and retired in disorder within the walls of the city.

Then Barnard turned to the Ridge overlooking Delhi, drove away the rebels posted there and encamped on a favourable position on the top. The rebels had lost 350 men, 26 guns and ammunition.

The next day the Guides, led by Colonel Daly, were cheered on their arrival. Let us give a few words about the Ridge and the city of Delhi

The Ridge rises 60 feet above the city; its left rested on the Jumna, generally too deep to ford, and wide enough to prevent our being enfiladed. On the right of the Ridge, bazaars, buildings, woods and garden walls afforded cover to the enemy when they made a sortie: the Ridge at this end was about 1200 yards from the city walls, at the Flagstaff Tower about a mile a half, and at the end near the river nearly two miles and a half.

The Flagstaff Tower in the centre of the Ridge was the general rendezvous for the sick and wounded; the tower was 150 feet high, approached by a winding staircase. The main piquet was established at Hindu Rao's house, a large stone building once belonging to a Mahratta prince. The city is surrounded on three sides by a lofty stone wall, five and a half miles long; the fourth side, two miles long, is covered by the river, and bridges and ferries gave the besieged means of procuring food from the country. The walls were mounted with 114 pieces of heavy artillery supplied with plenty of ammunition. In addition, the garrison of 40,000 sepoys had 60 pieces of field artillery, and their gunners had been trained by the English.

To meet this force the English general had at this time a little more than 3000 soldiers, some Gurkhas and the Guides with 22 field guns. On our rear was a canal with a splendid supply of water.

As we have stated before, the Guides had to fight on their first afternoon and lost Quintin Battye close up to the walls.

Lord Roberts says: "I spent a few hours with him on my way to Delhi, and I remember how his handsome face glowed when he talked of the opportunities for distinguishing themselves in store for the Guides. Proud of his regiment, and beloved by his men, who were captivated by his many soldierly qualities, he had every prospect before him of a splendid career, but he was destined to fall in his first fight. He was curiously fond of quotations, and his last words were 'Dulce et decorum est pro patriâ mori.'"

The few heavy guns were placed in position on the Ridge, but were soon found inferior to those of the enemy; ammunition, too, was so scarce that a reward was offered for every 24-pounder shot which could be picked up.

The rebels thought that they could persuade the Gurkhas to join them, and as the latter advanced they called out, "We are not firing; we want to speak to you, we want you to join us." The little, stubborn Gurkhas replied: "Oh yes, we are coming, wait a bit—we are coming to you."

Then, when within twenty paces of the sepoys they fired a volley and killed nearly 30 of them.

Every day attacks were made, sometimes on Hindu Rao's house in the centre of our position, sometimes on the Flagstaff Tower: on one occasion they crept up in a fog and nearly succeeded in taking the guns.

With so few men the work grew very toilsome, and the men were seldom off duty. General Barnard felt that his force was unequal to the task of taking Delhi by a *coup de main*, but he had written instructions from Lord Canning and Sir John Lawrence to make short work of Delhi. Those gentlemen, at a convenient distance, were sure that the city could be taken.

The perplexed general consulted his Engineers, and three of them drew up a plan of assault for the 12th June. The young officers were Greathed, Maunsell, and Chesney of the Engineers and Hodson of Hodson's Horse.

The scheme was kept so secret that even the commanding Engineer was not informed of it. Practically the whole force was to be engaged, divided into three columns—one to enter by the Kashmir gate, the second by the Lahore gate and the third was to attempt an escalade.

The troops assembled between one and two in the morning, but Brigadier Graves with his 300 Europeans was absent, and the assault was postponed.

Graves had received no written orders, and as the verbal

notice sent him would have involved his leaving the Flagstaff piquet in the hands of natives, he wisely declined to act upon it. All military critics agree in thinking this a merciful relief: the attacking party must have been repulsed; a repulse would have involved the destruction of the besieging force, and perhaps the loss of all India. This critical position was the result of civilians at a distance presuming to dictate to the general on the spot.

On the 14th June, General Reed arrived on the Ridge to assume command: for a time, owing to ill-health, he did not supersede Barnard.

But the question of a *coup de main* was discussed in Reed's tent for several days, and finally the senior officers voted against it.

On the 17th, we had to attack in two columns to prevent the enemy from completing a battery that would enfilade our position. Tombs had two horses killed under him, making five so far; he drove the rebels away and blew up a mosque which they had seized.

On the 18th, the rebels were reinforced by more mutineers with six guns: they celebrated the event by a fierce attack on our rear, which nearly succeeded; but Reed, the Gurkhas and 60th Rifles held on steadily and saved the situation.

The 23rd June, the hundredth anniversary of Plassey, was celebrated by a desperate attempt on the part of the sepoys to get their prophecy fulfilled: thousands rushed against a mere handful of men on our right; again Reed stood firm. After the 23rd the attacks were pushed home with less vigour.

On the 24th, Neville Chamberlain came from the Punjab to take the post of adjutant-general, and reinforcements raised our strength to 6600 men. On the 28th June, Roberts had come tired into camp and thrown himself down in the tent of his friend Norman.

Next morning he awoke, full of questions and eager to hear everything. He found that Harry Tombs, of the

Bengal Horse Artillery, was so far the hero of the hour—a handsome man and a thorough soldier.

After visiting the tents of Edwin Johnson and General Chamberlain and Sir Henry Barnard, to find out what his post was to be, it was settled Roberts was to be D.A.Q.M.G. with the artillery; which was the post he desired.

Once more the question of an assault was opened; the date 3rd July was fixed for it, and at 3 a.m. there arrived on the Ridge Baird-Smith, of the Engineers, destined to take a foremost place in the taking of Delhi.

But the assault had again to be postponed, as the enemy had planned a sortie for that day. On the 5th July, General Barnard was attacked by cholera and General Reed assumed command.

On the 9th July the rebels sent the regiment which had mutinied at Bareilly through the right of the British camp, by the rear; as their uniform was the same as our irregulars they were allowed to pass unchallenged. They had put to flight some young soldiers of the Carabineers when James Hills, one of the most daring soldiers in the world (later Sir James Hills-Johns) ordered out his two guns for action. But the enemy were upon him and he had no time to fire; so, determined at all costs to stop the foe and give his men time to load and fire a round of grape, he charged the head of the column single-handed, cutting down the leading men, and slashing at the second: then two sepoys rode at him and rolled over his horse. It had been raining heavily and Hills wore his cloak, which saved his life, for it was cut through in many places, as were his jacket and shirt! To pick himself up and find his sword was the work of a moment: but three men now came on, two mounted; the first sowar he shot, the second he ran through the body after seizing his lance in his left hand, the third man, on foot, wrenched his sword from him: twice his pistol missed fire, then Hills closed with the man and hit him in the face with his fists, but fell and would have been killed after all, had not Tombs cut his way through the enemy and, seeing

Hills' danger, taken a shot with his pistol at thirty yards, which killed the native trooper.

In spite of Hills' heroic attempt, his men never got a chance to fire a round; for the sepoys were amongst them, and riding off to the native horse artillery called upon the men to join them and bring away the guns. But the native artillerymen loyally refused to join the rebels: by this time the camp was roused and the irregulars rode off with some loss. Tombs and Hills both received the Victoria Cross for their gallantry.

At this moment Roberts was standing by his tent, watching with the interest of an owner his horses which had just arrived from Philour. They were crossing the bridge over the canal at the rear of the camp when the retiring sowars galloped over the bridge, not waiting to secure any loot. Roberts' servants had marched 200 miles through a disturbed country and had brought horses and baggage in good order.

Through the siege these servants behaved admirably: the khitmatgar never failed to bring his food under the hottest fire, and the syces (grooms) seemed quite indifferent to all risks wherever duty called them.

On the 14th July the rebels came out in great numbers, and had to be driven back: on reaching a wall lined with sepoys the troops stopped short, and Chamberlain, calling them to follow him, jumped his horse over the wall and got a ball in his shoulder. But the men did follow and the rebels were slowly driven away. Roberts was with two advanced guns on the grand trunk road: the subaltern was severely wounded, and a fine young sergeant being shot through the leg was being carried to a hut near the road.

"Don't put him in there," shouted Roberts, "he will be left behind."

Roberts, in the bursting of shells and crashing of branches, was not heard. The poor fellow was left in the hut, and, like other wounded, was murdered by the rebels.

As Roberts was helping the drivers to keep the gun-horses quiet (several of them being wounded) he suddenly felt a tremendous blow on the back, which made him faint and sick: he just managed to stick on his saddle until he got back to camp. He had been hit close to the spine by a bullet: his life was saved by the fact that a leather pouch for caps, which he usually wore in front, had slipped round; the bullet passed through this first and so was prevented from penetrating very far into his body.

This wound kept Roberts on the sick-list for a fortnight: his tent, fortunately, was pitched close to that of Campbell Brown, surgeon to the artillery. The medical officers were clever and worked hard; but the wounded had little shelter from sun and rain: chloroform was unknown, and antiseptics not yet heard of, and scarcely a single amputation case survived.

It was difficult to get rid of the festering carcases of animals; some were buried, and jackals and adjutants worked without pay to remove the nuisance. On the 17th July, General Reed's health broke down and he had to leave the camp. General Wilson assumed command, and was earnestly requested by Baird-Smith not to think of raising the siege: " We must maintain the grip we now have on Delhi." In consequence General Wilson ordered up a siege-train from Ferozepur; he also gave the troops relief by introducing order and method into their various duties, by caring for their health and recreation. He also put a stop to the practice of following up the enemy close to the city walls when repulsed—for this practice had led to many casualties from sharp-shooters.

About the 20th July, Roberts lost a cousin by an accidental shot. Captain Greensill of the 24th Foot was reconnoitring after dark, and on drawing near the enemy's position he halted his escort and went forward alone to examine the ground. He had given his men a signal by which they might recognise his approach; but this was apparently misunderstood, for as he came up in the dark the escort fired. The poor fellow died in great agony the next morning.

As to news, the besiegers regularly received letters from England by the Punjab, but for several weeks they had no news from the South.

Sometimes one of Hodson's spies would come in with a scrap of thin paper written on in Greek letters, sewn between the soles of his shoe, or twisted in his hair. How eagerly these missives were deciphered! A fight at Agra! Allahabad still safe! Lucknow holding out! troops at Calcutta from Madras, Ceylon, Mauritius! Lord Elgin diverts a force on way to China!

But they never heard a word from Cawnpur, nor of the death of General Wheeler, nor Sir Henry Lawrence; but thought Wheeler was coming to their aid. At length Norman, on the 15th July, addressed a letter written in French to Wheeler at Cawnpur: two sepoys of the Guides took it, delivered it faithfully to General Havelock at Cawnpur and returned with his reply on the 3rd August.

In this he acquaints General Reed with Wheeler's fate; states he has orders to relieve Lucknow; informs him that Sir Henry Somerset is commander-in-chief in India, and Sir Patrick Grant in Bengal; and speaks of his own victories.

Two days afterwards Colonel Fraser-Tytler's letter came from Cawnpur to Captain Earle: "Havelock has thrashed the Nana . . . will relieve Lucknow in four days . . . we shall soon be with you." This sanguine prophecy was a failure! Instead of four days it took four months to relieve Lucknow, and no troops from Cawnpur came to Delhi.

On the 14th August, Nicholson's column arrived, and hopes began to spring up; for this brought up the effective strength to about 8000 rank and file.

The rebels knew more than the British did: they knew Havelock had been obliged to fall back upon Cawnpur, and that a siege-train was not far off. So they decided to make a supreme effort to capture the big guns, and proceeded in the direction of Najafgarh on the 24th August.

The following morning at daybreak Nicholson started to catch the rebels and bring them to action; he had with him 16 horse artillery guns, 1600 infantry and 450 cavalry. Nicholson requested to have Roberts as his staff officer, but this was refused, as he was still on the sick-list.

A twelve hours' march through swamps and marches brought them, weary and wet, at 4 p.m. near the rebels, covered by guns and deep water.

But Nicholson, nothing daunted, led his men across the ford, breast-high: Tombs and Remington did good work with their batteries, and a plucky charge drove the sepoys from their strong position; they made for a bridge over the canal, but Nicholson caught them, killed 800 and took 13 guns.

Though reinforcements and able leaders had come to the Ridge, yet at the beginning of September there were 3000 sick in hospital!

Baird-Smith was emphatic and decisive for an assault before disease could still further weaken the attack. He said they must think of the Punjab which Lawrence had denuded of troops for their benefit. If delay should induce the native princes to take part against us, as was probable, then all India would be lost, at least for a time.

Wilson, ill and anxious, had long been hesitating, waiting for help from the South: now he knew that help would never come. Baird-Smith was strongly backed up by Nicholson, Daly, Hodson, Norman, and Alec Taylor.

Lord Roberts says he was sitting in Nicholson's tent before he set out to attend the council. In a confidential talk, Nicholson startled his friend by saying: "Delhi must be taken, and it is absolutely essential that this should be done at once; and if Wilson hesitates longer, I intend to propose at to-day's meeting that he should be superseded."

Roberts replied that as Chamberlain was *hors de combat* from his wound, Wilson's removal would leave him, Nicholson, senior officer with the force. To this Nicholson replied, he had thought of that and should propose that the command should be given to Campbell of the 52nd.

Fortunately so drastic a measure was not needed: Wilson agreed to the assault. For some time Taylor, second in command of the Engineers, had been scouting and measuring and drawing plans for the breaching-batteries: a battery was constructed to prevent sorties from the Lahore and Kabul gates; it was also there placed to make the rebels think our assault would be from the right of the Ridge, whereas it had been resolved to attack from the left, where the men could approach nearer to the walls under cover and where the river completely protected our left flank.

As Baird-Smith was ill, the responsibility fell on Taylor, a practical Engineer, alert and cheerful and trusted fully by all working under him. The evening of the 7th September was fixed for the tracing of the batteries. No. 1 battery was placed below the Ridge within 700 yards of the Mori bastion; this bastion was at the north-west corner of the walls, mounting eight guns. The right section of the battery to be commanded by Major Brind, "a real hero of the siege," as Malleson says; the left by Major Kaye.

The Engineers worked all night with such energy that on the morning of the 8th, when as yet only one gun was mounted, the enemy discovered Brind's section and opened upon it a deadly fire of shot and grape. By the afternoon, as new guns were mounted, the rebels' fire was crushed and the Mori bastion became a heap of ruins.

Kaye, too, was doing good work against the Kashmir bastion, until the half-battery caught fire from the constant discharge of guns. At once the rebels opened fire upon the burning battery, and it looked as if the hard work of three days would be thrown away. But the battery was saved from destruction by the gallantry of Lieutenant Lockhart, who, with two companies of the 2nd Gurkhas, carried sandbags to the top, cut them and smothered the fire with sand. Two of the Gurkhas were shot dead; Lockhart, shot through the jaw, rolled over the parapet; but the fire was extinguished.

No. 2 battery was erected in front of Ludlow Castle, nearer the river and about 500 yards from the Kashmir gate, in order to destroy the bastion, to knock away the parapet to the right and left that gave cover to the rebels, and lastly, to open a breach for the stormers.

By this time the enemy began to see that the assault would be on the left near the river, and did their utmost to check the erection of the batteries, mounting heavy guns along the northern face.

No. 3 battery, traced by Medley and commanded by Scott, was placed within 160 yards of the Water bastion and was finished by the night of the 11th. During the first night of its construction thirty-nine men were killed—Gurkhas. As man after man was knocked over, "they would stop a moment, weep a little over a fallen friend," says Forrest, place his body in a row along with the rest and then set to work again. No. 4 battery, half-way between 2 and 3, armed with ten heavy mortars, was commanded by Tombs.

It was to No. 2 battery that Roberts was posted, and he had charge of two guns. At eight o'clock on the morning of the 11th September they opened fire on the Kashmir bastion, and as the shots told and the stones flew into the air and rattled down, a loud cheer came from the artillerymen and others who had volunteered to work in the batteries.

But the enemy also had got the range very accurately, and as soon as the screen in front of the right gun was removed, a round shot came through the embrasure, knocking over Roberts and three others. "On regaining my feet," Roberts says, "I found that the young artilleryman, who was serving the vent while I was laying the gun, had had his right arm taken off."

In the evening, as they were taking a short rest in the shelter of the battery after the exhausting work and the heat, a shower of grape came down upon them, severely wounding the commander, Major Campbell: Edwin Johnson then took his place.

How terrible the work of bombarding was, carried on night and day, we may realise from the fact that these men never left their batteries until the day of the assault—the 14th—except to go by turns into Ludlow Castle, just behind the battery, for their meals. The roar of big guns and mortars was incessant, the rain of shot and shell on the city must have given the mutineers some sense of coming disaster.

But the rebels, on their side, had made an advanced trench in one night, only 350 yards from our left attack: this they lined with infantry and enfiladed our batteries: they sent rockets from their martello towers and left no part of our attack unsearched by their fire.

Three months' practice had made our men skilful in taking cover, but yet we lost 327 officers and men between the 7th and 14th September. On the evening of the 13th, Nicholson went down to see whether the gunners had done their work thoroughly enough to warrant an assault on the morrow. After a careful look he turned and said with a smile: "I must shake hands with you fellows; you have done your best to make my work easy to-morrow."

Taylor, too, who accompanied Nicholson, seemed well pleased with the results; for, soon after, he and Baird-Smith advised General Wilson that the breaches were sufficient: so Wilson ordered they should be closely examined. Four subaltern officers of Engineers were detailed to go to the walls after dark and report upon their condition: this dangerous duty was given to Greathed and Home for the Water bastion, Medley and Lang for the Kashmir bastion.

Lang wished to go and examine the breach while there was light: Taylor agreed. So, with an escort of four men of the 60th Rifles, Lang crept to the edge of the cover, and then running up the glacis, sat on the top of the counter-scarp for a few seconds, studying the ditch and the two breaches. He returned with the report that the breaches were practicable, but had to go again after dark with Medley to ascertain if ladders would be necessary.

Lang slipped into the ditch with a measuring rod, which gave 16 feet; Medley handed him the ladder and followed with two riflemen, four others remaining on the crest of the glacis to cover their retreat. By using the ladder they ascended the ditch and measured the height of the wall. In two minutes they would have reached the top of the breach, but in spite of all precautions they had been heard, and the noise of running sepoys came to their ears. Then they climbed up the ditch as quickly as possible and threw themselves down on the grass, hoping the sepoys would go away, and they might try once more to get to the top of the breach. But as the rebels remained chattering and listening, they resolved to run for it: a volley was fired as they dashed across the open, but fortunately no one was hit.

Greathed and Home reached the Water bastion and examined their breach successfully; and by midnight Baird-Smith made his report to the general, and at the same time advised him strongly to order the assault for the coming morning. So the order was given for the storming of Delhi a little before daybreak; and in every tent men were making ready, re-loading pistols, filling flasks, winding puggrees round their forage caps, and giving, friend to friend, instructions, "if I fall." A little after midnight they were bidden to fall in as quietly as possible, and by the light of a winking lantern the orders for the assault were read to the men. Any officer or man who should be wounded was to be left where he fell! for there were no men to spare. No plundering! all prizes to be put into common stock for fair division. No prisoners! No women or children to be hurt!

"No fear, sir!" murmured the men. Then in some cases a priest or chaplain came up and offered a short prayer for success as they waited till all were ready.

There were four columns of attack: Nicholson led the first; Brigadier W. Jones, the second; Colonel Campbell, the third; Major Reid, the fourth.

The fifth, or reserve column, was to support the first column, or any that required help, and was led by Colonel Longfield. Many of the sick and wounded were used for the protection of the camp.

A delay was caused by having to wait for the men who had been on piquet all night; also it was necessary to batter down some of the repairs made in the night to the breaches. While this was being done the infantry lay down under cover; the sun rose, the breaching guns ceased, Nicholson gave the signal, and the 60th Rifles with a cheer dashed forward in skirmishing order; meanwhile the other columns moved forward. But the rebels were on the look out and sent a storm of bullets into the mass; and officers and men fell thick on the crest of the glacis.

While our men stood at the edge of the ditch, waiting for more ladders, dusky figures crowded on the breach, hurled stones and insulting epithets and dared our men to cross. Then came a rush, a climb, a struggle; many fine men were ruined for life or killed in the breach, but the rebels gave way and the ramparts were ours.

No. 2 column also carried the breach at the Water bastion; but of the 39 men who carried the ladders, 29 dropped in as many seconds. The ladders were picked up by their comrades and placed against the escarp: the supports by mistake got on to the rampart; but Jones, seizing the situation, cleared the ramparts as far as the

Kabul gate, on the summit of which he planted the column flag, presented in 1877 to Queen Victoria.

No. 3 column advanced towards the Kashmir gate in the face of a heavy fire and halted.

Lieutenants Home and Salkeld with 8 sappers and miners and a bugler set out to blow the gate open; each carried 25 lb. of powder.

The rebels wondered what so small a party were going to do, and slackened fire; but very soon opened a deadly fire from the top of the gateway, the city wall, and the open wicket. The bridge over the ditch had been destroyed; a single beam remained, over which Home and his men crossed with difficulty.

How the gate was blown in has been already described in Chapter IV.

When Campbell got inside he found Nicholson's and Jones' columns, and together they poured into the open space between the Kashmir gate and the church.

The fourth column under Reid had to start without their four H.A. guns; Reid himself was wounded in the head, but managed to send for Captain Lawrence and gave him the command. But the rebels were strongly posted on the banks of the canal, and indeed threatened to break into our weakly-guarded camp, but just at the critical moment Hope Grant brought up the cavalry brigade, and No. 4 column were enabled to retire in an orderly manner.

Meanwhile Nicholson pushed on along the foot of the walls to the right towards the Lahore gate past the Kabul gate and Burn bastion. To do this he had to force his way through a lane 200 yards long where every building was manned with sharpshooters; the city wall was on his right, on his left flat-roofed houses with parapets sheltering rebels. He might have maintained his position at the Kabul gate, but thinking that the repulse of No. 4 would encourage the rebels, he cried, "Boys, storm the lane and take those two guns in front." They charged, recoiled, and charged again; Greville spiked the first gun, Lieutenant Butler got beyond the second gun. But the grape and round-shot were too much for mortal men. Jacobs of the 1st Fusiliers was mortally wounded. Wemyss, Greville, Caulfield, Speke, Woodcock, Butler were in turn struck down. The men, discouraged by the fall of their officers, were falling back a second time, when the clear-sounding voice of Nicholson called them to follow their general. But even as he turned to address them he was shot through the back and chest.

Though he felt the wound was mortal, nothing could yet quench the ardour of his spirit; he still called on his men to come on. But it was in vain; already 8 officers and 50 men had fallen in this attempt. The only thing was to fall back on the Kabul gate.

The result of the first day's operations was that we had won the entire space from the Water bastion by the river to the Kabul gate, being the north side of the city walls; while the fourth column, outside the city, held the batteries behind Hindu Rao's house. But the price paid was high.

In the day's fight we had lost 66 officers and 1104 men; the rebels were still very strong in numbers, in guns, in position; and they had had their measure of success and had no need to despair.

All this time Roberts was with General Wilson at Ludlow Castle on staff duty. Wilson watched the assault from the top of the house; and, seeing the success of the assaulting columns, he rode through the Kashmir gate to the church, and there stayed for the remainder of the day.

The general was ill and worn out with toil and anxiety, and as reports of disaster kept coming in, he grew more and more depressed. The failure of Reid and the 4th column, the fall of Nicholson, and the false report that Hope Grant and Tombs were killed—all this so distressed him that he began to consider the advisability of falling back again on the Ridge. Roberts was ordered to go and find out the truth of these reports and ascertain what had happened to No. 4 column.

While riding on his errand through the Kashmir gate

Roberts saw by the side of the road a dhoolie without bearers. He dismounted to see if there was a wounded officer inside, and perceived to his grief and consternation that it was John Nicholson, with death written on his face.

"The bearers—have gone off to plunder—I am in great pain—I should like to be taken to the hospital," the wounded man gasped out.

"Not seriously wounded, John, I hope?"

"I am dying; there is no chance for me."

"The sight of that great man lying helpless and on the point of death," says Lord Roberts, "was almost more than I could bear. Other men had daily died around me . . . but I never felt as I felt then—to lose Nicholson seemed to me at that moment to lose everything."

It took Roberts some time to find four men, whom he put in charge of a sergeant of the 61st Foot: he took down the sergeant's name, told him who the wounded officer was, and ordered him to go direct to the field hospital. Continuing his ride, Roberts came up with Hope Grant's brigade, and was very glad to find him and Tombs unhurt, and Hodson cheery and Probyn in high spirits at commanding his squadron.

So Roberts galloped back to Wilson with the good news, which did a little cheer him; but the heavy list of casualties came in later and seemed to crush all spirit out of him: he would have withdrawn from the city in spite of the opposing opinions of every officer on his staff, had not Baird-Smith come up, looking very ill and wasted by disease and suffering fearful pain from his wound.

"Now, Baird-Smith, shall we hold on or retire?" asked the general.

"Sir, we *must* hold on," was the reply given in so loud and determined a tone that Wilson shrugged his shoulders and said no more.

Neville Chamberlain, Daly, and Khan Sing Rosa, a distinguished officer of the Guides, all incapacitated by wounds,

LIEUTENANT ROBERTS FINDING GENERAL NICHOLSON

Riding through the Kashmir Gate after the capture of Delhi, Roberts saw a doolie lying at the roadside without bearers. He dismounted, and drawing aside the curtains saw, to his surprise and grief, General Nicholson lying mortally wounded.

were watching the assault from the top of Hindu Rao's house: to Chamberlain, Wilson sent two notes, asking his advice. Chamberlain urged the necessity for holding on to the last.

Nicholson, though slowly dying, when told of General Wilson's wish to retire to the Ridge, cried, "No! no! thank God I have strength yet to shoot him, if necessary!"

While such were the varying opinions of the besiegers, they little knew what emotions had been stirred in the hearts of the besieged by the capture of the walls and bastions and the calm bivouacking of the British within the city. The king and his counsellors were panic-stricken: the sepoys had had all the heart taken out of them by the terrible street fighting. If we had retired, all these advantages would have been thrown away. And they very nearly were!

But at length Wilson braced up his courage and decided to remain. In the afternoon of the 14th, Norman, Johnson, and Roberts were sent to visit every position occupied by our troops within the city.

They found great confusion naturally—men without officers, officers without men, and all without instructions. For three weak columns had been set to do the impossible; but they had done what was possible in gallant style. While riding along they were suddenly attacked from a side lane: but fortunately one of our piquets heard the firing and came running up to help. "In the scrimmage my poor mare was shot," says Roberts; "her death was a great loss to me at the time."

The magazine, the palace, and the fort of Salimgarh, all fortified, still remained in the enemies' hands, as well as the densely populated city. The general and his staff spent the night in Skinner's house near the church: whether the rebels were tired, or from whatever cause, the outworn troops were allowed to enjoy a peaceful and restful night, and awoke refreshed. The 15th was employed in restoring order, breaking wine-bottles, and preparations for shelling the city: the sepoys gave little trouble.

On the 16th the rebels evacuated Kishanganj, whence on the 14th they had repulsed the fourth column: the British stormed and took the magazine, so heroically defended, and partially blown up by Willoughby on the 11th of May.

On the 17th and 18th the bank was taken and the besiegers' posts were brought close to the palace: but it became necessary to take the Lahore gate, which was strongly held by the rebels, and was commanded by the Burn bastion. It was then that Alec Taylor besought the general to allow him to work his way from house to house to the Burn bastion.

The general assented, knowing now that what Taylor promised he would perform. Roberts was placed under Taylor, and they had with them 50 Europeans and 50 native soldiers, the senior officer being Captain Gordon of the 75th Foot. For hours these men worked like moles through houses, courtyards, and lanes, clearing all before them, where any natives were left, until on the afternoon of the 19th they found themselves in rear of the Burn bastion. Only one door now separated them from the lane leading to this bastion: Lang, of the Engineers, burst it open and the others followed at a rush up the ramp, surprising the guard and capturing the bastion without the loss of a man.

Early in the morning of 20th September, as they were sapping their way towards the Lahore gate, they came upon some 50 *banias* (grain merchants) huddled together and unarmed.

Instead of killing these inoffensive people, Taylor made a bargain with them, "Your lives shall be spared if you will conduct us safely to some spot from which we may observe how the Lahore gate is guarded."

After a long discussion among themselves they agreed that two of their party should guide Lang and Roberts, while the rest remained as hostages, to be shot if the two officers did not return.

In a panic the two guides led on from house to house and along secluded alleys, without meeting a single living person, until at last they brought the officers to the upper room of a house which looked out on the Chandni Chauk, or Silver Bazaar, the main street of Delhi, close to the Lahore gate. From the window of this room Lang and Roberts saw sepoys lounging about or cleaning their muskets, and sentries by the gateway and two guns.

The two *banias* were so afraid of anything untoward happening to the officers that they insisted on reconnoitring every house before entering: in consequence there was such delay that they found their friends ready to shoot the hostages, because they believed the guides had behaved treacherously.

Then the hundred men were guided along the same route and drawn up behind a gateway next to the house from which Roberts had seen the sentries. Suddenly the gate was flung open, the party rushed into the street, captured the guns, and killed or put to flight the sepoys.

This was a worthy achievement, for it gave possession of the street which led from the Lahore gate to the palace and the mosque.

Up this street Roberts and his men proceeded; finding it absolutely empty, except for the signs of looting, they pushed on to the Delhi Bank. A couple of guns outside the palace were sending round-shot about, but soon ceased firing: for the great Mahommedan mosque had just been taken by a column under Major James Brind, and Ensign M'Queen with one of his men had reconnoitred up to the chief gateway of the palace and reported only a few sepoys left. The 60th Rifles were allowed the honour of storming this last stronghold as they had distinguished themselves in the battle of Hindun, four months before. Roberts attached himself to the 60th on this occasion.

Home, of the Engineers, who blew up the Kashmir

gate, now advanced with some sappers and blew in the outer gate.

They waited for the smoke of the explosion to clear away and then rushed in, supported by the 4th Punjab Infantry: but a second door barred the way, which took some time to force open.

Then they saw crowds of wounded men in the recesses of the long passage leading to the inner rooms of the palace: a few fanatics only resisted. One of these, a Mahommedan sepoy, took aim and shot through M'Queen's helmet: he then charged madly along the passage, and was shot down.

"So ended the 20th September—a day I am never likely to forget."

We must add that Brigadier William Jones with 500 Sikhs helped Taylor to take the Lahore gate and the great mosque. Brind it was who asked permission to storm the palace: and a young lieutenant, named Aikman, had previously secured the Salimgarh.

That afternoon Wilson took up his quarters in the palace.

The poor old king had been advised by his commander-in-chief, Bakht Khan, to accompany the sepoys in flight and live to fight in the open. But the aged monarch had wives and sons to think of, so he sadly took refuge at the great tomb of Humayun, four or five miles away.

So ended the siege of Delhi: and a royal salute at sunrise on the 21st proclaimed that we were again the Masters of the Imperial City. But our triumph was honourably shared by the Gurkhas of the Himalayas, the frontier men of the Guides, the proud Sikhs, the daring Pathans. Heroes all—they had shown equally with the British soldier endurance of hardships, faith in their officers, and contempt of death. Lord Canning wrote in his dispatches home these words:—

"In the name of outraged humanity, in memory of innocent blood ruthlessly shed, in acknowledgment of the first signal vengeance inflicted on the foulest treason, the Governor-General in Council records his gratitude to Major-General Wilson and the brave army of Delhi. He does so in the sure conviction that a like tribute awaits them wherever the news of their well-earned triumph shall reach."

Nicholson just lived to know that his labours had not been in vain: his funeral took place on the 24th, and Roberts was marching out that morning with a mixed column to Cawnpur.

The victorious soldiers under Lieutenant-Colonel Greathed set out in the early morning light along Silver Street, now desolate and deserted: the gay bazaars all idle and forlorn and empty: not a sound was to be heard but the fall of their own footsteps. Dead bodies still polluted the air and stricken faces grinned a ghastly farewell: dogs and vultures were eating their loathsome breakfast: some dead sepoys lay with arm uplifted as if beckoning the column to come and see what war was like at closer quarters. The very horses felt the horror of the scene, for they trembled and snorted in disgust and fear, misliking the scent of blood.

It was a pure delight to gain the fresh air of the open country: but the taint of cholera had followed them; Captain Wilde of the 4th Punjab Infantry having to be sent back to Delhi apparently dying; but he made a good recovery and lived to fight again very strenuously.

It was not long before they came upon rebels strongly posted and had to storm a walled town; here Anson got surrounded by mutineers, performed heroic deeds of valour and won the Victoria Cross.

Here, too, Roberts' life was saved by his horse rearing and receiving in his head the bullet aimed at his rider: the horse survived and did good service. It had been John Nicholson's Wasiri stallion, a great favourite of his.

On the 1st of October another hero of the Mutiny lost his life: for it had been decided that Malagarh fort should be blown up. Lieutenant Home, who had been one of the Engineer officers to blow in the Kashmir gate, was engaged in laying the mine; the slow-match was lighted, but as no explosion followed, Home thought the match had gone out and ran forward to relight it. Just as he reached it the mine blew up and Home was no more.

When the column reached Khurja, a large Mahommedan town, the first thing that met the eyes of the soldiers was the skeleton of a white woman: it was placed against the side of the bridge, headless, the bones hacked and broken. The soldiers cried for vengeance and wished to burn the town; but as the townsfolk pleaded innocence, the houses were spared.

At the camping ground they saw a fakir sitting under a tree, vowed to silence, as a penance for sin; but when some officers drew near, he pointed to a wooden platter significantly—an ordinary plate, in which food had recently been mixed: still the fakir pointed: on closer inspection it was seen that a small piece of wood in the centre was loose; this on being lifted up revealed a tiny folded paper!

This was none other than a secret note from General Havelock, written in Greek letters, saying that he was on his way to Lucknow, and begging any commander into whose hands it should fall to hasten to his assistance.

Greathed, on reading this, decided to proceed at once to Cawnpur.

On reaching Aligarh they found a great crowd drawn up before the walls, blowing horns and cursing the foreigner: but these gentlemen catching a glimpse of the Horse Artillery, bolted within and closed the gates, leaving two guns in our possession. Thinking the city would be stormed and taken, they bolted out on the other side into the open country; but the cavalry had ridden round and were ready for them as they scuttled into the high crops and tried to hide.

The civil authorities of Aligarh welcomed the British rule again with alacrity and joy: for their taste of sepoy rule had not been sweet.

On the road to Cawnpur lived twin brothers, Rajputs, who had taken a prominent part in the rebellion:

the cavalry surrounded their village, and both brothers were killed in attempting to escape. In their house were found many articles which must have belonged to English ladies.

Pressing calls from Agra for help induced Greathed to turn from Cawnpur to Agra. What happened there can be given in detail in a later chapter.

The Agra authorities had assured Greathed on his arrival that the rebels were ten miles away: Roberts had got leave with Norman, Watson, and a few other officers to breakfast in the fort. They had scarcely sat down, full of delight at once more enjoying a charming meal in ladies' society, when the report of a gun startled them, then boomed out a second and a third!

The officers sprang to their feet: "What can it mean?—the enemy?"

The host ran to an angle in the terrace to see, and returned in hot haste, saying, "My God! an action is taking place, gentlemen!"

In a moment Roberts and his friends were down the stairs and on their horses galloping towards their camp: but their progress was stopped by an immense crowd of men, children, and animals, all rushing back to the fort with yells and screams of fear. They had flocked out to see the famous Delhi soldiers; and the surprise attack made by the rebels had sent them pell-mell back to the city. With difficulty the officers forced their way through the throng, and found their own men fighting in their shirt-sleeves, having been startled from their sleep by the round-shot, and not having had time to put on their accoutrements.

Roberts at this juncture was nearly killed by a dismounted sowar, who danced about in front of his horse, waving his turban in front of its eyes, so that Roberts could not get his charger to face the man: who held in his other hand a sharp sword that looked very business-like. However, a man of the 9th Lancers ran the rebel through and rescued his officer.

Though Greathed had been surprised, the rebels were

on their part more surprised: for they had supposed that the tents were those of the garrison whom they despised: a rumour had been spread abroad that the Delhi column was coming, but they had not believed it.

So when they charged into the camp on the parade-ground and were repulsed by the 75th Foot, they were heard to say to one another, "Arrah bhai! ze Delhiwale hain!" (I say, brothers, these are the Delhi fellows).

Hope Grant was put in command of the column in place of Greathed, and joined them in October soon after they left Agra. Grant was senior to Greathed, and knew much more of India and its customs; he was very popular with the troops.

They had some more fighting before they reached Cawnpur on the 26th October. Lord Roberts says: "Our visit to this scene of suffering and disaster was more harrowing than it is in the power of words to express; the sights which met our eyes, and the reflections they gave rise to, were quite maddening . . . tresses of hair, pieces of ladies' dresses, books crumpled and torn, bits of work and scraps of music, just as they had been left by the wretched owners on the fatal morning of the 27th June, when they started for that terrible walk to the boats provided by the Nana. . . . When one looked on the ruined, roofless barracks, with their hastily constructed parapet and ditch, one marvelled how 465 men, not more than half of them soldiers by profession, could have held out for three long weeks against the thousands of disciplined troops whom the Nana was able to bring to the attack."

The stay at Cawnpur was longer than had been expected, as they had to wait for the carts which had taken the women and children to Allahabad.

In a battle fought on the banks of the Kali Nadi, Roberts won his V.C. On the same day he did two daring deeds as they were chasing the flying foe: a batch of mutineers had faced about and fired into the squadron at close quarters. Younghusband fell, and Roberts waited to rescue a wounded sowar who was being attacked by a sepoy with fixed bayonet: one slash of the sword was sufficient: then Roberts rode on and saw two sepoys making off with a standard.

"This must be captured!" said Roberts to himself, and setting spurs to his horse soon overtook the rebels. One he cut down at once, and while he was wrenching the staff out of his hands, the other sepoy put his musket close to Roberts' body and fired.

Fortunately the musket missed fire and Roberts recovered the standard. As is the manner of English heroes, Lord Roberts only alludes to these actions in a summary way in his interesting *Forty-one Years in India.*

Roberts after this went on to Lucknow, meeting his old friend Sir Colin Campbell and General Outram at the Relief of Lucknow. We cannot now enter into details of that struggle, but Forbes-Mitchell gives us two sketches of what he witnessed concerning Lieutenant Roberts.

He tells us that the young lieutenant had been associated with the 93rd Highlanders in several skirmishes, so that the men had recognised his worth and familiarly spoke of him as "Plucky wee Bobs."

On the 14th November, as the 93rd were passing through the breach in the wall of the Dilkoosha Park, Roberts rode through, followed by a trooper, when suddenly a battery unmasked and opened fire: the second shot struck the trooper's horse, and horse and rider fell together in the dust. Someone cried, "Puir lad! plucky wee Bobs is done for!"

But as the dust cleared away, Roberts was seen to have dismounted and to be assisting the trooper to rise from under the dead horse.

As he remounted, the Highlanders gave him a rousing cheer, and he rode with the guns to the front, pointing the direction they should take.

"The young lieutenant who could thus coolly dismount and extricate a trooper from under a dead horse within point-blank range of a well-served battery of 9-pounder guns, was early qualifying for the distinguished position which he has since reached."[1]

After Lucknow, Roberts handed his office of D.A.Q.M.G. to Wolseley and returned to England. How our hero served his country in Afghanistan, Abyssinia, Burma, and South Africa must be learned elsewhere.

If Englishmen should ever awake to the duty of making themselves fit to defend their country, it will be mainly due to the unflagging exertions of our great field-marshal. He has never spared himself to defend us: but we are apt to be forgetful and ungrateful, until the approach of danger rouses us from a foolish lethargy.

[1] *Reminiscences of the Great Mutiny*, Macmillan.

In part from *Forty-one Years in India*, by kind permission of F.-M. Earl Roberts; and from Malleson's *Indian Mutiny*, by kind permission of Messrs. Seely, Service & Co.

CHAPTER VIII

JOHN NICHOLSON: THE HERO OF THE PUNJAB

LADY EDWARDES, Kaye, Trotter, Bosworth Smith, Lord Roberts, and others give many details of the life of John Nicholson. His earliest ancestors seem to have been of Cumberland descent; they went across to Ireland and settled in Derry and County Down.

John's father, Dr. Alexander Nicholson, was one of sixteen children. He married, in 1820, Clara Hogg, a sister of Sir James Weir Hogg, Bart., a very clever lawyer who went to Calcutta and made a fortune at the Bar. In time J. W. Hogg became chairman of the Court of Directors of the East India Company and was rewarded for his services by a baronetcy.

Dr. Alexander Nicholson worked his way up in his profession and won no small repute for his skill: his eldest son, John, was born at Lisburn in 1822. Sir John Kaye says of him: "He was a precocious boy, almost from his cradle; thoughtful, studious, of an inquiring nature; and he had the ineffable benefit of good parental teaching of the best kind. In his young mind the seeds of Christian piety were early sown and took deep root." John was only nine when his father died. It is said that his imagination was first fired by the war stories told him by an old drill sergeant. His mother moved him to the Royal School at Dungannon in County Tyrone: here he waxed strong and valiant in fight; though his father had been of Quaker descent!

For John had a fiery, imperious temper, and his

indignation was soon roused by any act of injustice: but as a rule he was modest and retiring, brave and generous, always ready to take the side of the weaker. In 1838 James W. Hogg obtained for him a cadetship in the Bengal Infantry: so at the age of sixteen he was whirled away from mother, friends, and home to London, took the oath of allegiance and set sail for the Cape and Calcutta.

His mother was poor, and John tried to economise: probably he drank no wine, and stinted himself of social amusements; for he thought much of the home folk.

His regiment, the 27th Native Infantry, was stationed at Ferozepur on the Sutlej; as he travelled by way of Meerut and Kurnal he was twice robbed in the night: forks and spoons, pistols, money, etc.—all were taken by skilful thieves.

At Ferozepur officers had to build their own bungalows, and his cost him two months' pay, entailing more sacrifice of pleasures. The station was a wilderness outside the town; neither tree nor grass grew in the place. Tigers were constantly on view in the neighbouring jungle, and in the cool season Nicholson tried to shoot them; but at first he found the great heat enervating to both mind and body.

He was now six feet high, but he added four inches more in the following years. Nicholson's regiment was ordered down to Peshawur to assist a convoy under Captain Broadfoot: the Sikh troops threatened to attack them, but Broadfoot's cool courage sent the Sikhs across the Indus and the convoy with many ladies arrived safely at Kabul.

They then went to Ghuzni to relieve the 16th Native Infantry; here Nicholson made a friend of Neville Chamberlain, his senior by two years, who thus describes the young Irishman:—

"He was then a tall, slender youth with regular features and a quiet, reserved manner: we became friends at first sight, as is common with youth, and we were constantly together during the short time that intervened between his regiment taking the fort and mine leaving for Kandahar."

For a few months Nicholson was able to study Oriental languages in order to qualify himself for a post in the Shah's service at Kabul or in the Company's. But his leisure was interrupted by the Afghan rising in 1841, when swarms of wild mountaineers, armed with long jezails, or matchlocks, surrounded Ghuzni in the winter: at last the water in the citadel failed, and Colonel Palmer had to make terms and surrender the citadel. Of course the Afghans broke their pledges to escort the garrison to Peshawur, and attacked the troops in their town quarters in March 1842. Lieutenant Crawford Burnett of the 54th and Nicholson saw from their roof next door the slaughter and havoc made among their sepoys by the Afghan fanatics; their house was set on fire, and they were driven from room to room, hungry and alternately frozen or baked by wind and raging fire.

On the second night they dug a hole through the back wall with their bayonets and escaped to the houses held by Palmer and his officers, and by many women and children. Poor, frost-bitten mortals! life was a misery to them.

On the night of 20th March, Palmer gave up all arms and surrendered. The young giant Nicholson, with tears of indignant fury in his eyes, thrice drove back the Afghan guard before he would give up his sword.

Nicholson gave his gaolers a second taste of his temper when they tried to rob him of the locket with his mother's hair: instead of giving it up he threw it passionately at the Sirdar's head.

"However," wrote Nicholson to his mother, "he seemed to like my act, for he gave strict orders that the locket was not to be taken from me."

The officers, kept in a small dungeon, in cold and filth and nakedness, suffered for some weeks: then, in April 1842, the news came that Pollock had forced the Khyber Pass, and their confinement became less severe. In August 1842 they were hurried on camels to Kabul, where Akbar Khan, the brave son of Dost, treated them very kindly and invited them to a public dinner: here they met Troup and

Pottinger and many polite Afghans. Next morning Akbar escorted them to the fort outside the city where Lady Sale, George Lawrence, and other prisoners were confined in good quarters. But their good fortune was not to last many days: when news came of the approach of Pollock and Nott, the prisoners were removed for security beyond the Hindu Kush. However, George Lawrence bribed the Afghan officer to accept a pension for life and let the prisoners go free.

So Lady Sale once more met her husband, whose regiment, the 13th Light Infantry, cheered the ladies as they returned to camp.

Nicholson and his fellow-captives were dressed as Afghans just now; and as Neville Chamberlain was passing a tent a stone struck him: he put his hand to his sword and angrily confronted the Afghan, who was stooping to pick up another stone.

"Good Lord! why, I'm blessed if you aren't John Nicholson!"

The two officers burst out laughing and shook hands heartily.

A second surprise meeting befell Nicholson on 1st November 1842 at the Afghan mouth of the Khyber Pass, as the army was returning to India. A young officer lately posted to one of Pollock's regiments began to talk to him: they seemed to be drawn together by some strange affinity: it was explained when they knew they were both Nicholsons—and brothers!

The third surprise meeting was mere tragedy: for three days later, as John was riding on rear-guard down the Pass with Ensign Dennys, they spied a naked body gleaming to the right: cantering to the spot, they found the mutilated body of a white man, with just a fragment of a shirt fluttering from the shoulder.

"That shirt seems too fine for a private soldier, doesn't it?" said Dennys.

There was no reply. Dennys looked up and saw his

friend's shoulders moving in suppressed grief: he had recognised his young brother! Poor Alexander! only just arrived from home and mother and kindred! but they had enjoyed one happy meeting before he was taken away.

The boy's remains were carried in a dhoolie to the next camping-ground: after solemn burial, a bonfire was lighted over the grave to save it from Afghan marauders.

John Nicholson felt this loss deeply, and the tears fell down his cheeks. His captivity in Afghanistan had won for John two good friends in George and Henry Lawrence: hence in 1847 he was appointed assistant to the Resident at Lahore, the Sikh capital.

His friend Dennys says of Nicholson: "In general he was reserved almost to moroseness in those days, and I was one of the very few who were in any way intimate with him. . . . Fear of any kind seemed unknown to him, and one could see there was a great depth behind his reserved and almost boorish manner." Indeed, Nicholson had tasted of sorrow very early.

It was on 20th April, when on his way to Multan, that John Nicholson met his young brother, Charles, whom he had last seen at the age of ten. Of course neither of them recognised the other: "I actually talked to him half an hour before I could persuade myself of his identity. He is as tall, if not taller than I am. . . . Our joy at meeting you will understand, mother, without my attempting to describe it to you."

There seems to have been a tragic fatality about the meetings of poor Mrs. Nicholson's sons—the lady who gave four sons to die for her country, John, Charles, William, and Alexander—for when Charles and John met at Delhi, they were both wounded, both lay side by side in the hospital tent, and exchanged the last words.

In the summer of 1848, Nicholson lay sick of fever; but when the news came that a very powerful Sikh chief had revolted, and George Lawrence, sitting on his bed, said, "John, if you had been fit for the work, I should have wished to send you; but that is out of the question."

"Never mind the fever," cried Nicholson, "I will start to-night." And he rose from his bed, made his preparations and started that evening with 60 Pathan Horse and 150 Mahommedans.

"Never shall I forget him," says a brother-officer, "as he prepared for his start, full of that noble reliance on the presence and protection of God which, added to an unusual share of physical courage, rendered him almost invincible."

He rode at a gallop and covered the fifty miles from Peshawur to Attock; but only thirty of his escort kept up with him as he crossed the Indus and dashed through the Sikhs at the gate of Attock.

Once inside the walls he cowed the sullen natives by his bold words and prompt action: for he arrested the leaders of sedition and stalked amongst the Sikhs like an angry god.

After securing Attock, Nicholson rode farther and checked the rising in other forts. We cannot follow him in his long rides and many fights. He was aide to Lord Gough in the battle of Chilianwala, that battlefield in which the Sikh gunners and camp-followers after the battle came down in the darkness of night, carried off twenty-eight guns, and stabbed every wounded man they found alive.

After the victories of Lord Gough, Nicholson was riding about every day, exploring for supplies, trying to protect the poor villagers from the cruel bands of plunderers: amongst these he caught some of Gough's soldiers, and had them soundly flogged. He asked for the powers of a provost-marshal, and wrote to Sir Henry Lawrence: "If I get them, rely on my bringing the army to its senses within two days."

Perhaps Sir Henry thought his subordinate a little too stern and severe, for he wrote about this time: "Let me advise you as a friend to curb your temper, and bear and forbear with natives and Europeans. . . . I admire your sincerity as much as any man can do, but say this much as a general warning . . . yet from what I saw in camp, I think you have done much towards conquering yourself."

At this time Nicholson lost another brother, William, who had come out recently as a cadet in the Bombay army. He was found in bed one morning in June 1849 with two ribs broken and many bruises: it was put down to sleep-walking, but the natives long after called his house "Murder House." He was only twenty.

At this time John Nicholson applied for leave of absence and went home with his friend, Herbert Edwardes, and John Lawrence's two little girls. He visited Russia, Prussia, and Paris, and studied foreign military systems; brought a new needle-gun to London; but the authorities saw little in it as an invention until later occurrences in war opened their eyes.

Nicholson's mother was now staying with Sir James Hogg, his uncle, and the boy Quintin, the future founder of the Polytechnic, listened open-mouthed to his tall cousin's wonderful tales of war and peace.

After a visit to Ireland, Nicholson returned in March 1851 to India. His friend, Sir Henry Lawrence, was still in power at Lahore; and as Reynell Taylor was leaving Bunnu for his furlough, he appointed Nicholson deputy-commissioner in his place.

Bunnu—the wildest corner of the north-west Punjab, and close to Afghanistan—was to be placed under the imperious, but sympathetic leadership of an Irish Hercules.

Taylor and Nicholson met and exchanged views in Bunnu. With Taylor was Richard Pollock (K.C.B.), who regarded Reynell Taylor as a saint upon earth, acting solely from duty and religion; while he was as yet somewhat prejudiced against the high-handed dealer of stern justice who was to succeed him. This prejudice was not lessened when he heard the loud, confident tone of Nicholson, and his expressed determination to do in so many months what the gentle, slow-working Taylor had only done in years.

The new warden of the marches, however, was a man of action: he was soon scouring the country at the head of 1500 mounted police, and he penetrated the homes of the

Wazirs, formerly believed to be inaccessible, and dealt stern punishment to thieves and marauders.

Night thefts in the cantonment were not rare. Men, well-armed, came across the border, sneaked up the dry beds of irrigation channels and killed any who resisted their robberies.

Their leader was the headman of a village just inside the Gumatti Pass. In the daytime was none so mealy-mouthed and respectable; by night he sent out his men to steal from friend and foe.

Nicholson had the canals patrolled by police, who lay down and waited for their man: the Waziri Malik came one night and got killed.

The next morning was market-day, and the natives gasped as they looked upon the dead body of the robber-chief exposed in the market-place, like a stoat nailed up on a barn-door.

Sir Herbert Edwardes knew what Bunnu was like, and what Nicholson had done. He wrote: "John Nicholson belongs to the school of Henry Lawrence. I only knocked down the walls of the Bunnu forts: John Nicholson has since reduced the people (the most ignorant, depraved, and bloodthirsty in the Punjab) to such a state of good order and respect for the laws, that in the last year of his charge not only was there no murder, burglary, or highway robbery, but not an attempt at any of these crimes. . . . A brotherhood of fakirs has commenced the worship of 'Nikkul Seyn,' which they still continue. Repeatedly they have met Nicholson since, and fallen at his feet as their guru, or religious teacher: he has flogged them soundly on every occasion and sometimes imprisoned them; but the sect of the Nikkul Seynes remains as devoted as ever." This was no other than the worship of Power: for these rude men thought that a man who could make all their world obey him must be divine. We may remember, too, that when the news of Nicholson's death at Delhi became known to his native worshippers in Hazâra, they came together to lament, and one of them cut his throat on the spot: for he said there was no profit in life when Nickilsyn had left it.

But another, more wise than he, averred that this was not the right way to serve their great guru, or teacher: but that if they wished to see him again in the great beyond, they must learn to love his God. Nicholson deeply regretted the removal of Henry Lawrence from Lahore, and for some time obstinately, with an ill grace, received the friendly overtures of Sir John Lawrence, his brother's successor.

But John Lawrence soon found out the worth of Nicholson, and heartily did he praise him in letters to Lord Dalhousie: "his presence among the wild men of Bunnu is well worth the wing of a regiment."

"He is the best district officer on the frontier. He possesses great courage, much force of character, and is at the same time shrewd and intelligent." [1]

The Governor-General was rather shocked at some of Nicholson's high-handed proceedings, and asked Sir John for reports of all incursions. "Don't send up any more men to be hanged direct," writes Sir John in 1853, "unless the case is very urgent."

But Nicholson was not to be bound by red tape: a friend once saw him sitting in his office with a bundle of papers on the floor.

"Government regulations—eh, Nicholson?"

"Yes—and this is the way I treat all these things," Nicholson replied with a sarcastic laugh, as he kicked them across the room.

In January 1854 the news came that Honoria, wife of Sir Henry Lawrence, had died after a lingering illness. This lady had exercised a softening and religious influence on Nicholson at Peshawur.

She had sent him a message through her husband in September 1853: "Tell him I love him dearly, as if he were my son. I know that he is noble and pure to his

[1] Bosworth Smith's *Life of Lord Lawrence*.

fellow-men, that he thinks not of himself; but tell him that he is a sinner, that one day he will be as weak and as near death as I am now."[1]

And yet this stern dispenser of justice loved children, he even sent for toys for some of the Waziri boys and girls.

Once a little boy was brought to him for having been put up to poison food.

"Did you not know it was wrong to kill?" asked Nicholson.

"Yes, sahib, I know it is wrong to kill with a knife or sword."

"Why, my boy?" asked the great man in gentle, sympathetic tones.

"Because, sahib, the blood leaves marks."

Nicholson had the child removed from his bad parents and adopted by a kind native. "I have seldom seen," writes Nicholson to his friend Edwardes, "anything more touching than their mutual adoption of each other as father and son; the child clasping the man's beard, the man placing his hands on the child's head."

One day a Mahommedan was brought to him for having murdered his own brother—it was a very hot evening, and the criminal looked dreadfully parched and exhausted after a forced march of many miles. "Why!" said Nicholson, "is it possible you can have walked in, fasting, on a day like this?"

"Thank God!" said the murderer, "I am a regular faster."

"But why have you killed your brother?"

"I saw a fowl killed last night; the sight of the blood put the devil into me."

The man had chopped up his brother in cold blood, stood a long chase, and been marched into camp: but he was religiously keeping his fast—thank God!

In January 1856, Nicholson was nearly assassinated by a fanatic, who rushed at him with a drawn sword as he stood at his garden gate.

[1] Kaye, *Indian Officers.*

A native orderly with a sword ran in between them. The fanatic shouted, "Stand aside, Chuprassi; I want to kill the sahib, not a common soldier."

"All our names are Nikkul Seyn here!" replied the Chuprassi.

But as the fanatic pressed on, Nicholson snatched a musket from a passing sentry, and presenting it, said, "Put down your sword, or I will fire."

"Sahib, either you or I must die," answered the madman.

Nicholson then shot the fellow through the heart, and the ball passed through a religious book which was tied as a charm across his chest.

No wonder that with such experiences Nicholson had grown grave and somewhat stern in expression, for the dark devilry of the Bunnuchis demanded an iron will and an imperious temper.

At this time his face was partly concealed by a long, dark beard and moustache; while he walked, like his brothers, with a firm, vigorous step, holding his head high and looking very masterful. But it was just this masterful look and relentless insistence on obedience which gained for him the awe and respect of the natives, though such imperious ways did not always commend him to his equals.

He said once to Sir Neville Chamberlain: "There is one thing in life I have failed in, which I wished to attain—that is to be popular with my brother-officers; I know I am not, and I am sorry for it."

However, even his brother-officers found out his true worth before he died. But the rod of iron tempered by sunny humour won the savage heart, for he was always just; and they recognised his justice, and loved his smiles One day, as he was riding through a Bunnuchi village with his escort, he noticed a Mullah, or Mussulman priest, forbore to salaam as he sat in front of his mosque and scowled as they passed. When he reached camp, Nicholson sent two orderlies to fetch the Mullah, and with him the village barber.

"Shave off that priest's beard, Master Barber," ordered Nicholson. This, the direst insult to a Mahommedan, was speedily carried out; and the culprit humbly returned to his mosque a sadder and, let us hope, a wiser man.

Sir Richard Pollock says of Nicholson's rule at Bunnu: "Edwardes found Bunnu a valley of forts and left it a valley of open villages. Nicholson found it a hell upon earth, and left it probably as wicked as ever, but curbed to punishment." Nothing seemed to tire Nicholson; he could ride twenty miles before breakfast to investigate a crime, and then sit in court through the heat of a summer day hearing cases for judgment. A Peshawari said of him, "You can hear the ring of his horse's hoofs from Attock to the Khyber Pass."

With all his stern severity he loved children, and they, looking up into his dark lustrous eyes, trusted the big sahib who gave them so many toys. His generosity extended to all; when he found a man suffering poverty from no moral fault, he would hand him his bag of rupees and say, "Here, my friend, God knows you have done your best; take a handful."

In 1856, Nicholson was transferred to Peshawur as deputy-commissioner. He writes in March 1857: "Old Coke tells me that the Bunnuchis, well-tamed as they have been, speak kindly and gratefully of me. I would rather have heard this than have got a present of £1000, for there could be no stronger testimony of my having done my duty among them. . . . I can't help a feeling of pride that a savage people, whom I was obliged to deal with so sternly, should appreciate and give me credit for good intentions."

Sir Herbert Edwardes had told Lord Canning when he was at Calcutta: "My lord, you may rely upon this, that if ever there is a desperate deed to be done in India, John Nicholson is the man to do it."

The time was rapidly drawing nigh when Britain in India would need this hero. In January 1857, Dost Mohamed, Ameer of Afghanistan, renewed his treaty with the British

Government at Jamrud, and concluded with these words: "Happen what may, I will keep it faithfully till death."

But John Nicholson made an excuse for not attending Sir John Lawrence's durbar; he had suffered so much at the hands of treacherous Afghans, he had found them so utterly false and faithless that his whole soul revolted against the idea of making them our friends and allies.

Fortunately Herbert Edwardes was right in trusting them this time, for during the Mutiny they might have taken a great revenge, but instead of that they loyally kept faith and lent us trusty fighters.

In May 1857, Nicholson was deputy-commissioner at Peshawur, General Sydney Cotton commanded the troops, and Colonel Herbert Edwardes was the commissioner in political charge. With these were Brigadier Neville Chamberlain, commander of the Punjab Irregular Force, and Major-General Reed, who commanded the Peshawur division of the army.

As we have seen in a former chapter, the officers were sitting at mess on the evening of 11th May, when the fatal telegram came which told how the mutineers from Meerut had entered Delhi and killed many Europeans. Next morning came the telegram sent from Meerut at midnight on the 10th: "Native troops in open mutiny: cantonments burnt: several officers killed: European troops under arms defending barracks."

At Peshawur they could at first hardly believe that the mutineers could get safely away from a camp guarded by two strong white regiments and several batteries of artillery! It was a thing to gasp at!

We have already described how Chamberlain was chosen to lead the movable column, and how Nicholson rode down the disaffected and helped to disarm the native regiments.

In June the death of Colonel Chester at Delhi called Chamberlain to fill his place, and Nicholson was chosen to command the Irregular Horse with the rank of brigadier-general.

Soon after Nicholson took up his command he moved to Jullundur, in which city the sepoys had been allowed to go off with their muskets and much treasure. The Rajah of Kapurthala offered to garrison Jullundur for us with his own troops: though the Rajah himself was loyal, his officers and men swaggered about rather offensively. When Nicholson came with his column *en route* for Delhi, the commissioner, Major Edward Lake, invited the officers of the Kapurthala troops to a durbar with Nicholson at his house.

All went well until the end, when General Mehtab Sing, a relation of the Rajah's, took his leave, and as the senior in rank was walking out of the room first, but Nicholson stalked with long strides to the door, waved Mehtab Sing back with an imperious air, while he let the rest of the company pass out. When they had all gone, Nicholson said to Lake: "Do you see that General Mehtab Sing has his shoes on?"

Now a native in native dress politely removes his shoes as we take off a hat. Then, speaking in Hindustani, Nicholson went on:—

"There is no possible excuse for such an act of gross impertinence. Mehtab Sing knows perfectly well that he would not venture to step on his own father's carpet save barefooted, and he only commits this breach of etiquette to-day because he thinks we are not in a position to resent the insult." Mehtab Sing stammered out some kind of apology; but Nicholson, still unappeased, politely turned to Lake and said: "I hope the commissioner will now allow me to order you to take your shoes off and carry them out in your own hands so that your followers may witness your discomfiture."

The native general, completely cowed, meekly did as he was ordered. We have this story on the authority of Lord Roberts, who was present on the occasion, and five years after had a good laugh with the Rajah about it. "We often chaff our general about that little affair," said the Rajah, and tell him he richly deserved the treatment he received from the great Nicholson Sahib.

Major Lake soon admitted the wisdom of Nicholson's action; for the manner of the Kapurthala people changed at once, disrespect vanished, and they ceased to swagger about as masters of the world. We cannot give details of the masterly way in which Nicholson proceeded to disarm native regiments, and how he punished the Sealkote mutineers for killing their brigadier and many women and children. In all these movements he showed the skill of a consummate general. But for his strategy the Delhi garrison would have been strengthened by four thousand good native soldiers. Sir John Lawrence, knowing the importance of taking Delhi, consented to Nicholson leading his column down to help the men on the Ridge.

The author of *The Siege of Delhi*, an officer who served there, writes: "A stranger of very striking appearance was remarked visiting all our pickets, examining everything and making most searching inquiries. His attire gave no clue to his rank; it evidently never cost the owner a thought. It was soon made out that this was General Nicholson, whose person was not yet known to camp; it was whispered at the same time that he was possessed of the most brilliant military genius. He was a man cast in a giant mould, with massive chest and powerful limbs, and an expression ardent and commanding—features of stern beauty, a long black beard, and sonorous voice."

On the 7th of August this stranger dined at the head-quarters mess; he sat silent and grave, and evidently damped down the gaiety of the younger officers. Sir Harvey Greathed says: "If we had all been as solemn and as taciturn during the last two months, I do not think we should have survived: our genial, jolly mess-dinners have kept up our spirits."

We must remember that Nicholson had only recently heard of the death of his great friend Sir Henry Lawrence; then the news from Cawnpur and Lucknow must have shocked him: he knew that Sir John Lawrence was sending down from the Punjab his last man and his last gun: no wonder he looked grave and stern.

Next day, when he visited Major Reid at Hindu Rao's house, the post which he and his sturdy Gurkhas had defended so gallantly for two months, Nicholson gave unconsciously some offence by his close questioning.

"I don't like his lofty manner and overbearing style of address," said the major to Baird-Smith, the chief Engineer.

"That wears off," was the reply; "you'll like him better when you have seen more of him." Kaye tells us that Reid's dislike soon turned to admiration, and the two men became excellent friends.

On the morning of the 12th, Nicholson rode away from Delhi to join his movable column: they had expected to be attacked by a sortie from Delhi, but there was a swamp on either side of the road, and they met no resistance. But they heard the roar of cannon, and at night the flash of guns told them how constant was the struggle.

On the morning of the 14th August they marched on to the Ridge with bands playing and colours flying, 3000 strong, while cheers welcomed their arrival.

We have already given some description of Nicholson's doings before Delhi: his routing of the enemy who had gone out to cut off the siege train, when at one time in fording a canal the water was over the horses' backs; his daily rounds with Taylor of the Engineers in search of a site for the new batteries; his impatient appeals to General Wilson to fix a day for the grand assault; his riding round at night to see that the sentries were on the alert; his last advice when the officers were consulting how they should proceed after they had carried the breaches in the wall:—

"Don't press the enemy too hard: let them have a golden bridge to retire by." For he knew there were many Sikhs in Delhi who had been unwillingly fighting the British: many sepoys who were there by compulsion. And he thought it unwise to render the enemy desperate by giving no hope of mercy.

On 1st September, Nicholson had written to Herbert Edwardes: "If it please Providence that I live through this business, you must get me alongside of you again, and be my guide and help in endeavouring to follow Sir Henry's example; for I am so weak and unstable that I shall never do any good of myself." So, then, this strong hero of war knew his own moral weakness and was not ashamed to confess it to a real friend.

He thought of the welfare of his soldiers in all the stress of battle. Thus he writes to Edwardes: "A poor orderly of mine, named Sâdat Khan, died here of cholera the other day. He has a mother and a brother, and I think a wife in the Usafzai country. Should I not be left to do it, will you kindly provide for the brother, and give the women a couple of hundred rupees out of my estate?"[1]

The storming of Delhi on the 14th September we need not dwell on now: the fighting in narrow streets, the fatal shot that laid Nicholson low in the act of calling on his men to try once more, the removal of the wounded general by Colonel Graydon and a sergeant, and later by his aide-de-camp, Captain Trench, who went for further assistance: all this has been already described. But one thing more we must add.

As he lay in a recess in the street, Captain Hay of the 60th Native Infantry, with whom Nicholson was not on very friendly terms, happened to bend over him. "I will make up my difference with you, Hay," gasped Nicholson, "I will let you take me back": so, with Captain Hay by his side, he was borne slowly back to the Kashmir gate; but when the captain left him with instruction to the bearers to go to the field hospital, these worthies put down the dhoolie and bolted, and then it was that Lieutenant Roberts found him as already described.

It was late in the afternoon when John Nicholson was carried into the field hospital. As he lay awaiting his turn, fate decreed that his brother Charles should be brought in wounded and set down by his side. Charles had just had his shattered arm amputated, and he, like his brother John, lay cold and white: they might have been two statues

[1] Kaye.

carved in marble. Sadly they recognised each other and murmured a last good-bye.

In the evening Neville Chamberlain came over from Hindu Rao's house to see him: the wounded man, shot through the lungs, would talk about the day's doings; this increased the danger to the wounded lung. But the strong man lingered on in great pain for nine days: in this time he sent loving messages to old friends and to his mother. Edwardes wired to Chamberlain: "Give John Nicholson our love in time and eternity. God ever bless him! I do not cease to hope and pray for him as a dear brother." At half-past nine on the morning of 23rd September the hero passed away.

It is a relief to know that Charles Nicholson lived some five years longer: he was removed to Umballa, whence he wrote with his left hand a long letter to Sir James Hogg, his uncle; he it was who gave John and Charles Nicholson the great opportunities they had seized so well. Early in 1858 Charles left India on sick leave for Ireland, and visited his mother at Lisburn. In October he went to the United States, married his cousin, Miss Gillilan, and brought her back to Ireland.

In 1862, Sir Hugh Rose offered him the command of a Gurkha regiment in North India; but on his way up country he broke a blood-vessel and died at the age of thirty-three.

John Nicholson's mother died at the age of eighty-eight, having outlived six of her seven children. Before she died, Mrs. Nicholson at her own cost placed a monument to John's memory in the Parish Church at Lisburn; this was designed and executed by J. H. Foley, R.A. The upper part of the tablet is a scene representing the storming of the Kashmir bastion carved in clear relief on white marble. Sir Herbert Edwardes wrote the inscription, in which were these words: "In all he thought and did, unselfish, earnest, plain and true . . . soldier and civilian, a tower of strength; the type of the conquering race."

CHAPTER IX

GENERAL SIR A. TAYLOR, G.C.B.: THE MAN WHO TOOK DELHI

ALEXANDER TAYLOR was a Scot by race and an Irishman by birth: many of his ancestors had been distinguished engineers, both civil and military, and they hailed from Aberdeen.

Alexander's grandfather, Captain George Taylor, began life as a civil engineer at Aberdeen: he planned and superintended the construction of the Aberdeen-Inverurie Canal, and the harbour of Howth (Dublin).

In 1779 we find him fighting as a volunteer in the British Army under Sir Henry Clinton, and distinguishing himself at the Siege of Charlestown: he received a commission as captain in the Duke of Cumberland's regiment in Jamaica. On his return he married Barbara Thompson, bought the family place, Anfield, and became captain of the Aberdeen Volunteers.

Soon after, he left Scotland for Dublin and undertook the management of high roads between Dublin and the south-west of Ireland.

The Taylors were the great road-makers: Alexander inherited this faculty. William Taylor, George's youngest son, the father of Sir Alexander, devoted himself to the introduction into Ireland of the new steam-engine, and owing to his energy and enthusiasm the Southern and South-Western Railway was speedily opened.

Alexander Taylor was this William's eldest son and was born in Dublin in 1826. At the early age of twelve the boy was sent to the famous school at Hofwyl, near

Berne, which was managed by Pestalozzi's friend, Herr Von Fellenberg.

The basis of the teaching was love to God and love to man: the education of the body and the character came first; hands, eyes and ears were carefully trained before the pure intelligence was instructed.

Alexander remained here till he was fifteen: he rapidly rose in the school, became a good gymnast, skater, rider and fencer. It was a splendid school for one who was to become an Engineer.

In August, 1841, Taylor entered the military college at Addiscombe, where he gained the friendship of George Fulton, killed at Lucknow in 1857. When the young lieutenant arrived at Calcutta he joined the headquarters of the Sappers at Meerut, and was shortly after sent to Ferozepur. As he had done much sailing at Chatham, Lord Ellenborough gave him charge of a flotilla of fifty boats for military bridging on the Sutlej. On the outbreak of the first Sikh War, Taylor was ordered to sink these boats and fall back on Ferozepur: here he was put in command of the Sappers and Miners, though only a young subaltern.

When the Sikhs withdrew Taylor had orders to raise the boats, and they afterwards formed the bridge across which the British Army marched to Lahore after the battle of Sobraon.

When fighting began at Multan (1848) he carried down the heavy Engineer train required for the siege in these same unwieldy boats. No doubt he enjoyed it vastly; for 200 miles he was fending them off shoals, or guiding them through foaming rapids; but he brought them safely to Multan, and won the praise and esteem of his only passenger—Robert Napier, his chief Engineer, and later known as Lord Napier of Magdala.

Modesty, promptitude, a huge appetite for work, resource in the time of peril, great cheerfulness—all these qualities were duly marked by his chief, who afterwards gave him his life's work—the construction of the grand trunk road between Lahore and Peshawur. Taylor was in charge of the Engineers' Park in both sieges of Multan, and distinguished himself by preparing all kinds of contrivances for facilitating siege operations, as well as by making brilliant and hazardous reconnaissances. For, in exploring the ground, as afterwards at Delhi, in taking measurements of walls, etc., many lives were saved. The writer has just heard from a Mutiny veteran how mistakes were sometimes made when besieging cities. In estimating the height of walls, ladders would not reach to the top, or the coping had not been knocked off by the guns: in consequence valuable lives were lost, as the attacking party were shot down before they could escalade the ramparts. It was such defaults as these which Alexander Taylor never permitted; he knew what to do, and how to do it well.

When the breaches in the walls of Multan were completed, Robert Napier allowed him to guide the party assaulting the left breach: in doing this Taylor was severely wounded.

At the battle of Gujerat (February 1849), being orderly officer to General Sir John Cheape, Taylor had his horse killed under him. He was with Gilbert in the pursuit of the Sikhs to the mouth of the Khyber, and was thanked for his services in dispatches.

In May 1849, Robert Napier entrusted Taylor with the construction of a new military road destined to connect Lahore and Peshawur—290 miles through a wild country that possessed no roads and little organised labour, and of which there were no maps. The Lahore-Peshawur road is now the first military road in India, and from the trunk line radiate branches in every direction.

On this work Taylor with his subordinates and roadmakers was employed unremittingly from 1849 to 1857.

The viaducts over the five rivers, the Sutlej, the Beas, the Ravi, the Chenab and the Jhelum, were to be postponed; but bridges over all lesser rivers were to be built, and a good and clear passage made through the rugged country between the Jhelum and the Indus.

For a few miles wide on each side of these rivers of the Punjab (five rivers) there lies a narrow belt of fertile land, irrigated by overflow waters. All between the rivers, with this exception, is jungle of tamarisk and thorn, haunted by wild beasts or wilder men, assassins and cattle-lifters.

The heat here is terrible amid these rocks and deserts and scanty grasses.

The Punjab is as populous as Bengal in the rich country, healthy and pleasant in the hill districts; but in the plains, as at Lahore and Multan, the heat is well-nigh intolerable. Hence an Indian proverb arose: "When God had Multan ready for His purpose, why did He make Hell?"

Of the different peoples among whom Taylor was working, come first the Sikhs, tall and lithe and bearded, the bravest and most chivalrous race in India: they had fought well against us in two great wars and taken their beating like men, and were soon to show how their good faith was as strong as their valour.

The aboriginal Goojurs and Gukkurs together with Rajputs made up a sixth part of the population; the rest, in the country round Multan, Hazâra and Peshawur, were mostly Mussulman: the farther west, the wilder the tribes —all ready to swoop down on the industrious nations of the richer valleys and slay with robbery under arms.

Such were the men amongst whom Taylor and his subordinates had to work: and when they first began, there was not a road or a map existent.

Taylor had to work single-handed: he had to be his own draughtsman, surveyor and leveller: he had to collect labourers from the district, not always by persuasion: he had to keep his own accounts and send them up punctually to Sir John Lawrence, who came once a year to inspect progress, and was more given to find fault than to praise.

Soon rumours began to come to him of sepoys shooting

their officers, of horsemen hurrying south towards Delhi, and of a great siege beginning. Still he toiled on amid the pickaxes and spades, wondering if his siege experiences at Multan might some day soon be thought useful down at Delhi! Then, one day, the commissioner of the district, Edward Thornton, came to see him, and said gaily, "Hello, Taylor! you here, still making roads! Why, you ought to be at Delhi, working in the trenches."

"I would give my eyes," replied Taylor, "to be there; but my work is here, and I do not think it right to volunteer."

Thornton rode off, musing on the strange throwing away of a good engineer, when he was so much wanted elsewhere.

The next time he saw John Lawrence he told him what he had seen, and what he had thought. And John Lawrence said curtly, "Send him!" So Thornton rode out again to Alexander Taylor and said:

"I have come from the chief commissioner: he says you are to go to Delhi."

"Oh!" said Taylor, "any of you fellows got a sword?"

In a quarter of an hour the road-maker was ready to start, and, joining Neville Chamberlain, he reached Delhi on 27th June. There Captain Taylor found Baird-Smith nominally chief Engineer, but his important staff duties and his increasing illness compelled him to delegate the actual duties of chief Engineer to the younger man from the Punjab, who had come to the camp with so brilliant a reputation.

As General Sir F. R. Maunsell has ably set out in his pamphlet on the siege of Delhi, the British force on the Ridge had just enough ammunition to form practicable breaches, and if the city could not be taken by surprise when this was expended, there was no other hope of success. The only site suitable for such an attack was covered with buildings, trees, copses and ruins, and was occupied more or less by the enemy.

Captain Taylor, from the first day of his arrival, began to examine the ground at the risk of his life and with many hairbreadth escapes. In these hazardous scoutings he was frequently accompanied by General Nicholson, who loved the audacity of such adventures.

For some time no one knew what he was studying or planning, for Taylor was the most modest and retiring of men.

Any one who might be informed that the Engineer was seeking a site for his batteries in the very ground occupied by a watchful enemy would say at once, how can he survey the site, take measurements and mark the position of the guns in the face of the enemy? The thing is absurd.

But Taylor was doing all this long before the siege guns arrived. Owing, however, to Baird-Smith being ill, no full report of the Engineer's part in the siege was written, and the earliest histories scarcely mentioned Taylor's name. But Sir John Kaye, after the publication of his *History of the Mutiny*, asked Sir Alexander Taylor some direct questions, and Sir Alexander's reply will probably be printed in full when the Engineer's *Life* by Miss Taylor is published.

General Maunsell writes: "I knew Taylor first at Multan and afterwards at Delhi. These defensive replies were forced from him by those who demanded the facts from him directly. Never was he one to claim more than his due. At Delhi he humbly let others take the credit and honour really due to him."

In Sir Alexander's letter, dated 29th November 1875, he states that he and Baird-Smith often discussed how the assault was to be made; they agreed that economy of time would be the chief point. It must be a surprise, and give no time to the enemy to prepare a counter-attack.

An attack in full form, with trenches, etc., was out of the question. There must be no room for error, but all must be actually seen and measured.

There was a great house called Ludlow Castle between our lines and the walls of the city, in which the enemy kept a large piquet of several hundred sepoys. As Taylor one day was watching Ludlow Castle with his glasses, he thought the old piquet had been withdrawn and the new one had not yet arrived. Ludlow Castle is set on the crest of a ridge sloping down towards the city walls. "Now's my chance to examine the ground," he thought: thereupon he threw down sword and belt, seized his pistol, ordered a piquet of sixteen men from the Guides to follow him, and passed between Ludlow Castle and the river; he even went as far as Khoodsia Bagh, an old summer palace of the Mogul kings.

Leaving the men in extended order outside this building, with strict orders on no account to fire, Taylor entered the walled enclosure with the havildar, or native officer, and explored it thoroughly; then, mounting on the wall next the city, he could see the sentry on the ramparts apparently quite close.

The Custom House, one hundred and eighty yards in front of him, and lower down, was between him and the city wall. Taylor lay on his face on the top of the palace wall behind a small shrub, and carefully examined the Custom House for more than an hour. They effected their retreat without being observed. It was risky work, because on their right when in the old palace there were dense groves of orange bushes, and to their rear was the enemy's piquet in Ludlow Castle. Taylor had ascertained that the roof of the Custom House had fallen in, but that the brick walls remained standing, and that the site was good for a battery. It, in fact, became the site of Battery No. 3.

He also learnt that Ludlow Castle was the only place near, and outside the walls, which was occupied in force; in other parts the vegetation was untrampled. Throughout July and August Taylor seized other opportunities to examine the ground and make plans for batteries.

Once he was going with twenty men far in front of our advanced posts, and had come to within sixty yards of a stone wall which crossed their path at right angles, when suddenly a couple of hundred sepoys sprang up, delivered a volley in their faces, and jumping the wall, tried to close with them.

Taylor and his men, thinking discretion the better part of valour in a case like this, turned and bolted like rabbits into the brushwood. Fortunately the fire had been bad, and no one was badly hurt, but they had to run half a mile to get clear, and escaped into Metcalfe's piquet.

On another occasion, Taylor says, Ludlow Castle seemed to be unoccupied and he ran down to it alone, and was taking observations from the flat roof when he suddenly perceived the head of a regiment entering the gateway beneath him: quietly the Engineer officer crept downstairs, went out at a door on the other side of the house and climbed the garden wall unnoticed.

By these close observations made in broad daylight Taylor was able to find out where the breaching batteries could be most successful.

Every night he unfolded his facts and plans to Baird-Smith, who at length laid them before General Wilson at headquarters.

The general read the report with astonishment, and some show of doubt. "Very important, Baird-Smith, if true and exact: but I question whether Captain Taylor has really gone so far as Ludlow Castle, let alone the Khoodsia Bagh." Upon this General Nicholson broke in: "Look here, general, I will undertake to go with Captain Taylor to Ludlow Castle and will report the result." Accordingly Taylor conducted John Nicholson at midnight into Ludlow Castle, which happened to be unoccupied, for the sepoys often left it empty for an hour between the relief of the garrison.

Then Taylor took his friend down to the old palace, and finally got him safely back to camp: no doubt he felt a little sore at his word being doubted. But Taylor was not a man to complain or feel a grievance.

Nicholson made such a report, that General Wilson made no more objections to Taylor's plans and projects; and, being an artilleryman himself, he must have fully realised the importance of a close examination of the ground and the lie of the guns.

After this Nicholson used to go every day on the works for the batteries, very often from an hour before dawn until sunset: he did this partly that he might arrange for any movement of troops which Taylor desired. How the batteries, when finished, did their work we have already seen in a previous chapter: Taylor's chief trouble was in removing the old brick walls of the Custom House which partly blocked one battery.

On the evening of 7th September they began to trace the assailing batteries, and worked so hard that by the next morning they had mounted one gun: the sepoys noticed it and sent out a sortie from the Lahore gate, which was defeated; and as the enemy's guns could not fire while their own men were out, it gave the Engineers time to complete five platforms and mount five guns which immediately opened fire. Brind and Kaye soon rendered the Mori and Kashmir bastions harmless. By dawn of the 11th, No. 2 battery had been completed—the third battery under Captain Medley, placed only 160 yards from the Water bastion, was armed by the night of the 11th.

A fourth battery under the gallant Tombs, for throwing shells, was traced near the old palace and completed on the 11th.

Then the two sides proceeded fiercely to pound one another, until on the afternoon of the 13th Wilson and Baird-Smith thought the breaches sufficient.

But Taylor did not consider his work over even when his batteries had made the breaches, and our men had won the ramparts of the city. On 18th September, when he saw how Nicholson, and after him Colonel Greathed, had failed to carry Burn bastion, Taylor applied for a large body of men, and with these he occupied a large block of houses between the workshops and the Begum's gardens; it was Wilde's regiment that took possession. Sir John Kaye writes: "Ever to the front, ever active, ever fertile in resources, the Engineer brigade had much to do, and did it well. It had been terribly shattered during the assault: few had escaped"—(on the 14th Lieutenant Tandy had been killed, Lieutenant Salkeld died a few days after, when blowing in the Kashmir gate, and eight other Engineer officers were wounded).

It was Taylor who suggested to the commander-in-chief that, instead of fighting in the open streets, the Engineers should work through the sheltered houses to the Burn bastion. A little friction arose at first with the brigade officers, but this soon passed away. We have seen in the chapter on Lord Roberts how successful this plan was, and how economical of life. Kaye writes: "Taylor was one who thought nothing impossible; all men worked under him with the heartiest goodwill, for he animated and inspired all who came into contact with him in battery or in trench. The younger officers of the Engineers swore by him."

Sir John Lawrence wrote to Lord Dalhousie on 14th January 1858: "Up to the capture of Delhi, the scales were trembling in the balance. The Punjabis of all classes have behaved admirably . . . still, if Delhi had not fallen, we must have been ruined. Had the troops retreated, all must have been lost. To Nicholson, Alexander Taylor of the Engineers and Neville Chamberlain the real merit of our success is due. Alexander Taylor, though only the second Engineer before Delhi, was really the officer who designed and arranged all the scientific operations which led to the success of the assault, and in the actual attack was as forward as any man that day."[1]

General Sir F. Maunsell, the Engineer officer in charge of the right attack, writes: "I can frankly state that none of us were capable of doing what Taylor did: we doubtless all thought ourselves fine fellows—more or less—but as to a mastery or control of the great questions and issues involved, we were nowhere as compared with him . . . we all believed in him as a first-rate man."

[1] Bosworth Smith's *Lord Lawrence*, vol. ii. p. 251.

It is only of late that the importance of the siege of Delhi has been recognised: the great anxiety as to the fate of Lucknow with its women and children took all the public attention at the time, and Delhi was almost ignored.

Sir Henry Norman writes: "Throughout the operations Taylor seems to have been omnipresent, and to bear a charmed life . . . the plan of the attack was bold and skilful. . . . Pandy can fight well behind cover, but here he was outmanœuvred; his attention was diverted from the real point of attack until the last (by the feint on the right) and then the cover on the left was seized at the right moment, without loss, and all its advantages turned against him."

Taylor himself pays a tribute to the services of his chief, Baird-Smith: "He did all that could be done by a chief Engineer of great capacity, but crippled by heavy sickness; took a sound view of our position and its requirements, and gave firm and wise council to General Wilson, more than once. . . . For all this grand work he deserved the thanks, not only of the Delhi field force, but of every white face to the north of Delhi, whose fate depended on our success."

After the fall of Delhi, Colonel Baird-Smith left in a bullock-cart, being too ill to ride on horseback: Taylor took up the command, and was told to restore the battered fortifications and strengthen the bastions.

Taylor would rather have served with one of the columns destined to put down rebellion in the North-West Provinces; but duty was duty to him. However, his plans, which were approved by General Wilson, were thought by Sir John Lawrence too ambitious: probably Sir John thought that the time for rebuilding had not yet come, and that Taylor was wanted elsewhere. So, in November, Taylor went to Agra in command of the Engineer Brigade, and on the 10th of December joined Seaton's column at Alighur, south-east of Delhi, just in time to take part in the brilliant cavalry engagement at Khasgunge, in which the Carabineers and Hodson's Horse so ably distinguished themselves.

Colonel Sir Edward Thackeray, V.C., who was attached to Seaton's column, gives a vivid picture of Hodson thoroughly enjoying himself as a Paladin of the olden time.

It was early in the morning of 17th December, while the dawn was yet cool and grey, the column was near Puttiali, when distant shots were heard. Taylor and Hodson, attended by some of his troopers, rode forward to reconnoitre: they reached a village which seemed to be deserted; there was no sign of life, the gates were built up, and there was no admittance.

Taylor sent two men back for some powder-bags to blow up one of the gates: meanwhile both officers dismounted; and, while Taylor and Thackeray lay down under a tree for a short nap, Hodson took a hog-spear and wandered about on a voyage of discovery.

He happened at length to stray into an enclosed yard, at one end of which was a long, low one-storeyed house: the door was fast bolted. Taking a run and a kick Hodson forced open the central door, but found not what he had expected. Instead of an empty house, he saw dimly in the darkness of the room ten swordsmen in front of him; and he remembered too late that he had left his pistol and sword elsewhere.

In a moment the sepoys stepped forward to attack him!

Hodson seized the situation in a flash, stepped back one pace into the yard, and, as each swordsman came through the narrow doorway, so low that he had to stoop and could not immediately use his sword, Hodson met him with a spear thrust.

Taylor says that this occurred within a few yards of where he had been lying down: Hodson came back to Taylor and said, "Come and have a look at what I have found in here."

They went together, the troopers following, and Taylor

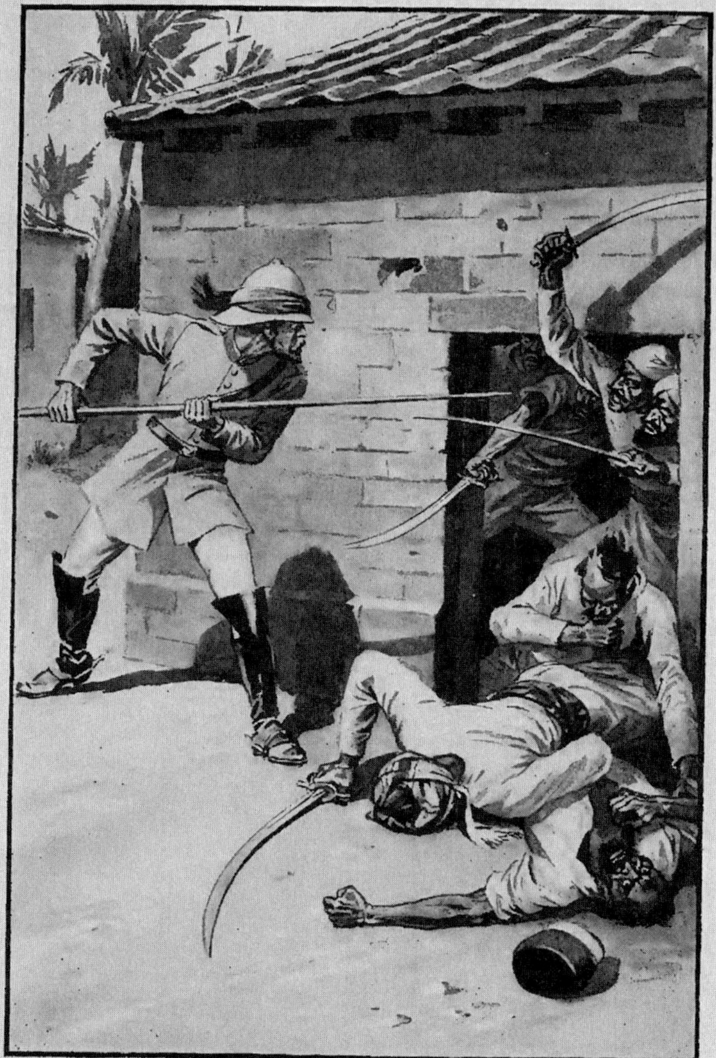

HODSON AND HIS BOAR-SPEAR

While wandering through a village with a boar-spear in his hand, Hodson came across a low building with locked door. He burst it open with his foot, and discovered ten armed men. Instead of making a judicious retreat, he laid each one low by a spear thrust as he emerged from the doorway.

was rather horrified to see ten armed men, dead or dying, stretched about the floor of the room.

"Either their lives or mine, Taylor—theirs for choice."

It was wonderful to see how cool and resourceful the great scout was in sudden danger. Taylor did not know that his own trial was near at hand; for, after going to the gateway to ascertain how best to dispose of the powder-bags, he began to stroll along the foot of the village wall.

There was a low round tower springing out of this wall and covered with creepers: into this Taylor climbed, got through a narrow window and found a staircase which brought him on to the flat, mud roof. There was not a sound to be heard nor a soul moving.

He began to advance slowly and cautiously, as he had so often done at Ludlow Castle, when he suddenly spied a man on a neighbouring roof on the other side of a very narrow street! This man was kneeling, but not saying his prayers: no, for Taylor perceived a long matchlock levelled at him.

Resourceful as Hodson, but not perhaps quite so cool, Taylor gave a wild shout, rushed straight at the sepoy and cleared the narrow passage at a bound (had he not learnt to jump in Switzerland?). The dark man did not wait for more; he thought a white devil was coming, dropped his gun and vanished.

So, Taylor had a story to tell Hodson while the powder-bags were being placed close to the gate: the village was found to be deserted after all. When they came next morning to Puttiali, Taylor, riding along the front, easily ascertained the position of the guns, as each foolishly fired on him when he came opposite; then Taylor sent a plan to General Seaton and suggested where his guns could enfilade the fort. In consequence, the enemy, although some 5000 strong, broke and fled before our infantry could arrive, leaving all their guns and carriage in our hands.

Towards the end of the year Taylor joined the force under the commander-in-chief, and was sent to Cawnpur to prepare an Engineer Park for the siege of Lucknow, and a bridge of casks for the passage of the Gumti River. He was in command of the Bengal Engineers at the capture of Lucknow, and was wounded at the taking of the Begum Koti, or Palace, by the 93rd Highlanders and 4th Punjab Rifles, led by the chivalrous Adrian Hope.

Taylor never completely recovered from his wound: for the bullet passed through the leg a few inches above the knee.

In a letter to a friend Taylor writes: "We had got into the palace and had made good headway. I had mounted up to the highest pinnacle to see what was ahead of me, and what further could be done. Pandy, in an adjoining house, took advantage of me."

It was on this day, 11th March 1858, that Hodson was mortally wounded. Colonel Chalmers wrote: "Captain Hodson, the best cavalry officer in this, or indeed I think in any other service, is very dangerously wounded. . . . Major Taylor of the Engineers is also wounded, and has had to lie up, and is a great loss. As in reality he was the man who planned the taking of Delhi, so here . . . he has pushed on in the face of opposition. . . . The consequence of his wound was the giving up of a quarter of a mile of street we had got."

But even when our men had got through the breach at the palace and crushed the main opposition, there still remained hundreds of sepoys hiding in the various rooms and cellars. One encounter of Lieutenant MacBean with eleven men won him the Victoria Cross.

Forbes-Mitchell in his *Reminiscences* gives the story.

Paddy MacBean, as the men called him, met a havildar, a naik, and nine sepoys at one gate of the palace, and killed ten of them one after the other. The havildar was the last to come out, and by this time several of our men had come up to help their comrade.

"Stand back, boys; fair play for the havildar," shouted MacBean: thereat he made a feint to cut, but instead lowered his point and ran his opponent through the chest.

It is said that this strong young man had been an Inverness-shire ploughman before he enlisted, and rose from the ranks to command the regiment, dying a major-general.

Next morning the Begum Palace presented a strange spectacle with its enormous mirrors, lamps and chandeliers, with dead Highlanders and sepoys lying about on the rich carpets: the smell of burnt clothing and hair was horrible, and large parties of camp-followers were brought in to drag out the dead. For on our side we had lost 75 officers and 800 men killed or wounded.

As soon as Taylor was well enough he took his first furlough to Europe after an absence of fifteen years.

Lord Canning wrote to thank him for his great services, and that was his only reward for some time.

In 1861 he returned to India and was offered the post of Chief Engineer of the Central Provinces: but the family instinct was strong in him; he chose rather to return to his old work in the Punjab, the completion of the grand trunk road.

However, he saw some more active service under General Neville Chamberlain; was appointed Chief Engineer in the Punjab, and in 1876 was designated Quarter-Master-General at Simla: but as an affection of the eyes threatened him with loss of sight, Taylor went to Europe and consulted a famous German occulist, Dr. Meurer, who effected a cure.

In 1876 he returned to India and was appointed Secretary to Government in the Public Works Department, but soon resigned, and on coming home succeeded Sir George Chesney as President of the Royal Engineering College at Cooper's Hill; this post he filled for sixteen years. Taylor became at once a favourite with all members of the College staff: he regarded the professors as his colleagues and consulted them without reserve. Being intensely religious, he looked upon moral discipline and example as the highest ideal to aim at, and insisted upon regularity in attendance at the Chapel services. He still kept his interest in yachting and athletic sports, and though old in years acted as though he were young.

The obituary notice in the *Cooper's Hill Magazine* says: "Sir Alexander was loved and respected by every one with whom he came into contact: he was a firm friend, and always did his best to help those who were in any sort of trouble. He was a strict disciplinarian, but generally had a strong tendency to take a merciful view of a case. But in the event of anything of grave importance taking place, he was the very last person any student of Cooper's Hill cared to meet."

He died on 25th February 1912, at the ripe age of eighty-six.

From a memoir by Col. Sir Edward Thackeray in the *R. E. Journal*, by kind permission of the Editors, from papers by Gen. Sir F. R. Maunsell and from other sources.

CHAPTER X

SIR HENRY AND JOHN LORD LAWRENCE: THE GREAT TWIN BRETHREN

THE Lawrences were sprung from the mixed races of Scot and Irish that we find in Ulster. The cool caution of the Scot mixes with the more genial humour of the Irish Celt, and sometimes one member of a family inherits the one characteristic and another inherits the other.

Henry was five years older than John and had more of the Irishman in him: John was at heart a Scot, sometimes rather hard and dour, but with lovable qualities.

Their mother, Letitia Catherine Knox, was a business-like woman, who kept the family together when her husband, Colonel Alexander Lawrence, by his habit of speaking his mind too freely, failed to make his mark as he might have done.

In 1813 the three elder sons, Alexander, George, and Henry, were sent to the Grammar School of Londonderry, now Foyle College, presided over by their mother's brother, the Rev. James Knox. There they drank in something of the daring spirit of old Derry, whose watchword "No surrender!" seems to have been before Sir Henry's mind in his last agony at Lucknow. Mr. Huddlestone, a connection of Mrs. Lawrence, kindly gave some of the boys cadetships in the East India Company.

Henry went to Addiscombe, being selected for the artillery. In 1822 he arrived at Calcutta and was quartered at Dum-Dum, where he stayed three years, when the Burmese war broke out and Lawrence was summoned to serve under Colonel Lindsay. Fever caught in the swamps of Arracan compelled him to go to the sanatorium at Penang, and thence to Canton.

Here he began to study surveying—a knowledge which was to serve him in good stead; for on going home he joined the Irish Survey, and here he met his cousin, Honoria Marshall, a young lady of deep religious feeling and artistic instincts, whom Lawrence afterwards married.

On his return to India he passed in the native languages at Cawnpur, and Lord William Bentinck, at George Lawrence's request, appointed Henry assistant to the Revenue Survey of India.

This was the final and most important element in his education: for while engaged on survey work he got into touch with the real natives, with the peasant proprietors and the landowners, and thus grew to sympathise with them in their troubles and distress. His wife lived with him now in a tiny hut or tent and became his helper in every work of justice and mercy.

Here he learnt the good policy of making light assessments so that the poor cultivator might have a chance of gaining a profit out of his toil; in making roads and bridges and putting the native usurer out of countenance.

Here, too, they conceived the idea of the Lawrence Asylums, to save the children of our soldiers from early death in the heat of the plains.

In 1841, Henry Lawrence marched with a Sikh contingent to Kabul, but won no honours from Government.

However, soon after this, Lord Ellenborough made him Resident at the Court of Nepal. Some articles he wrote from here for the *Calcutta Review* attracted the notice of the new Governor-General, Sir Henry Hardinge. He soon appointed Henry Lawrence to be political officer on the frontier; at Lahore Henry trusted the Sikhs as some thought dangerously, but kept the turbulent natives in check, and exerted such a good influence on Golab Singh, the Jummu chief, that that worthy abolished suttee and slavery throughout his dominions. In 1847, Lawrence went home, and the Queen made him a Knight Commander of the Bath.

After his return to India, Lord Dalhousie annexed the Punjab, and made Sir Henry president of a governing Board, having for his colleagues his brother John and Mr. Mansel.

Sir Henry's policy was to be lenient, merciful, and kind: twice he visited all the stations in the Punjab, riding thirty or forty miles a day. Good authorities say that his work at this period did much to quell the Mutiny that was coming. For he made the Sikhs our true and faithful friends. John Lawrence sent them to Delhi to help us on the Ridge, and he has been deservedly praised for all he did. But if it had not been for his brother's generous policy, he could not have sent a man from the Punjab.

Montgomery, a friend of Sir Henry, joined the Board; but it happened that he more often sided with John, for both of them felt that Henry's chivalrous spirit led him into extravagant measures. The condition of the Sikh nobility grieved Sir Henry and he longed to help them. The friction between the brothers came to Lord Dalhousie's ears, and when both sent in their resignation, he determined to dissolve the Board and appoint Henry's younger brother, John, sole ruler in the Punjab. He offered Henry the Agency to the Governor-General in Rajputana. Sir Henry accepted this with a bitter sense of injury done him, and with the feeling that he had been right in his dealings with the native princes, and his brother had been wrong.

"To know Sir Henry was to love him," said one of his friends.

Bosworth Smith writes: "Nobody has ever done so much towards bridging over the gulf that separates race from race, colour from colour, and creed from creed; nobody has ever been so beloved, nobody has ever deserved to be so beloved, as Sir Henry Lawrence"[1]

When the time came for him to quit Lahore, in

[1] *Life of Lord Lawrence*, Smith, Elder & Co.

January 1853, a long procession of weeping native chiefs followed his carriage, some for ten miles, some for twenty, from the city. His sun was set, and they could not be expecting favours to come: but they wished to testify their grief and their gratitude for one who had protected those that were down. Robert Napier (Lord Napier of Magdala) was the last to take leave of him and bade him an affectionate farewell. So to Rajputana Sir Henry fared. First he visited the gaols and made them more healthy; many prisoners he released. The Rajput princes he incited to put down widow-burning and think a little of the welfare of their subjects.

But a great trouble came upon him when his beloved wife, who had done so much to help him with his work and to cheer him in his hours of depression, sickened and died.

Then he was all for going home, to see his old friends in Ireland: but a new governor-general, who had heard of the wonderful and engaging qualities of the man, offered him the commissionership of Oudh.

The disappointed man plucked up health and spirits at the honour done him and the recognition it showed of the important work he had already effected.

But the appointment was made a few years too late: Sir Henry found Oudh seething with discontent; the princes were in the dust, and kept there in abject poverty, so that their ladies were forced to drive out after dark in order to sell their shawls and jewels in the bazaars.

The stipends of the old nobility had been neglected, and one of the first things Sir Henry did was to invite them to the Residency and pay up what was due.

The country was full of disbanded soldiers, every man an enemy of the Company; for their future had been ruined. The sepoy's privileges had been taken from him, his pay was poor, his pension—if it came at all—could only be obtained when he was too old to enjoy it: many rajahs believed that the English Government had broken faith with them, and were ready to listen to the agitators who swore the Christians were resolved to do away with caste and change their religion. In the Punjab, Henry Lawrence had won the trust and confidence of the Sikhs, chiefs and people alike.

As long ago as 1843, he had written a paper on the condition of the native army, insisting on the importance of the sepoys being well paid, disciplined, and rendered absolutely reliant on the good faith of the Government. He had predicted all that followed at Delhi and elsewhere, if the dangers should be overlooked. But his paper was lost in the waste-paper basket: now they expected him to stay the Mutiny!

Sir Henry Lawrence arrived at Lucknow and took charge of his province about 20th March. He found brigandage on the increase and took steps to crush it. Then the chiefs and princes were called to durbar, or spoken to in private, and assured of justice being done them.

But, knowing the native mind as he did, Sir Henry perceived that things had gone too far for gentle measures only.

There was an old Sikh fort, square and castellated, near the Residency, a tumble-down building on a site thirty feet above the road, which had long been used as a storehouse. This fort Sir Henry had quietly cleared out and put in repair, that it might be a place of refuge in time of sudden *émeute*.

On 1st May the 7th Oudh Infantry, stationed in a suburb of Lucknow, refused to use their cartridges: next day the regiment was surrounded and disarmed: the ringleaders were tried and punished, the loyal officers were promoted and rewarded.

On 11th May the telegraph ceased to work and the postal service was disorganised: people began to feel uneasy.

On the 14th, news came of the outbreak at Meerut and Delhi, and of the restoration of the old Mogul dynasty.

Sir Henry at once placed troops and guns in the old fort, and desired all English families to assemble in the Residency grounds. He also held the southern end of the cantonments with British troops. The Residency site was extensive, healthy, and supplied with water; it possessed much house accommodation and shelter, and commanded the river face for half its circle.

Lucknow is about five and a half miles long and two and a half broad, lying mainly along the southern or right bank of the Gumti, and encircled on its three other sides by a deep canal: it is forty-two miles east of Cawnpur. The Mutchi Bhown and the Residency lay close to the river, on its north bank, to the east of the stone and iron bridges.

After 23rd May, the Sikh fort being now secured, batteries and defensive works were begun on the Residency, parapets and breastworks were raised, streets were blocked up which interfered with the defence, and many buildings were barricaded and loopholed.

Meanwhile food and supplies came pouring in from the country, and none of the rebels thought of stopping them!

Sir Henry called in two bodies of pensioners, one of sepoys and one of Oudh artillerymen, both of whom gave loyal service during the siege, together with a body of trusty Sikhs.

On 30th May, as the staff were at dinner, a faithful sepoy rushed in with the news that the sepoys had just broken out at evening gun-fire from their lines: they were gutting and burning the officers' houses and firing muskets wildly.

At the main picket they had killed the officer in charge, Lieutenant Grant, and a stray shot had killed Brigadier Handscombe!

Sir Henry rose from dinner and moved to the Government House near the cantonment, which was guarded by the 13th Native Infantry, who had remained loyal. Captain Hardinge with his irregular cavalry patrolled the streets of the cantonment.

Next morning the mutineers were attacked, defeated, and chased away ten miles or more: the city police dispersed a large body of bad characters who were trying to cross the river.

The flight of the mutineers took off some of the strain of anxiety, and enabled the besieged to know who were their friends.

From 3rd June onward the news came of mutinies at Seetapur, at Faizabad, and elsewhere, and the conduct of the large landowners proved that they sympathised with the rebels.

Kavanagh, writing about the night of the 30th, says: "Sir Henry was without fear for himself, and his noble nature melted at the thought of the danger in which we were soon to be involved.

"A more unselfish man never breathed, he would willingly have walked to death to avert the doom that threatened his countrymen."

It was indeed a fearful night for a sick man to pass who felt the heavy weight of responsibility upon him.

The screams of the mutineers in their lines, stealthy, gliding figures passing in the streets from glare to shadow as they fired the thatched bungalows around, the crackling of blazing bamboos and the crash of falling roofs, all must have contributed to weaken the health of Sir Henry.

By the 9th of June, under medical advice, he gave over temporary charge of his duties to a Council, with Mr. Gubbins at its head. But two days later, hearing that his policy of retaining native troops was being set aside, he resumed command and recalled many that had been sent away.

On 11th June he wrote to Brigadier Inglis and informed him that now he was of opinion there should only be one position to defend: all the treasure, guns, stores, etc., in the Mutchi Bhown must be withdrawn into the Residency; for the condition of Cawnpur troubled him, and he pushed on the defences of the Residency.

About 12th June cholera appeared and carried off many valuable lives and some children. On the same day the military police mutinied, and were pursued by volunteers from the Residency under Captain Forbes: this officer did valuable service with his volunteers in the surrounding country before the siege. But on the 28th the news came of Sir H. Wheeler's capitulation at Cawnpur, and at once everything was changed.

The poor ladies in the Residency heard and discussed the awful tidings with white faces and reeling heads and sickened hearts. The men turned to thoughts of vengeance, and "Cawnpur" became the war-cry for severities which British soldiers of a later generation would be glad to disown.

Meanwhile the Governor-General was writing home: "Sir Henry Lawrence is doing admirably at Lucknow; all safe there." On receiving this approval the Court of Directors named Sir Henry governor-general, in case Lord Canning should die.

An honour paid to merit, and never known by Sir Henry: he, for his part, was preparing for his own death,—perhaps half wishing it might come soon.

"If anything happens to me, I recommend that Colonel Inglis should succeed me in command . . . there should be no surrender. I commend my children and the Lawrence Asylums to Government." The Derry note of "No surrender!" was continually sounding in his ears.

As soon as the mutineer regiments heard of the Cawnpur massacre they began to flock back to Lucknow. Sir Henry ordered a reconnaissance for 30th June to check their movement. He took a third of his garrison, ten guns, and one howitzer. But the enemy were in force, and defeated him at Chinhut with the loss of four officers, many men, and five guns; the howitzer also was taken.

Sir Henry, seeing his native artillerymen cut the traces of their guns, was heard to exclaim, "My God!—and I brought them to this!"

As our wounded men struggled back many natives came from the houses along the road and offered them water and milk.

Hundreds of people had been engaged at work in the Residency that day, but suddenly they all disappeared, as if by magic! A few minutes after, the first fugitives from the fight came in with their tale of disaster.

In a moment gates were shut and barred and batteries were manned: in the dark of the night of 1st July, Colonel Palmer silently withdrew his men from the Mutchi Bhown, and Lieutenant Thomas lighted a twenty-minute fuse to blow up the magazine.

Thus the siege of the Residency began on 2nd July, and lasted till Havelock and Outram reinforced the besieged on 25th September. Kavanagh says that at first the higher and airy rooms were given to the officers' families, amid some competition for places. But the lofty rooms proved more dangerous, and soon the common peril levelled all distinctions of rank: for as the servants had deserted, the ladies had to do their own cooking, nursing, etc. During the whole siege there was food enough, owing to Sir Henry's forethought. The 32nd Regiment formed the backbone of the defence, and contained many Cornish miners who were very useful.

On the morning of the 2nd of July, Sir Henry went round early, inspecting every post and encouraging the garrison, telling men what they had to do, and steadying all in their duty.

Sir Henry had chosen an upper room in the Residency, into which already one shell had penetrated.

He would not change his room, because from it he could command a wide view over the city.

A little before eight o'clock a.m. he lay down for a short rest after his labours, while he discussed business with Captain Wilson, his nephew George being on another bed at his side.

At eight a shell burst in the room, bringing down part

of the ceiling and filling the air with blinding smoke. George Lawrence was unhurt, Wilson's shirt was torn from his back.

"Are you hurt, uncle?" asked George Lawrence after a brief silence.

"I think I am killed," was the reply.

They carried him out under the verandah, and Sir Henry said to the doctor after he had examined the wound in his thigh, "How long have I to live, doctor?"

"Three days perhaps, Sir Henry."

"I think not so long," murmured the shattered man. Then he turned his thoughts to the defence, and after giving instructions and naming Major Banks his successor in the civil administration, and Brigadier Inglis in the military command together with Major Anderson his chief Engineer, he repeated again and again, "No surrender!": and to one of his friends he said, "Bury me simply, with just a stone saying, 'Here lies Henry Lawrence, who tried to do his duty.'" He died on the morning of 4th July after hours of great agony, and his loss was lamented by many of all creeds and colours. "I feel as if at Lucknow and Delhi (Nicholson) I had lost the father and the brother of my public life," wrote Sir Herbert Edwardes to John Lawrence. "His loss just now will be a national calamity," was the reply. The brother who represented chivalry, generosity, and sympathy was gone: the stronger character of John Lawrence remained, to stamp out the last sparks of mutiny and to secure the English rule.

John Lawrence, five years younger than Henry, like his brother was sent to Foyle College, where such heroes were educated as Lord Gough, "the most reckless of generals"; Sir George Lawrence, the Afghan prisoner; Sir Henry Lawrence, Sir Robert Montgomery. The last was John's intimate companion there, and in India, and writes of Lawrence as "determined and quick-tempered, recording that in their walks he used to entertain him with long stories of sieges and battles." For as a boy Lawrence read history and biography, knew a good deal of the campaigns of Hannibal, was thoroughly conversant with Plutarch's *Lives*, and infinitely preferred reading about live men to studying dead languages. He tells us that at his preparatory school he was flogged every day, except one, when he was flogged twice.

Even at Haileybury College, where he was sent to study for the Indian Civil Service, his industry was fitful; but he passed out third for Bengal without having attracted much notice from his professors. Indeed, Principal Batten scolded his son for "loafing about with that tall Irishman" who seemed to be of no particular merit. At this time John Lawrence looked rugged and uncouth, but he had some Irish humour and plenty of keen intelligence: he did not much care for games, but would go long walks in the country or drive tandem.

Henry, who was home on furlough, used to coach him up for his examinations. John was eighteen when he went to India with his brother Henry, and arrived at Calcutta in February 1830. Here they separated, Henry going to Kurnal, north of Delhi, John to Fort William College to study native languages.

After passing in Hindustani and Persian he obtained a post at Delhi as assistant judge. Even at this time he had an old look in his face, an expression of hunger and care, with strong lines like Sir Colin Campbell's; he was restless and eager to be doing something strenuous.

One of his first discoveries was to catch the King of Delhi's Lord Chancellor forging deeds to his great profit.

That swarthy nobleman was condemned to five years' labour on the public roads; we doubt if the punishment did not appear to his countrymen unjustly severe. There are such things as privileges which seem venerable by their long usage.

After four years at Delhi, Lawrence was transferred to a more northern district and nearer to his brother's post.

Here he mixed freely with the natives, redressed wrongs,

punished wrong-doers severely, and, where Henry would have made himself beloved, John was feared and respected.

Once when Lawrence had fever and felt depressed, a friend dropped in for a chat. Lawrence heard him listlessly, until he happened to say he had just met a fakir.

"Anything new?" I asked the beggar.

"Indeed there is," replied the fakir; "old Sahib is gone, we all sorry! for one Larens Sahib is come in his place."

"What! you don't like the new Sahib?"

"No, no! such a change in my poor country! all the rogues get punished now—all the revenue is collected—it is terrible—terrible for the country."

John Lawrence sat up and laughed; the fever was quickly going, the man's unwilling testimony acted like a tonic; he began to mend from that hour.

One friend gave Lawrence the nickname of Oliver, because he was so like Cromwell, severe but just. A native officer said of him: "When he is in anger his voice is like a tiger's roar, and the pens tremble in the hands of the writers all round the room."

In 1844, John Lawrence married Miss Hamilton, the daughter of a plucky justice of the peace in Donegal.

As they were travelling in Italy the news of the Afghan rising came and of George Lawrence being held captive.

They arrived at Bombay in November 1842 and went through the Central Provinces to Cawnpur, where they stayed with Richard Lawrence, the youngest of the Lawrence brothers.

As John had at present no billet, he bought tents and horses and encamped about gipsy-fashion. One day they came upon a large encampment in the jungle; and as they gazed in wonder, a man in Afghan dress came out of a tent, shaded his eyes with his hand and then suddenly shouted—

"Is that you, John?"

"Yes—but who on earth are you, sir?"

"Well—I am your brother George—free after a long captivity."

"What a chance—absurdly improbable," we should say if we met the story in fiction; but reality has a habit of giving us rare shocks of joy and sorrow and of fear.

George had much to tell of his perils among the Afghans, and John had his young wife to introduce. They spent a day together, and as they went on their way John heard he had been appointed civil and sessions judge at Delhi.

It was owing to the years spent at Delhi, when he took stock of the yielding nature of the population, that John Lawrence advised an immediate assault on the city at the outset of the Mutiny. Here in 1845 the new Governor-General, Sir Henry Hardinge, met him, saw his strong points, and, after the Punjab had been annexed, made him ruler over the Jullundur Doab, a country lying between the rivers Sutlej and Beas.

Here he enforced his three commandments: "Thou shalt not burn thy widow": "Thou shalt not kill thy daughters": "Thou shalt not bury alive thy lepers."

In 1853 he was made chief commissioner of the Punjab, and gradually collected near him a coterie of strong men: Richard Temple, Nicholson, Chamberlain, Edwardes, Montgomery, Lumsden, Daly, and others.

At this time we are told he was curt in his speech, very sharp in mastering details, used no complimentary phrases to the chiefs, and used to sit in his room with his shirt-sleeves turned up, to the horror of his Indian attendants.

In 1851, Lord Dalhousie pressed him to go home to recruit his health; but John Lawrence declined, saying that in 1855 he would have served his time and be entitled to his annuity: "I do not think I have more than three or four years of good honest work left in me."

Yet this man was to work on in the Punjab seven years longer, meeting the sepoy mutiny with strong, unflinching resolution; he was to serve four years at home in the Indian Council, and return to India as Viceroy for five years of hard work, and then return to work in London as chairman of the School Board!

Perhaps the long apprenticeship to the strenuous labour of governing a people many of whom had been robbers and murderers from their cradles, steeled this man's heart and mind and purpose to work on till the night came.

His wife, too, possessed much the same spirit of resistance; for in 1855, though she was very ill and was ordered home by the doctors, she stoutly refused to quit her husband's side, and thus was enabled to support him by her sympathy through the trying months of the Mutiny.

Even that tower of strength, John Nicholson, gave his chief much anxiety at times by his overbearing and wayward conduct.

Nicholson resented having to account for his punitive measures.

The following was his official report to the chief commissioner of one of his prompt sallies:—

"SIR,—I have the honour to report that a man came into my compound to-day, intending to kill me, and that I shot him dead.—Your obedient servant,

"JOHN NICHOLSON."

On 4th May 1857, John Lawrence visited Sealkote, a depôt for the new military instruction; he wished to see for himself the feelings of the sepoys, and wrote to Lord Canning a favourable report! On 12th May came the telegram from Delhi announcing the outbreak of the Mutiny! Henry Lawrence, the man of sympathy, had foreseen this result many years before. But when Sir John Lawrence had the scales dashed from his eyes, he acted promptly, and so did Montgomery, disarming the sepoys at Lahore before they could think twice about mutiny.

Lawrence at this time was suffering from neuralgia, but when the news came from Delhi he left his bed of pain and sent off letters and telegrams in all directions, taking upon him to stir up and direct the commander-in-chief, General Anson. "Everything now depends on energy and resolution: a week or two hence it may be too late." Even to the Governor-General, Lord Canning, Lawrence wrote in peremptory style: "Send for our troops from Persia. Intercept the force now on its way to China and bring it to Calcutta. Every European soldier will be required to save the country."

To his subordinates Sir John wrote: "Disarm the regulars if you suspect them, hunt them down if they mutiny, enlist the Sikhs, collect camels, remove Hindustanis from posts of trust, arrest all fakirs, examine sepoys' letters; don't wait to be directed, but act on your own responsibility."

Sir John could trust his brilliant colleagues, and the Punjab under their instant and fearless action saved India.

But we must remember that the gentle, sympathetic rule of Sir Henry Lawrence had won over the allegiance of the Sikhs and made it possible to send the Guides and other forces to help the army before Delhi.

With all Sir John's sternness, he never lost his head in the day of danger, never called for indiscriminate vengeance. "I would not hang a bird on such evidence," he once remarked as some charge was being pressed against a native.

While praising the active, he thundered against the inefficient. Writing to Sir Bartle Frere, he complained: "I do assure you, some of our commanders are worse enemies than the mutineers themselves."

Sir John trusted the old Sikh gunners who had fought against us in the two Sikh wars: he sent them down to Delhi and they fought loyally: he even picked out a body of the despised "sweeper" caste, and sent them as sappers and miners: they deserved well, won the esteem of their officers, and thus a noble self-respect redeemed them from their traditional degradation.

In short, it was from the Punjab, and at Sir John's suggestion, that siege trains were fitted out, that transport trains were organised, that horses, saddles, tents, ammunition were dispatched when they were needed. And all the time the danger of mutiny was at his own door! but Lawrence thought of the safety of India first, and of the Punjab afterwards.

He braved the peril of the Mutiny as much in his lonely office as the most dashing officer on the field of battle. Therefore we must count Sir John Lawrence a hero of the Indian Mutiny.

CHAPTER XI

F.-M. SIR HENRY WYLIE NORMAN: THE ORGANISER OF VICTORY

HENRY WYLIE NORMAN was born in the parish of St. Luke's in London on 2nd December 1826. As a boy he was left much to himself, and never saw his father until he landed in India in 1842. Norman's mother followed her husband to Cuba and other West Indian islands, only revisiting England at rare intervals. She left her son in charge of her own parents, Henry and Charlotte Wylie, who lived sometimes at Bridlington Quay, sometimes in Ireland, Mrs. Wylie's native country.

Norman's education was intermittent: three private schools played a part in moulding his mind and character, but he seems to have been more beholden to his own love of reading at every spare minute.

"My favourite subjects," he writes, "even when I was very young, were naval and military histories, voyages and biographies."

Of his father Norman wrote: "My father was a sailor, and when only twenty-two years of age went as supercargo of a ship, eventually settling in Havana as a merchant. It was usual for merchants in those days to send a vessel on a sort of cruise in charge of a supercargo, who traded on his employer's account, and when he had a full cargo, came home.

"My father had many adventures when trading, and once his vessel was in the hands of pirates, when he narrowly escaped with his life, and showed so much adroitness that the pirates left his ship without discovering a quantity of specie hidden on board."

SIR HENRY WYLIE NORMAN

In London, the boy Norman saw the festivities at the accession of Queen Victoria, and was inspired with a desire to emulate the great soldiers. He says: "I rejoiced to see with my own eyes the great duke, Marshal Soult, Lord Lynedoch, and others well known to me *from my reading*."

In Ireland he saw the parades at Limerick, while the faction fights in Tipperary stirred his blood, and perhaps his sense of humour.

In June 1842 he accompanied his mother to Calcutta in the frigate *Ellenborough.* The long voyage round the Cape prompted him to ask if he might take the duties of a midshipman, having learnt how to determine longitude and latitude. By the time they reached Calcutta, Norman was yearning to join the mercantile marine, but talks with his father and the news of the day—of the advance of Pollock and Nott into Afghanistan—turned the thoughts of the sixteen-year-old boy into new channels.

He was now eager to join the army, and frequently attended the parades of the 10th Foot quartered at Fort William: he also studied Hindustani and military history during the enforced leisure of eighteen months which elapsed before he got his nomination.

The doctor who examined him laughed at his small size and weight: "You are thin and must fill out," he remarked. But this Norman failed to accomplish. Seven stone and a half were all he owned of bone and flesh, but he had a good brain and constitution! Norman chose the 1st Bengal Native Infantry, because it was the senior native corps at the largest garrison, and he hoped to be able to learn his military duties better at a large station.

In June 1844, Norman left Calcutta for Dinapur by palanquin: on the third day, while waiting for a change of bearers, his old bearers decamped, and he fell asleep owing to the great heat.

He was roused from his slumbers by an English voice: a planter named Renshaw asked him to his bungalow and procured him fresh bearers.

Eleven years later it fell to Norman's lot to command a detachment of troops for punishing some Santals who had murdered this same planter and his son.

On joining the steamer at Rajmahal, he made friends with Lieutenant R. A. Yule of the 16th Lancers, who was afterwards killed before Delhi.

At Dinapur, Norman joined his regiment, then under Major Rowcroft, and spent his time in learning his profession until March 1845, when a vacancy occurred in the 31st Native Infantry, to which he was posted. This change saved him a terrible doom, for the first regiment which he left was destined to be stationed at Cawnpur, mutinied and shot its officers. At the time Norman regretted the exchange.

By 25th March he reached Almora, the headquarters of the 31st, placed on the lower slopes of the Himalayas, north-east of Delhi. Almora was a very attractive station; from this point excursions were made to the glaciers, or to tea plantations in Kumaon.

At the close of the year news came that the Sikh army had crossed the Sutlej, and the 31st were expecting to go to the front.

Colonel Weston chose Norman, to his great surprise and delight, as adjutant of the wing sent off under Major Corfield to Bareilly. He was still a few weeks under nineteen!

At Bareilly he used to take walks with his munshi, or teacher of languages, and through him he learnt reports of what had occurred in the war before the same came to the ears of the general.

Always Norman was on good terms with native officers, and from some of these he gathered information of the desire in the hearts of the people to restore the native chiefs and bring down the British Raj.

Fortunately Sir Henry Smith's victories at Aliwal and Sobraon in January and February 1846 convinced those meditating mutiny that the time had not yet arrived.

SIR HENRY WYLIE NORMAN

In 1847, Norman's regiment was ordered to Lahore, where Colonel Colin Campbell was in command of the garrison: hence the lifelong friendship between Lord Clyde (Sir Colin) and Norman had its origin.

The Sikhs had been beaten but not vanquished. All the gates of Lahore had to be held by strong guards under British officers.

"Brigadier Colin Campbell," writes Norman, "always made me breakfast and lunch with him when on guard, and often employed me to copy out confidential letters. In this way I learned thoroughly to admire this kind-hearted, but quick-tempered old soldier. To me it was delightful to hear his stories of the old wars, and listen to his doctrine of the duty the officer owed to his men. . . . May we have more men like him when our next great struggle comes!"

During this year Norman got to know the three brothers Lawrence, and Lumsden, Herbert Edwardes, Reynell Taylor, and Nicholson: with such friends the young man quickly increased in knowledge, if little in stature.

In January 1848, the 31st Regiment left Lahore for Ferozepur. On his arrival the doctor diagnosed small-pox, and he was assiduously nursed by one of his own sepoys. Then on recovery he was sent to Simla for six months.

Norman had just been promoted to the rank of lieutenant and was regretting his being placed on the sick list when the news of the murder of Vans Agnew and Anderson at Multan reached his hill-station. He heard at the same time that he was recommended as adjutant of his regiment. He felt no longer sick, and hurried down to the hot plains: but his regiment was not ordered to Multan until October.

The prospect of fighting acted as a tonic on all the soldiers: the hospital soon grew empty. Only three sick men stayed behind; for the 31st were all proud to serve under so good a soldier as Sir Hugh Gough.

Norman, too, felt the magnetic influence of a general

brave and yet tender, whose deep religious feeling, chivalry, and care for his men appealed to all.

The second Sikh War of 1848 gave Norman his first experiences in big battles and long pursuits. As adjutant he had many hours of work in his tent when others were resting: but he loved the work.

We cannot enter into the details of the battles in which the Sikhs fought so bravely, and nearly gained decisive successes more than once.

He served under Gilbert and General Penney in the crowning victory of Gujerat in February 1849, and took part in the final pursuit of the Sikh army.

Norman's regiment then returned to Peshawur, whence in 1850 Norman, as brigade-major, accompanied Sir Colin Campbell against the Afridis. He served also in similar expeditions for keeping down the robbers of the frontier, and was thanked by General A. Roberts, father of Earl Roberts, as "being possessed of all the qualifications for a good soldier and a first-rate staff officer."

In 1853, after going out against the Afridis, Norman married the daughter of Dr. Davidson, a lady of great character and devoted to her husband.

In 1854, General A. Roberts retired, and thanked Norman in a letter for his talent for detail combined with suavity of manner.

From such hints we can build up the character of the man: religious, conscientious, painstaking, and—the opposite of Nicholson—courteous and pleasing in manner: a lover of the natives, careful of his men, and winning their love in return; above all, learned in his profession. From Peshawur and frontier wars Norman was transferred to Ambala, and manœuvres under Sydney Cotton.

Just as he was feeling the change irksome, news came of a rising of the Santals in Bengal: his own regiment was ordered out from Barrackpur, and Norman got leave to join it. He disliked the methods to which they were obliged to have recourse in order to drive the brave, but ill-armed Santals out of the dense jungle, where no cavalry or infantry could penetrate. Bows and battle-axes against rifles was an unfair fight; but these men had been maddened by the extortions of the moneylender and tax-gatherer, and were slaying all they met of either sex. The only thing was to draw a cordon of troops round them, and leave the tiger and wild boar and the pangs of hunger to do the rest.

But what Norman did like was the oppórtunity of living in close and familiar association with his native soldiers, some of whom he had known well six years before. He remained with this detachment until January 1856: in this way he became intimately acquainted with the native character and language, and learnt from his men how the annexation of Oudh had estranged them from us.

Both English officers and their native men disliked the work of firing volleys into ill-armed villages. At last the rigours of climate and disease left few Santals available for resistance. Norman went back to Peshawur and to General Reed and Sydney Cotton: the latter was carrying out a series of instructive field manœuvres with his brigade, and Norman asked permission of General Reed to attend those field days. Sport and social attractions had never taken him away from the post of duty: his superior officers noted his enthusiastic interest in his profession, and he had not long to wait for promotion. The post of second assistant to Colonel Chester, adjutant-general, became vacant, and Norman was chosen to fill it.

This entailed a long and weary journey to Calcutta with his wife and three small children—and that, too, in the fatal month of May. Twenty-nine painful days of travelling by road brought them to Raniganj, where Lord Dalhousie's new railway conveyed them on. At Calcutta, Norman met the new commander-in-chief, General the Hon. George Anson, with whom he left Calcutta in September by river for Allahabad on a tour of inspection, visiting in turn Cawnpur, Aligarh, Lucknow, and Meerut.

At Meerut, Norman was left behind to work up reports

until March 1857, meeting many officers, ladies, and gentlemen—all in the highest spirits, unconscious of coming evil, —and he was for a time the guest of Captain MacDonald, who three months later was killed, together with his wife, by his own men rising in mutiny.

Thence Norman went on to Simla, and learnt of the murder of Colonel Finnis at Meerut: but even he had no suspicion of what it meant, though he said later that he knew the General Service Order of Lord Canning, issued in 1856, had much to do with the sepoy unrest. This order made them liable to serve across sea—a thing they dreaded, for most of them were of high caste, and life on board ship offended their caste rules and customs: secondly, the rule that sepoys could not be promoted to be non-commissioned officers unless they could read and write, was now to be enforced: the result of this was that many excellent soldiers, possibly of good family, who had served twelve or fourteen years, saw themselves deprived of all hope of gratifying their worthy ambition.

Norman tells us that in his old company several men who had distinguished themselves greatly in the Punjab came to him with tears in their eyes, deploring their cruel misfortune. "No, sahib, we are too old to learn to write now," they explained.

It only shows how high authorities should not presume to introduce sudden changes without carefully consulting the men who, like Norman, Daly, and Hodson, had studied intimately the minds of the Indian. While Norman was at Simla, it being Sunday, 10th May, as the residents were quietly going to church, a native mendicant outraged their feelings by presenting himself quite naked—a form of insult.

Other signs and symptoms of discontent followed: then on 12th May an officer rode in from Ambala, where the telegraph line ended, bringing a copy of the message received from Delhi by Sir Henry Barnard. It was dated 11th May, from the signaller, W. Brendish, at Delhi, to the signaller at Ambala, and was repeated thence to all stations.

"We must leave office: all the bungalows are burning down by the sepoys of Meerut: they came in this morning: we are off: don't call to-day: Mr. C. Todd is dead, I think. He went out this morning and has not returned yet: we heard that nine Europeans are killed: good-bye."

This was a terrible and startling message to receive: the scales now fell from the eyes of the blind, and Norman had plenty to do arranging for the departure of regiments. We may explain that Todd was the telegraph master at Delhi, who had gone out to repair a wire: it may be remembered that the Meerut mutineers met a European on the bridge of Delhi and killed him. Taking a hasty leave of his wife and family, Norman left Simla with Colonel Chester for Ambala.

From Ambala he wrote to his wife on 16th May, saying he was overwhelmed with work, and had only ladies to copy orders and dispatches: no horses or carts or dhoolie-bearers. Later he tells her that many Europeans were butchered in Delhi Palace. "Providence has tried us sorely, but with God's aid there is not the slightest cause for despondency." Already many men had died of cholera; amongst them General Anson on 27th May. Norman felt some sharp twinges, but a little brandy and laudanum and a sharp walk set him right.

On 7th June, Wilson's force from Meerut joined Reid's Gurkhas and the Ambala troops at Alipur. "The 60th Rifles came swinging along after their sixteen-mile march singing splendidly in chorus." Norman was with Colonel Chester at Badli-ki-Serai when he was killed as he sat on horseback upon a mound 800 yards from the enemy's guns: only that morning as they rode along together the colonel had been expressing his delight at soon meeting the mutineers. "He was in the act of replying to a remark I had made when a cannon-shot struck him, and passing through his horse they both sank to the ground."

We will not weary the reader by going over again the details of the siege, but a few points made in Norman's letters or journal will fill up the picture and make it more easy to realise.

He states that nearly every dead sepoy was found to have about him a number of gold mohurs (seventeen rupees each): one rifleman gained eighty gold mohurs (£136) in this way: for so many treasuries had been plundered and the proceeds had been divided amongst the mutineers.

When the besiegers knew that 300 heavy guns were mounted on the walls and bastions of Delhi, and that the mutineers outnumbered them ten times or more, they talked less of making an immediate assault. Abbot's famous gunners, too, were in Delhi after 17th June with the guns on which was engraven the mural crown ordered by Lord Ellenborough for their great glory won in the holding of Jellalabad. Yet people at home soon began to wonder why our forces did not retake Delhi. No one realised then that the full strength of the Mutiny had been drawn to Delhi, and that our forces were decimated by illness.

On 18th June, Norman heard of the death of an officer at a distance whom he much liked. As usual, this officer trusted his men too much. He with his wife and some officers had escaped from Shahjahanpur; when a mutiny broke out there on 31st May during time of service in church, they were all shot by their escort a few days later, men and women together while kneeling in prayer.

Norman knew how his friend had trusted and loved many of his men, and how many of the sepoys of the 25th Native Infantry loved their leader: it seemed to him incomprehensible, and only to be explained by religious madness.

Another friend whose loss he deplored was Lieutenant Alexander of the 3rd Native Infantry, who had only been in camp on the Ridge a few days. He was just a boy, of charming manners and appearance, and had come with a company of his regiment, escorting a long train of carts laden with ordnance stores. On reaching camp after his hot march of 200 miles the poor boy had to be told that his regiment had mutinied and his company must be disarmed.

All the bright, enthusiastic delight in soldiering left him, and he wandered from point to point disconsolately. Norman often met him and tried to cheer him and make him see the rosier side of things; but his heart was broken, and he sought danger for its own sake.

One afternoon Alexander's native soubhadar came in tears to Norman's tent: "I was with my officer, sahib; a waggon blew up and I see him no more. I must find him, sahib; may I take unarmed sepoys to search for my sahib?" The poor fellow could scarce speak for sorrow. Norman gave him leave.

Later, when Norman had lain down to sleep, the soubhadar came back saying, "We have found his body—no life, sahib—master gone!"

Utterly broken down was the faithful Indian as he told his tale; since his love for his sahib was as that of Jonathan for David.

It is only right to remember the splendid instances of good faith and devotion in the sepoy when we are moved to anger by atrocities. "How easy it is for people at a distance to criticise," wrote Norman to his wife in July. "No one who is not here knows the difficulties that beset this force. To my mind no troops have ever deserved better of their country, or could be more ready and willing for any enterprise."

Even Lady Canning, who might have known more than others, wrote in August: "At Delhi they do nothing but repel attacks; why they dread to assault we cannot understand."

Perhaps one reason why we did not assault was the ominous fact that Delhi was armed with our best guns and 30,000 well-drilled soldiers, while the men on the Ridge numbered 3700, many being sick or wounded; and already, in July, the 18-pounder ammunition was almost expended! Fortunately these brave, patient besiegers knew not at the time what severe criticism was being levelled at them by ignorance dwelling in security. Amongst the casualties we find one wound at least which proved wholesome.

Blair of the Fusiliers was shot while carrying an armful of ammunition to his men. It seemed a bad case: "He can hardly survive," said the surgeon. But the bullet had tapped an abscess in Blair's liver, and so prolonged his life, for he did not die until 1907!

Packe of the 4th Sikh Infantry was shot in the ankle while kneeling behind a stone breastwork, the enemy being in front. That looked suspicious. A few days after, Hodson came to Norman's tent with a sepoy of the Guides and said—

"I say, Norman, I should like you to hear what my sepoy has to say."

The sepoy then declared that in a skirmish in the suburbs he had seen men of the 4th Sikhs hang back and fire at the backs of their officers.

"What! Sikhs do so treacherous a deed?"

"No, sahib, no! Many Hindustanis hiding in this regiment."

The man was cross-examined and stuck to his story: also the adjutant had been shot through the back.

In the end, the Hindustanis, a fourth of the regiment, were disarmed and sent out of camp.

In July, Chamberlain's wound threw upon Norman again the duties of adjutant-general: the death of General Sir H. Barnard by cholera would have led to Chamberlain being commander, had he not been laid up.

On the afternoon of 17th July a native from Benares was brought to Norman's hut: he was allowed to ramble on about Allahabad and Benares, when Norman, anxious to know how soon General Sir Hugh Wheeler could come to their relief at Delhi, lightly asked the men, "What news from Cawnpur?"

"Cawnpur, sahib? you have not heard that?" Then

dropping his voice, he murmured, " Every white man, woman, and child has been put to death."

"A thrill of horror passed over me," writes Norman, "for his bearing and tone convinced me that what he said was true."

Norman took the native to Colonel Becher and they examined his report; then to the civil commissioner, Mr. Greathed: but for many days they dared not let the troops know the horrors of what had happened.

An amusing incident befell on 18th July, when, after driving some sepoys from cover on the right flank, a prisoner was brought in.

" It's a woman, sir," said the sergeant of the 60th; "so we did not kill her."

A very masculine dame she looked, and her language was Indian Billingsgate of a virulent type. The more the riflemen laughed, the fiercer the beldame grew in her denunciations.

Some officers came round to see her; one, tall and well-built, suddenly attracted her attention: her manner changed and she whispered coyly, "A very nice man to look at! never saw such kind eyes before! if he likes me well enough, I don't mind marrying him."

" It need hardly be said that the officer in question had to endure a considerable amount of chaff": but history does not say what became of the relenting prisoner.

On 18th August a Mrs. Leeson escaped from the city: she had been severely wounded on 10th May; the bullet passed through her child whom she held in her arms, and then through herself. Both her other children had their throats cut in her presence. A citizen of Delhi out of pity concealed her, had her wound cured and helped her to escape.

In describing to his wife the work of constructing the batteries in September, Norman writes: " You may judge of its magnitude when I mention that 1000 camel-loads of fascines and material had to be taken down, besides 100 camel-loads of powder, shot, and shell: all available men took part in the construction: on the 18th, 300 Europeans and 100 natives went on duty; and two days later no fewer than 800 Europeans and 400 natives with twenty-four officers were engaged on the work.

After the capture of the walls and gates, Roberts and Norman went exploring in the streets and had some narrow shaves from stray bullets: the sepoys wore net purses round their waists under their clothes, and often had them full of looted gold. In one street Norman found a European soldier and a Punjabi struggling together over one of these purses torn from a dead sepoy. Neither of them would let go first, and Norman was obliged to beat them with all his force on the knuckles with the hilt of his sword.

The purse was full of rupees, and as their comrades stood round grinning, Norman said, "I shall distribute the rupees amongst you all; for these others have done good service while you have been intent on loot." So, he dealt them out one by one all round like a pack of cards, keeping for himself the mutineer's medal for service in the Punjab.

Johnson, Stewart, Roberts and Norman, friends inseparable at this time, were with Taylor pushing on from house to house.

Edwin Johnson was a very clever officer, with a caustic wit and amusing. Stewart had come to the Ridge with Ford from Agra, having volunteered to carry dispatches: it was a most perilous and adventurous journey and won him great renown. He died a Field-Marshal.

In passing from house to house Roberts says they found curious things, such as magic lanterns, musical boxes, and half-starved, deserted wives.

On 21st September, headquarters were removed to the palace, and the officers established their mess and sleeping cots in the famous Diwan-i-Am, or Hall of Audience. But the joy of victory was almost drowned in the lamentations for the slain. Three friends Norman mourned for in especial: Lieutenant Salkeld, hero of the Kashmir gate, was now rapidly sinking: the general had sent his aide-de-camp to tell him he would receive the Victoria Cross; but he could only smile faintly as he drifted away. John Nicholson was found by Norman unconscious, with heaving chest and a vacant, distressed look in his eyes.

Charles Nicholson, Norman's dearest friend, had spent the last week in command of Coke's Rifles, day and night on constant duty, and now lay with a smashed arm. "I am not ashamed to say that when we parted, as we expected, for the last time, we exchanged a loving kiss." Another friend was Charles Reid, the gallant holder of Hindu Rao's house during ninety-nine days of attack.

In speaking of Hodson and the shooting of the princes, Norman writes: "I don't believe in 'the threatening crowd': they were mostly terrified townspeople. . . . I believe Hodson shot them because he believed they deserved death; and was apprehensive, if he brought them in alive, their lives might be spared. In doing this he did what I think was in the highest degree wrong. . . . I am bound to say, however, that many officers thought he did right, and had displayed commendable vigour and resolution."

We ought not to leave Delhi and its brave besiegers without once more bearing testimony to the heroic deeds of Colonel H. Tombs, R.A., V.C., whom one and all admired for his wonderful handling of his battery, as well as for his valiant exploits.

Lord Roberts writes: "As a cool, bold leader of men Tombs was unsurpassed: no fire, however hot, and no crisis, however unexpected, could take him by surprise; he grasped the situation in a moment and issued his orders without hesitation, inspiring all ranks with confidence in his powers. He was somewhat of a martinet, and was more feared than liked by his men until they realised what a grand leader he was, when they gave him their entire confidence, and were ready to follow him anywhere."

Delhi had been taken after tremendous fighting, suffering from wounds and disease, months of anxiety, depression and hope deferred. For some time there was a feeling of soreness amongst the officers and men left alive to tell the tale; "from Calcutta not one word of thanks or encouragement has ever been vouchsafed to us," writes Norman. However, Norman was attached to Greathed's column as a staff officer on his way to report himself to the commander-in-chief, and marched away from the smells and dust of "the accursed city" on 24th September.

The transport animals had been worn out at Delhi, and the men in rags and ill-fed were very prone to sickness. But Lucknow called for them, and all ranks, native and European, pressed forward willingly.

As they travelled through townlets and villages they noticed that trade had ceased; dâk-bungalows, police-stations, telegraph wires were all destroyed: the people, believing that the English rule was over, had begun to fortify their villages against men of their own race—as though justice had fled the earth.

It has been mentioned before how Agra had called for help, and the column had gone to assist them, and had been surprised by the enemy owing to misleading information given by the Agra authorities. Sixty or seventy of our force were killed and wounded, while the country for miles was strewn with dead sepoys. Norman speaks bitterly of "the imbecility of these wretched Agra people."

On 21st October, as Norman was riding by the side of Hope Grant, who had relieved Greathed of the command of the column, the brigadier's horse lashed out and struck Norman on the shin bone: he was thus compelled to continue his journey to Lucknow in a litter. A few words may be necessary to explain the events which had taken place at Lucknow while the siege of Delhi was being conducted.

On 30th June, Sir Henry Lawrence retired to the Residency on the bank of the Gumti after a repulse at Chinhat. The little garrison of under 2000, including 163 civilians, now stood at bay against a city of 300,000 inhabitants.

On 2nd July, Sir Henry died of his wounds and Colonel

Inglis took command; death by shot and shell and fell disease and weariness reduced their numbers to 577 Europeans and 402 sepoys, until on 25th September, Havelock, with Outram serving under him, brought the first relief.

But Havelock's force had suffered so much that they could not carry away the sixty-one ladies and forty-three children: all Havelock could do was to leave 200 men under Outram to strengthen the garrison; he then posted the sick and wounded under MacIntyre at the Alumbagh: here they suffered great hardships and many died of starvation.

Sir Colin Campbell, the new commander-in-chief, left Calcutta on 27th October, and made forced marches to Lucknow, joining the Delhi column on the way early in November.

Norman was warmly welcomed by Sir Colin and General Mansfield, the chief of the staff: he now resumed his duties in the adjutant-general's department.

One morning, as he left Sir Colin's tent before daybreak, Norman was jostled by a native: angrily he ordered the fellow in Hindostani to stand away from the entrance at his peril. To his surprise the native replied with a touch of Irish brogue: "I am one of the garrison of Lucknow—Kavanagh—I have come out of the Residency with letters for the commander-in-chief."

One can imagine the changed tone in which Norman replied: "Come in! come in! excuse my mistake. You are so well disguised, I took you for a native—and the old man too—you are welcome indeed!"

Yes—a dangerous journey these two men had successfully completed through the teeming city and the enemy's lines: for this exploit Kavanagh won the Victoria Cross. Kavanagh brought something more important than letters: he had been for some years employed in the office of the chief commissioner of Oudh, and knew the streets and by-lanes of Lucknow: he brought a map of the city and its surroundings and pointed out to Sir Colin the best way of reaching the Residency.

On 11th November, Sir Colin reviewed his force of 5000 men with 26 guns on the plain about five miles in front of the Alumbagh, and especially commended the Delhi column.

When the Sikh regiments first saw the Highlanders, "bonnets and plumes and a'," they could hardly be got past them, so great was their admiration: and when they heard the bagpipes, it reminded them of the Afridi's music —"the best music we ever heard," was their verdict.

Not less interesting to all were the stalwart tars of the Naval Brigade under Captain William Peel with 24-pounder guns drawn by bullocks: the native drivers were vastly perplexed when ordered to go "starboard."

The 93rd, with feather bonnets and dark waving plumes, formed the extreme left of the line, and as the old chief, commencing with the right, halted and addressed a short speech to each corps, he slowly drew near his old regiment, 1000 strong; some 700 of them wore the Crimean medal on their breasts.

Forbes-Mitchell, who was in the 93rd, says: "The men remarked among themselves that none of the other corps had given him a single cheer, but had taken what he said in solemn silence. At last he approached us; we were called to attention, and formed close column, so that every man might hear what was said. When Sir Colin rode up, he appeared to have a worn and haggard expression on his face; but he was received with such a cheer, or rather shout of welcome, as made the echoes ring from the neighbouring woods. His wrinkled brow at once became smooth, and his wearied features broke into a smile, as he acknowledged the cheer with a hearty salute."[1]

Sir Colin then spoke of the dangers they had encountered in the Crimea; told them they had to rescue women and children from a fate worse than death: they must come to close quarters and use the bayonet.

[1] *Reminiscences of the Mutiny* (Macmillan & Co.).

"Ninety-third!" he ended, "you are my own lads: I rely on you to do the work."

A voice from the ranks called out: "Ay, ay, Sir Colin, ye ken us and we ken you; we'll bring the women and children out o' Lucknow or dee wi' you in the attempt!" Thereat the whole line burst into another ringing cheer.

When at length the Alumbagh was reached, the sick and some surplus stores were left in it, to be protected by the 75th Foot. Then they marched on to storm the Secundrabagh, when nearly every staff officer was wounded. "My horse was hit in three places in a charge of the 93rd led by Sir Colin," writes Norman, who himself seemed to have a charmed life.

The men at this time had no baggage or tents, and the cold at nights was terrible.

On 14th November, the Dilkusha, or garden house of the King of Oudh, was reached by a wide circuit made through difficult ground—Kavanagh doubtless showing the way. Havelock had threaded his way through the densest part of the city and lost many men in street fighting.

They reached the walls of the King's Park as the sun was rising: the infantry halted until a breach was made in the walls.

The men lay down in a field of carrots, and began eating them raw. The Park swarmed with deer, black buck and spotted: but they had not time to enjoy the beauties of nature, for 9-pounder shot came bowling along as they formed into line and cut down several men.

Old Colonel Leith-Hay called out, "Keep steady, men: close up the ranks."

But MacBean, the adjutant, as he stood behind the line, said in an undertone: "Don't mind the colonel: open out and let the round-shot go through—and watch the shot."

Then Roberts led the artillery to the front, and took the guns of the enemy in the flank: whereupon the sepoys bolted downhill to the Martinière.

There the sailors quickly threw up a battery in front of their guns and escaped with trifling loss owing to their good use of the spade: their cheery ways amused and gave heart to the rest, for they were full of fun and good temper. The natives described the sailors as "little men, four feet in the beam; always laughing and dragging about their own guns."

When the Martinière was carried by brilliant fighting, in which Lieutenant Watson distinguished himself, Norman and Sir Colin mounted to the top of the college, when Kavanagh pointed out the rebels' main positions. A semaphore was erected and communications established with the Residency.

On 16th November the advance began at 9 a.m.: every man carried his greatcoat and food for three days. First they crossed the canal and passed through a village on their way to attack the Secundrabagh.

This was a high-walled enclosure of strong masonry, loopholed all round, and flanked by circular bastions; in the centre was a two-storeyed house from which a strong fire was kept up.

Here Sir Colin was struck on the thigh by a bullet, Blunt thrown to the ground under his dying horse, and Norman's horse was twice hit. After an hour and a half of fierce attack a hole was found big enough to let the 93rd and 4th Punjabis storm through in close rivalry.

As Norman was approaching the gateway over heaps of dead, he received a violent blow on the head: it was not a bullet this time, but the body of a dying rebel thrown at him from above!

Norman and Roberts then entered the house and found the floors strewn four feet deep with the bodies of the dead and dying. There was no doubt that the sepoys had on their side fought desperately for victory.

Norman writes: "My horse reared on receiving his second blow, and just then a bullet struck him in the side, but I managed to ride him for half an hour longer: the troops lay down in the Park, after capturing the Shah Nujeef, a strong domed mosque with a walled garden: and a nice cold night we had of it with a soaking dew."

But Norman in his modesty did not tell his wife how, when a battalion recoiled and was thrown into disorder, he had ridden amongst the men, rallied them and led them again to the attack.

Sir Colin had been sitting in the saddle with knit brows, anxious for the result of the evening's work; but no sooner did he hear the yell of his pet Highlanders than all trace of care vanished: he turned to his bivouac in the open air and slept as his men did, with his staff around him.

The Secundrabagh was indeed a fierce retaliation for Cawnpur: it is said that 3000 dead sepoys, all slain by the bayonet, there met their fate. Forbes-Mitchell tells us the 93rd were ordered to attack with bayonets in groups of threes: the sepoys, after firing their muskets, hurled them like javelins, bayonets first, and then drawing their tulwars, which were as keen as razors, they slashed in blind fury, shouting Deen! Deen! (the Faith!)

With regard to Adjutant MacBean's advice, to let the balls go through: Sir Colin, during the attack on the Secundrabagh, kept turning round, when a man was hit as they sheltered behind a low mud wall, and cried, "Lie down, 93rd, lie down! Every man of you is worth his weight in gold to England to-day."

We do not often remember this in the selfish hours of peace! We let men fight for us, and leave them after all to the degradation of the workhouse. As the men lay down on the cold ground to get rest and sleep, they plainly heard the pipers of the 78th playing inside the Residency as a welcome to cheer their rescuers on their perilous way.

On 17th November, Norman took a last look at the interior of the tomb of the Shah Nujeef: to his surprise he saw that the glass ornaments had been broken, and the beautiful marble pavement cracked. Presently he met a man of the Naval Brigade with a 24-pounder shot.

"Yes, sir, it's me did it all! I couldna stand any of their idolatry."

It was not until the afternoon of the 18th that the mess-house was taken, as Sir Colin had to secure his left from attack: after this the Moti Mahal was taken; they were now near the English position, and by knocking a hole in the wall communications were opened, though the space between was exposed to the enemies' fire.

Thus, when Sir J. Outram and Sir H. Havelock crossed this zone to confer with Sir Colin, three of their staff were wounded.

It was a critical time and the problem set was difficult: at Cawnpur the Gwalior army was threatening to overcome Windham and his troops: there must be no delay in returning to help Windham. But Lucknow swarmed with rebels and could not be taken in a short time.

Sir Colin decided to withdraw the troops and the 1500 women and children from the Residency, and leave Outram with 4000 men to hold the Alumbagh.

From 19th to 22nd November the women and children were withdrawn under cover of darkness, the rebels being quite ignorant of the movement, as Peel's guns kept up a "command performance" to give the rebels something to do and to think about. Norman saw Havelock before he left the Residency. He was lying on his bed in his blue uniform coat, very weak, suffering from dysentery, and "on the point to die."

The troops from the Residency were told to stream noiselessly away without military formation to the Martinière. Sir Colin's men, under the Hon. Adrian Hope, lined the road, silent as spectres.

When all had passed, Sir Colin lay down to sleep by a fire which the Highlanders had piled up for him. The enemy were so skilfully deceived they they fired on the Residency long after it had been abandoned.

On the 24th, our men marched to the Alumbagh, and there Sir Colin left his sick and wounded and large stores.

It was on this morning that the heroic Havelock breathed his last: happily he had lived long enough to know that his countrymen and women were rescued, and his end was peace: his earthly remains were buried in a grave in the Alumbagh.

On the morning of the 27th, Sir Colin started for Cawnpur with soldiers worn out by fighting and watching, but cheerily bent on saving their comrades. The train of men extended along ten miles of road, three abreast: they soon heard the distant sound of guns thirty miles away, and an order was given that they must reach the bridge of boats at Cawnpur on the next day.

It was 11 p.m. when they reached Bunnee Bridge, 17 miles from Lucknow: here the soldiers halted till daylight of the 28th November: but the women and children had started under guard at 2 a.m.

About five miles farther on, Sir Colin, attended by Norman and his staff, ordered the 93rd to-form up; when he took them into his confidence as usual. He told them that General Windham had been attacked by the Nana and the Gwalior contingent, and had been forced to retire within the fort.

If the bridge of boats were cut, it would be a serious position for the British: 50,000 enemies in the rear; a river and 40,000 well-armed men in front, and all the sick and women to guard! "So, 93rd," said the old chief with emotion, "I don't ask you to undertake this forced march, in your present tired condition, without good reason. We must reach Cawnpur to-night at all costs."

"All right, Sir Colin, we'll do it," was the resolute reply.

So, on they went, footsore and weary, but roused by the tonic of a good cannonade in front. The wounded, says Norman, were nearly jolted to death in hackeries, and the women in their strange surroundings looked frightened and wide-eyed.

About noon on the 25th, a native sprang out of the

long grass and held out a letter: it was written in Greek characters to Sir Colin, or any officer commanding troops, and asked for prompt succour. Sir Colin ordered Roberts to ride forward and see how they sped at Cawnpur: at the bridge-head an excited officer met him with the remark, "We are at our last gasp!" "All right!" answered Roberts, "we are just here!"

He rode across the bridge of boats under fire and entered the fort; many came crowding round to ask the news. General Windham he found cool and collected: Captain Mowbray Thomson had kept 4000 coolies daily employed on the defences from dawn till dark, and the fortifications were not to be despised. There was to be no second Cawnpur Massacre!

But the force that went to relieve Lucknow had left all their spare kit and 500 tents, harness, etc., in Cawnpur: all this the rebels had seized and were burning on the bank of the Ganges. It was the first sight that greeted the eyes of the relieving force: they had not changed their clothes since the 10th, and the sight did not soothe their feelings.

Sir Colin, irritable and anxious, could not wait for Roberts to return. Taking Norman with him and a few more he rode to the bridge-head. The same officer made unfortunately the same remark he had made to Roberts. "Sir Colin, we are at our last gasp!"

"D—n you, sir; how dare you say such a thing to me!"

The poor officer fell back in dismay; the chief and his staff rode over the swaying bridge and entered the fort.

At once some of the Rifle Brigade recognised Sir Colin, and their deafening cheers soon showed what they thought of the value of his presence amongst them.

Next day Sir Colin transferred his headquarters across the river: gradually the men marched across, and on the night of 3rd December the women and children with 500 sick and wounded were secretly sent off to Allahabad.

On the 6th, news came by telegraph that the party

had arrived at the railway station and would soon be safe within the fortress of Allahabad.

It was not until the reception of this news that Sir Colin ordered an advance against the rebels: Norman in this fighting had several fortunate escapes, while Sir Colin and General Grant were both hit by musket-balls.

Norman, beside his work in the field, had heavy duties to perform. A new native army was being raised, and the Deputy Adjutant-General of the Bengal Army had much to do in instructing and organising. "I sometimes complained that the work almost killed me," he writes.

What Norman had been to General Wilson at Delhi he now proved to be to Sir Colin Campbell. "Norman is the life and soul of the Force," wrote Edwin Johnson at Delhi. Blunt, writing from Cawnpur, says: "Old Norman is the same as ever, only fighting fattens him. He is all in all to Sir Colin, and is worth his weight in gold."

In March 1858, our army once more set out for Lucknow: the Dilkusha Palace was taken, and the Martinière attacked and taken on the 9th. Here Peel, K.C.B., was wounded and laid up for the rest of the siege. Outram was co-operating successfully and by the evening of the 10th the enemy's first line of defence was carried. The entrenchments along the canal were stupendous, and in the rear every building was strongly entrenched and loopholed.

On the 11th March, Norman visited Outram's camp and the naval battery: he found Outram attempting to secure the bridges which spanned the Goomtee: but he had to hurry back to headquarters to receive the Prime Minister of Nepaul, Maharaja Jang Bahadur. The interview took place with an accompaniment of musketry and artillery: before it was over news came that Adrian Hope had captured the Begum's Palace. Norman hurried off to this—"the sternest struggle in the siege."

The fight, in which the 93rd, the 4th Punjab Rifles and the Gurkhas had played so heroic a part, had raged for two hours from court to court and from room to room; while the pipe-major, John M'Leod, walked about playing the pipes as calmly as if he had been at a mess-dinner.

It was in this attack that Hodson, the Prince of Scouts, was killed. Of him Norman writes: "Though not without serious faults, he was a most accomplished and gallant officer, and as a leader of irregulars in our time probably unsurpassed": and again, "Poor Hodson was buried last night: it was quite dark, a lantern being held up to enable the chaplain to read the service."

On the 17th, Norman ascended one of the minarets of the Imambara with Hope Johnstone, and became the target for various bullets. He was able to inform the chief that the Musabagh must be attacked. On this day Mrs. Orr and Miss Jackson were rescued by Captain M'Neil and Lieutenant Boyle: these ladies had been in prison since the previous May. On 21st March, the city of Lucknow was in our hands—the rebel loss being about 4000, the British under 800.

After the siege still more work for Norman, headaches and low fever! His friends were scattered—Roberts to England, Hugh Gough to the hills, Watson to the Punjab, Probyn invalided.

Then came the list of Delhi honours; but Norman's name was not there! Wilson a K.C.B., Daly a C.B., Norman apparently forgotten. He felt it keenly, not knowing the reason, and wrote to his wife: "I am not included, though every A.D.C. who was a captain is a brevet-major. Having been in nearly eighty actions and skirmishes, it seems odd that I cannot be rewarded, even though head of the adjutant-general's department in a large army."

However, Sir Colin showed him in his dispatch of 22nd March these words: "I must draw very particular attention to the services of Major Norman, who has performed the very onerous duty of adjutant-general of the army in the field throughout the campaign."

SIR HENRY WYLIE NORMAN

It was not that the War Office had forgotten him: only they had bound themselves by rules they dared not break: Norman was too young to be rewarded!

At last the Gazette gave him the local rank of Lieutenant-Colonel in the East Indies and a C.B.

We cannot follow him further. After the Rohilkhand campaign, Norman became a military secretary at the Horse Guards, a member of the Viceroy's council, governor of Jamaica, governor of Queensland, governor of Chelsea, Field-Marshal.

Lord Roberts, in estimating his character, notes three great qualities: (1) A natural liking and aptitude for work; sport and games had no temptations for him. (2) An extraordinary memory: he seemed to know the Army List by heart; he had a wide knowledge of military history. (3) He possessed sound soldierly instincts, was always on the spot, courted danger, yet was cool and brave always: he was very cheerful, and apt to see the bright side of things. He died on 26th October 1904.

From a *Memoir of Sir H. W. Norman*, by kind permission of Sir W. Lee-Warner, G.C.S.I., and Messrs. Smith & Elder.

CHAPTER XII

THE HEROES OF CAWNPUR

NO memorial of the heroes of the Indian Mutiny would be complete which did not give some account of the men, women and children who suffered, fought or died at Cawnpur.

Those of them who may not be designated heroes were veritable martyrs. Cawnpur lies on the right bank of the Ganges, 270 miles south-east from Delhi, 684 from Calcutta by land, 954 by water; from Allahabad, some 120 miles: it is the principal town in the Doab, which lies between the Ganges and the Jumna.

The cantonments, quite distinct from the native city, were extended along the bank of the river six miles from north-west to south-east and contained an area of about ten square miles. Here hundreds of little white bungalows, the homes of the officers and their families, stood in their three-acre compounds or gardens, each surrounded by a low and crumbling mound and ditch, or hedge of prickly pear.

Forest trees abounded and gave a pleasant shade—each regiment had its own bazaar, whether the men lived in the barracks or under canvas. On higher ground stood the church and assembly rooms; farther on was the theatre for amateur performances, and a café.

In the officers' gardens vegetables of all kinds thrived, while peaches and melons, limes, oranges and custard apples formed a healthy addition to the diet. In summer, Cawnpur is one of the hottest stations in India; in winter, water will freeze in shallow pans if left out at night.

Boating on the river, horse-racing, polo and billiards were the chief amusements. In the dry season the Ganges is about five hundred yards wide, but in the rains it swells to more than a mile across: it is navigable for boats of light draught down to the sea, or one thousand miles: while up-stream one can travel by boat for three hundred miles.

The ghaut, or landing-place, is usually the spot where strange creatures congregate—traders, hucksters, fakirs, beggars of all kinds.

A bridge of boats constructed by the Government was open to all who wished to pass over into, or from, the province of Oudh: a small toll being charged for the up-keep. Hundreds of vessels with thatched roofs were moored near the shore, looking like a swaying village, while country boats like stacks adrift were constantly being urged up or down by their smoking and singing rowers.

The native city, closely packed in teeming huts and houses, contained sixty thousand inhabitants, having only one wide street or boulevard, called the Chandnee Choke, or Silver Street. This name dates from the time when there were no banks, and natives who possessed capital were fain to convert it into fantastic belts and rings, and hang their wealth for security about the ears and ankles of their families: this street abounds in the shops of silversmiths. The city swarmed with cut-throats escaped from smaller cities after they had murdered and robbed some industrious and saving countryman.

Of course the city gaol was tolerably full of the worst specimens of humanity, poisoners and adepts in the fine art of strangling and stabbing. We must now give a short account of the two men who are notorious for having urged the mutineers to make war upon our women and children. Nana Sahib, as he is usually called, was the adopted son of Bajee Rao, who had been Peishwa of Poonah, and the last of the Mahratta kings.

The Government at Calcutta had dethroned the Peishwa for his repeated acts of treachery, confiscated his lands and made him live at Bithoor, twelve miles up river from Cawnpur. Here he resided in princely state near the banks of the sacred Ganges, having from the Company an annuity of £80,000 wherewith to supply himself with luxuries and keep contented his host of splendid retainers.

But the ex-Peishwa had no son: so, according to Hindoo custom, he adopted Seereek Dhoondu Punth, or "Nana" (grandson) for short.

The old man died in 1851: his heir, the Nana, at once presented a claim upon the East India Company for a continuance of the pension allowed to the late Peishwa. Lord Dalhousie curtly refused it; but the Nana still came into possession of the old man's savings, and his wealth was very conspicuous amongst the richest Indian landowners. His palace was furnished expensively, his stables contained well-bred Arabs, elephants and camels; his ladies were tricked out with costly jewels; his little army, horse and foot, paid four rupees each man a month, eked out their pittance by plundering peasants or ryots and extorting blackmail from the merchants of Cawnpur.

Yet the Nana never forgot, or forgave, Lord Dalhousie's stern denial of his claim. He sent his vakeel, or agent, to London in 1854 to press his demand in Leadenhall Street. This man was Azimoolah Khan, a clever, witty and good-looking young Indian.

It is said he had once been a kitmutgar, or butler, in the house of an Anglo-Indian: here he learnt to speak English and French fluently. Then he became a teacher in a Government school at Cawnpur, and later became a trusted adviser of the Nana.

This man, then, went to London with plenty of money, posed as a prince, was accepted as one of the lions of the season, and made influential friends of both sexes. However, he could not induce the Company to grant his master the pension: yet he took home important news, for he passed through Constantinople just when our fortunes in the Crimean War were at the lowest ebb: he was thus able to tell his Bithoor master that the power of England was shattered: now was the time for revolt!

The Nana Sahib was at this time about thirty-six years old, very corpulent, sallow, clean shaven, as all Mahrattas are: he treated the English officers with generous hospitality, for he never allowed any suspicion of his loyalty to arise from look or word or deed. No doubt Azimoolah's account of the decadence of England was spread abroad in all the great cities of India; and this, together with the anniversary of Plassey, decided the time of revolt.

Azimoolah, the fêted prince, was perhaps more cruel and bloodthirsty than his master: it was he who ordered the massacre of the women and children.

The Cawnpur garrison in 1857 consisted of about 3000 sepoys. The Europeans consisted of about 300 fighting men, their wives, children and native servants; 300 half-caste, or Eurasian children of the Cawnpur School; merchants, shopkeepers, etc., and other civilians: these amounted in all to more than a thousand Europeans.

Major-General Sir Hugh Wheeler, K.C.B., was in command of the Cawnpur division: he had spent more than fifty years in India, and was supposed to understand the native mind as well as any one. Like most of the old officers, he worshipped his sepoys, chatted with them in their own language and could not believe they would prove unfaithful. He was short and spare, active for his years, and inspired confidence. But sinister news from Meerut and Delhi began to leak out from the bazaars, and came to the ears of the general.

Sir Hugh had always found the Maharaja of Bithoor, or the Nana, full of genial courtesy: he had no reason to suspect his loyalty, except that Sir Henry Lawrence had misliked the Nana's manner on his late visit to Lucknow. He now, at the suggestion of Mr. Hillersden, the resident magistrate, asked the Nana to take charge of the treasury and the magazine, whilst this temporary unrest was upsetting his sepoys.

Nana Sahib rode over, attended by his bodyguard, and offered to send a force of 200 cavalry, 400 infantry and two guns to protect the revenue.

This was considered exceedingly kind and generous: the Nana had even offered to take charge of all the English ladies at his palace; but some of the officers scrupled to go so far, and the (apparently) chivalrous offer was not accepted.

The treasury was distant from the cantonments about five miles, and was on the other side of the native city: it contained more than a hundred thousand pounds in silver. The magazine was well stocked with powder, shot and shell: the general felt relieved when these valuable buildings were safe under the charge of the polite and gracious Maharaja.

It was time something was done: for alarming news kept coming from Delhi after the 14th of May, and the north road was infested with dacoits and liberated convicts; but the sepoys remained quiet and obedient.

Then there came a visitor to the cantonments who frightened all the ladies by her terrible tale of woe.

This was Mrs. Fraser, the wife of an officer in the 27th Native Infantry, who had travelled by dâk from the city of Delhi. The native driver had taken her up in the suburbs of Delhi and brought her safely 266 miles through a country excited by passion, disturbed by marauders and thronged with mutineers on their way to the capital of the Moghul.

Her carriage had been pierced by bullets, but the lady had escaped. Poor woman! she drew a breath of thankfulness as she found herself safe once more and amongst friends and loyal sepoys.

Captain Mowbray Thomson in his *Story of Cawnpore* places this lady in the forefront of the many heroines that the perils of the siege called forth to do and dare for the sake of the weaker.

He says: "During the horrors of the siege she won the admiration of all our party by her indefatigable attentions to the wounded. Neither danger nor fatigue seemed to have power to suspend her ministry of mercy. Even on the fatal morning of embarkation, although she had escaped to the boats with scarcely any clothing on her, in the thickest of the deadly volleys poured upon us from the banks, she appeared alike indifferent to danger and to her own scanty covering; while she was entirely occupied in the attempt to soothe and relieve the agonised sufferers around her, whose wounds scarcely made their condition worse than her own. Such rare heroism deserves a far higher tribute than this simple record."

Mrs. Fraser was one of the ladies who were recaptured from the boats, and is said to have died of fever in the massacre house; and so she escaped that last awful scene arranged by the Nana and Azimoolah.

As day followed day, so evidence accumulated that the sepoys at Cawnpur would follow the example of their comrades elsewhere.

The sergeant-major's wife of the 53rd, an Eurasian, was accosted by a sepoy while she was marketing in the native bazaar: "You will none of you come here much oftener," he said; "you will not be alive another week."

She reported this story, but it was not thought worthy of belief.

Some officers tried to persuade the ladies to retire to Calcutta.

"Why should we?" was the reply; "General Wheeler's family are here."

But Sir Hugh had heard enough to make him nervous about the women and children. He began to consider a good site for a fort: the magazine was too far off: there was no building large enough on the river-bank: he decided to strengthen the old dragoon hospital, which consisted of two brick buildings, one thatched, the other roofed with masonry, and a few outhouses. A mud wall, four feet high, was thrown up round this hospital: it was hard work digging in the rock-like ground, but they did what they could in the time.

On the 21st of May the women and children were ordered into this enclosure; the officers still slept in the native lines with their corps, lest the sepoys should think the officers suspected their loyalty.

A few days later Lieutenant Ashe of the Bengal Artillery arrived from Lucknow with two 9-powders and one 24-pounder howitzer. So the garrison now had ten guns placed in wide embrasures that gave no cover, but exposed to the enemies' fire all who worked them.

General Wheeler ordered supplies to last twenty-five days: surely they would be relieved before that! Also the regimental mess sent in beer, wine and tinned food. Ammunition was plentiful, two thousand pounds of powder and plenty of round-shot.

During the last days of May many of these doomed sons and daughters of Britain were busy writing the last letters they would ever pen. They were eager to catch the home mail—and some of them foresaw it would in all probability be their last.

Colonel Ewart, sitting in his tent amongst the swaggering, insolent sepoys whom he had given many years to teach and train and improve, writes thus: "I do not wish to write gloomily, but there is no use in disguising the fact that we are in the utmost danger; and, as I have said, if the troops do mutiny, my life must almost certainly be sacrificed; but I do not think they will venture to attack the entrenched position which is held by the European troops. So I hope in God that E—— and my child will be saved. . . . I know you will be everything a mother can be to my boy. I cannot write to him this time, dear little fellow. Kiss him for me: kind love to M—— and my brothers."

Had he some glimmer of the last procession to the river, when his own men would stop his litter, taunt him and slash him to pieces in presence of his wife, ere she met the same cruel fate?

And Mrs. Ewart, writing in the stuffy room of the

barracks on the 1st of June, was sending her last message home by the Calcutta mail: "My dear little child is looking very delicate: my prayer is that she may be spared much suffering. The bitterness of death has been tasted by us many times during the last fortnight; should the reality come, I hope we may find strength to meet it with a truly Christian courage. It is not hard to die oneself, but to see a dear child suffer and perish—that is the hard, the bitter trial, and the cup which I must drink should God not deem it fit that it should pass from me."

If we only could read more of the letters in that last mail-bag from Cawnpur, we should be able to realise more fully the sterling worth of those heroes, great and small, who were beginning to tread the hard road that led through fear and thirst and suffering to a cruel death.

"We must not give way to despondency," writes the same brave lady, "for at the worst we know that we are in God's hands. . . . He will be with us in the valley of the shadow of death also, and we need fear no evil."

It is so difficult for us to realise that it is not the life of the body, or its preservation, that the providence of God takes charge of. Perhaps in the few weeks of painful, agonising endurance which these poor mortals went through they were training their spirit life for higher duties in a better world hereafter. That must be our chief consolation when we follow with indignant sympathy their earthly trials in the next three weeks.

On the night of the 6th of June what all feared suddenly happened. The sowars of the 2nd Cavalry arose in the night with shouts, set fire to the bungalow of the English riding-master, attacked the soubahdar-major, or native colonel, who tried to defend the colours and treasure, and called upon the 1st Native Infantry to join them in mutiny.

Colonel Ewart, hearing the tumult, ran across to his men, crying in Hindostani, "My children! do not so great a wickedness—oh! my children!"

It was useless to recall the sepoys to their duty: they were fired by the lust of loot and sped away to the treasury. The 56th Native Infantry followed the next morning: the 53rd stood firm against evil counsel, until Sir Hugh Wheeler made the mistake of ordering Ashe's battery to open upon them; the sepoys of the 53rd could not believe they were being fired upon at first, but at the third round they broke and fled. Their native officers had been called within the entrenchments before this: these and eighty men of the 53rd who came in later gave their help to the white folk, until after nine days' fighting they were asked to depart, because there was not enough food to keep so many men!

There were a few hours of stillness before the storm; the faithful sepoys were now employed in collecting and carting muskets, ammunition, etc., which had been left about in the native lines. The English officers drew a long breath of relief: the mutineers had doubtless gone off to Delhi. At present they had only gone as far as the treasury, when the Nana met them with an escort and many elephants, swore fidelity to the national cause, and distributed much of the silver among the four regiments. Then the sepoys broke open the gaol and let out a motley host of God-forsaken rascals, who set to work at once and burned and sacked every European house, making a bonfire of all the records in the court-house, civil and criminal alike. The mutineers had travelled on the Delhi road as far as Kullianpur when they were overtaken by the Nana, his two brothers, Bala and Baba Bhut, and Azimoolah.

"Return to Cawnpur, destroy all the Europeans, and I will give every man a gold anklet and license to pillage"; so spake the Nana.

The sepoys agreed, saluted the Nana as their Rajah and chose Teeke Sing chief of their cavalry, and other Hindoos as colonels of the 53rd and 56th.

Next morning Sir Hugh Wheeler received a polite letter from the Nana, intimating that he was about to commence the attack.

Sir Hugh at once summoned all the officers from the native lines within the entrenchment without delay: they came, leaving their breakfast coffee, their clothes and valuables, and hurried into the fatal precincts of the Dragoon hospital, which was exposed on four sides to attack, and was commanded by some half-finished barracks at distances varying from 300 to 800 yards. A small detachment was placed in No. 4 barrack, consisting chiefly of civil engineers, who were good shots and judges of distance.

Captain Moore of Her Majesty's 32nd Foot assisted General Wheeler in arranging for the defence, and gradually became the practical chief. It was Sunday morning, about 10 a.m., when the first shot fired by the mutineers came from a 9-pounder; it struck the crest of the mud wall and glided over into the smaller barrack, where it broke the leg of a native servant.

A large party of ladies and children were sitting in the shade of the verandahs, when the whizz of the round-shot, and the bugle-call sending every man to his post, awoke all to the stern reality which was coming upon them. The children screamed with fright and ran into the dark rooms for safety. By noon the mutineers had placed many guns in position and the entrenchment was raked by 24-pound shot from every quarter.

All through this first day the shrieks of the women and children were heart-rending, as often as the balls struck the walls and windows; while a low wailing cry formed a piteous undertone of sad despair, but it was only on that first day that such sounds troubled the hearts of the brave defenders: after that, Captain Mowbray Thomson tells us, they had learnt silence and never uttered a sound except when groaning from the horrible mutilations they had to endure. Had their mothers taught these tiny heroes to suppress all cries of fear? had they told them that if God willed they should die, He would welcome them in His arms to a better world than this?

Anyhow, the children grew used to the horrible noises and

the fearful sights, and even ran and played about on the exposed ground between the mud walls of the entrenchment.

Before the third evening every window and door had been battered in; screens, piled-up furniture, partitions—all went down, and shell and cannon-ball ranged freely through the naked rooms. Grape and round-shot, bullets and falling timber killed many ladies and children in those first days, while the gunners at their guns fell mortally wounded in large numbers.

But wherever there was pressing danger or direst misery, Captain Moore was not long before he came with encouraging sympathy to strengthen and comfort the sufferer. He was a tall, fair, blue-eyed Irishman, full of cheerful animation and intrepid as a young lion.

"Wherever Moore had passed," writes Sir G. Trevelyan, "he left men something more courageous, and women something less unhappy."

The three civilians in No. 4 barrack outside the walls, Heberden, Latouche and Miller, with a few others had the most severe time: for after fighting all day they were assaulted in the dark by hundreds of sepoys who crept up to take them by surprise.

To aid these gallant civil engineers Captain Jenkins of the 2nd Cavalry was given them as commander: and here the little company of sixteen held the key of the position. Lieutenant Glanville afterwards held No. 2, and when dangerously wounded was succeeded by Mowbray Thomson. Lieutenant Sterling, an expert shot with the rifle, did good service here: for Thomson contrived a sort of perch twenty feet up the wall in which Sterling used to sit and wait upon the unwary.

Sometimes prisoners were brought in at night: on one occasion eleven sepoys were captured, and as no sentry could be spared to guard them, they were at a loss how to keep them.

"Give me a sword, sir: I'll undertake to mind they don't get out."

The officer turned in surprise, for it was a woman's voice surely.

Yes, Bridget Widdowson, a stalwart dame indeed! wife of a private in H.M.'s 32nd regiment. The prisoners were roped together, wrist to wrist, and sat motionless for more than an hour while the strong and brave woman marched with drawn sword before them.

It is a pity—but when she retired and a male guard took her place, they all managed to slip away in the dark. After that no more prisoners were brought in.

After a week's siege food began to grow scarce and the Europeans were put upon rations: once a lean horse allowed himself to be shot, and once a sacred bull went down before Mr. Sterling's rifle. But as his sanctity fell some three hundred yards away from the wall, to fetch in the beef might entail loss of human life.

Yet beef was beef: so Captain Moore and eight others ran out with a strong rope, hauled in the bull at the cost of a few wounds and were rewarded by the cheers of the ladies.

Alas! Captain Jenkins, when carrying some horse-soup from No. 2 barrack to his wife, was shot dead.

The heat was so intense that a gun-barrel left for a few minutes in the sun could not be touched, and many died of sunstroke. The well in the entrenchment was a great source of danger, as the rebels fired grape upon that spot as soon as any one came to draw water. At night they knew by the creaking of the tackle that water was being drawn and instantly opened with their artillery.

Privates were paid eight shillings a bucket: but they were willing to draw water for nothing, to help the poor women and children. Soon John M'Killop, of the Civil Service, gallantly constituted himself captain of the well. For a week he drew water cheerfully for all: then a grape-shot wound in the groin removed him from the scene. The dead were thrown at night down a well outside the walls. By the end of the first week fifty-nine artillerymen had been killed at their posts: sunstroke had killed Major

Prout and Captain Kempland. Lieutenant Eckford was struck on the heart by a cannon-ball while resting under the verandah, Dempster was shot dead, and Martin had a bullet in his lungs: then untrained volunteers came forward to do what they could, firing 6-pound balls from damaged 9-pounders. At last only two guns could be fired, and for these the ladies gave up their stockings to supply a sort of cartridge-case. On the eighth evening of the bombardment a shell settled among the rafters of the thatched barrack and it was burnt to the ground. There were sick and wounded within; long after midnight men and women were working to get them out; but in spite of all, two wounded artillerymen perished in the flames.

The enemy advanced that night by hundreds with yells of defiance to storm Ashe's battery. Ashe held his fire until they came within sixty yards, and then let them have a charge of grape. Every man round the wall had eight or ten rifles which he fired in quick succession; in half an hour a hundred sepoys lay dead. In the burnt barrack all medical stores and surgical instruments were consumed; and from that time no bullets could be extracted, no mutilations dressed.

Amongst those who distinguished themselves during the fire was Lieutenant Ward, a son of Admiral Ward, "a model soldier," says Captain Thomson. That night of horror who can describe? The men were either saving the wounded from the flames, or beating back the enemy. The poor children, huddled together in the ditch, were crying softly, the women, tired out, at last flung themselves down in the ditch too, for there was no room for them in the other barrack.

Unshod, unkempt, ragged and squalid—for they had not had a pint of water to wash in for a week—they herded together in their misery. All good looks and signs of youth had fled: want, exposure, sorrow, depression had drawn awful lines upon faces recently so fair: fever and apoplexy and dysentery brooded over what shot and shell had spared.

Not less than two hundred women and children now had to pass twelve days and nights upon the bare ground without a roof over their heads. The cold by night, the heat by day, were wearing them out slowly: but many of them braced themselves up to help the fighters; they carried round ammunition, they tended the sick and wounded, they encouraged all by brave smiles and the appearances of indifference to their wretched state. Once a shell fell into Whiting's battery and killed seven soldiers' wives, who were sitting together in the trench.

Mrs. White, a private's wife, was walking beside her husband carrying her twin children, one on each arm; they were well under cover, they thought, but a bullet killed the man and passed through the wife's arms, so that father, mother, and babes fell in a heap together.

Thomson says: "I saw her afterwards in the main-guard lying on her back with the children laid, one at each breast, while the mother's bosom refused not what her broken arms could not administer."

Mrs. Williams, after losing her husband, Colonel Williams, early in the siege, was herself shot in the face: her daughter, who was also suffering from a bullet-wound, attended to her till she died.

An ayah had both her legs taken off by a round-shot: the babe was picked up smeared with blood, but unhurt.

It is too harrowing to go through the fatal list of sufferers: Miss Brightman, Mrs. Evans, Mrs. Reynolds and many more were killed. But those who were not killed became the greatest martyrs.

One poor woman must have had some premonition of this; for she ran out with a child in each hand, courting sudden death; but a private bravely went after her and dragged them back to cover.

Mr. Hillersden, the magistrate of Cawnpur, was standing in the verandah talking to his wife, who had only recently recovered from her accouchement, when a round-shot cut him in two. Mrs. Hillersden died three days later under a fall of bricks. Thomson says: "She was a most accomplished lady, and by reason of her cheerfulness, amiability and piety a universal favourite."

The general's son, Lieutenant Wheeler, was sitting on a sofa, faint with a wound just received: his sister was fanning him when a round-shot passed through the room and carried away his head. Father, mother and two sisters were in the room at the time.

Lieutenant Daniell was among the bravest of the young officers. He had been a favourite of the Nana, and had often been invited to the palace at Bithoor: once the Nana took a valuable diamond ring from his own finger and gave it to Daniell. He was scarce twenty years old, a splendid rider and good in all field sports, full of fun and enthusiastic love of life.

One day, as Thomson and he were dashing round to clear the out-buildings of sepoys, they heard sounds of a struggle going on within. They entered and saw Captain Moore lying on the ground, a powerful native kneeling over him with tulwar raised. In a moment Daniell had run the sepoy through with his bayonet.

"Thanks, old fellow," said Moore, rising stiffly; "my broken collar-bone has a bit disabled me: that was a touch and go."

In the multitude of terrible accidents this was as nothing: Daniell survived the siege, but was wounded during the embarkation by a musket-shot in the temple, and probably fell into the river.

About ten days after the beginning of the bombardment, very early in the morning mist, the sentinels saw some one riding up at a gallop. A shot was fired and the horse was hit, but rose at the wall and cleared it like a bird.

"A white man, by Jove!" The excitement spread through the camp.

"I am Lieutenant Bolton of the 7th Cavalry—excuse my feeble voice, friends. Yes, I was sent out with a detachment of the 48th from Lucknow to keep open the road from

Futteyghur to Cawnpur: our men mutinied; Major Staples and I rode away—pursued—poor Staples shot—fell from his horse. They cut him to pieces. Three troopers chased me for sixteen miles, one gave me this bullet-hole through my cheek. I gave them the slip last night, got through the Nana's camp unobserved. Didn't know where you fellows were, so slept out in the plain all night. At daybreak I spotted the entrenchment and rode for safety, as you see."

Safety! an ironical smile must have passed round the listening group. Well, this Lieutenant Bolton proved a valuable addition to the garrison. He joined the out-picket under Captain Jenkins and lived through the siege to perish in the boats.

The 23rd of June, being the centenary of Plassey, the rebels showed signs of keeping the eve thereof by a series of night assaults. After repelling two or three attacks, Captain Moore and Delafosse came across to Thomson's barrack, and the former said: "Thomson, I think I shall try a new dodge; we are going out into the open, and I shall give the word of command as though our party were about to commence an attack."

Forthwith out they went into the dark space beyond the walls, Moore with a sword, Delafosse carrying an empty musket. The gay captain shouted in stentorian tones, "Number one to the front!" Thereat, like rabbits scuttling to a warren, hundreds of sepoys bolted out from their cover behind heaps of rubbish to the safer shelter of the barrack walls.

With a hearty laugh at their success in clearing out the hiding foe, they returned to their posts. But by dawn the sixteen men in No. 2 had shot eighteen sepoys just outside their doorway.

On the 23rd, great efforts were made to break into the entrenchment; cavalry rode up winded and retired in confusion after a dose of grape. General Wheeler grew less and less able to superintend the posts of defence: his short, spare figure was seldom seen now: the death of his son seemed to have taken all the vigour out of him. Mrs. Moore often accompanied her husband in his visits to the various posts: the men fitted up a bamboo hut for her. Alas! she lived long enough to endure the last torments in the house of massacre.

Mr. Moncrieff, the station chaplain, had been very devoted to his work all through, spending most of his time in the hospital, but going round the post and batteries to read a prayer or psalm; the men would bow head for a minute or two, and think on these things.

Meanwhile the Nana had managed to intercept a few stray travellers, families going down stream and others: all these he ordered to be shot, though they had nothing to do with Cawnpur.

On the twenty-first day of the siege the look-out men in the crow's nest of the barrack shouted to Captain Thomson, "There's a woman coming across." The captain knocked up a man's arm who would have fired at her, only just in time to save her: the poor thing had neither shoes nor stockings, and held a child to her breast.

As Thomson lifted her over the barricade he recognised her as Mrs. Greenway, wife of a wealthy merchant in the city. Her husband had paid the Nana £30,000 to save the lives of the whole household. The monster took the ransom and killed all save this lady.

As soon as she had recovered herself, Mrs. Greenway (or, as some assert, Mrs. Jacobi, a friend of the Greenways), handed Captain Thomson this letter:—

"To the subjects of Her Most Gracious Majesty, Queen Victoria,—

"All those who are in no way connected with the acts of Lord Dalhousie, and are willing to lay down their arms, shall receive a safe passage to Allahabad."

It was unsigned, but the handwriting was that of Azimoolah.

Thomson took the letter at once to Captain Moore,

who, together with General Wheeler and Captain Whiting, deliberated over the contents.

Sir Hugh, fearing treachery on the part of the Nana, for a long time opposed the idea of making terms. But when the others reminded him that they had only three days' rations left, that the rains were due and would inevitably wash away the ramparts and level the hospital, he gave in. It was the thought of the women and children that made the younger men agree to treat: if they had only had men to consider, they would have made a dash for Allahabad, and Moore would have led the forlorn hope.

As Mrs. Greenway waited for the reply, she answered inquiries as to how she had been treated: very cruelly, she said, on a starving allowance of chupatties and water, stripped of all clothing but a gown; her ear-rings had been pulled out roughly; and she cried bitterly as she mentioned her wrongs. She was sent back in the afternoon with the message that the general was in deliberation as to his answer. The Maharaja heard the lady's message and sent her back to her prison: he needed her no further.

Next morning Azimoolah, accompanied by Jwala Pershad, the brigadier of the Nana's cavalry, walked up to within 200 yards of the outer barrack and met Moore, Whiting, and Mr. Roche, the postmaster, in conference. It was agreed that the English should surrender the fortification, treasury and artillery, should go forth armed with sixty rounds of ammunition per man; that carriages should be provided for the sick and wounded, and that boats furnished with flour should be ready at the ghaut.

To this the native delegates agreed, and one graciously added: "Yes, and we will give you sheep and goats also."

The Nana read over the terms and sent a trooper to say that the entrenchments must be evacuated the same night.

After some haggling and threats, the Nana consented to put it off till next morning. Then Mr. Todd, who had been the Nana's tutor, went over to get the Nana's signature: he was courteously received, and returned with the signature affixed. As if to show their good faith, the rebels sent three men into the entrenchment to stay the night as hostages. One of these was Jwala Pershad: this gentleman made a parade of condoling with General Wheeler upon the privations he had undergone, and assured him that no harm should come upon any one to-morrow.

A company of the Nana's artillerymen stood guard by the guns all night. Meanwhile Captain Turner and Lieutenants Delafosse and Goad were deputed to go down to the river and see if the boats were being got ready: they went on elephants with an escort of native cavalry, and found about forty boats moored near the bank. But to their vexation the boats were in a very dilapidated state; so, four hundred workmen were set to work repairing the thatched roofs and making a flooring of bamboo. As the officers waited, provisions were brought on men's heads and stored on board: all seemed to be in a fair way for the departure. But one thing perplexed them not a little: Captain Turner had listened to the idle talk of some men of the 56th Native Infantry who were lying on the river's bank: he distinctly overheard the word "kuttle" repeated, and everytime with a sardonic laugh. Now "kuttle" means *massacre*, and it made him uneasy; but he made no report of it, because it was not evidence strong enough to bring a charge of treachery.

And now the little garrison lay down for their last sleep in the entrenchments: all was quiet, except the well and bucket: quite a little queue of waiting children stood by it, and every one enjoyed a good drink of the cloudy water. Double rations were given round. The faces of the women grew less anxious: the children laughed and played till they dropped down that Friday evening in a pleasant, peaceful sleep.

The women whispered together as they rested after collecting their few valuables: "Will it be all right to-morrow, think you?" or "Will they really let us go down in safety to Allahabad?"

The strange stillness of the night, in contrast to the usual pandemonium of shot and shell, kept many of the men awake till long past midnight: perhaps their confidence in the Nana and in Azimoolah was not so strong as they had pretended during the day. They could hear the jackals barking as they prowled around amongst the dead bodies outside; and the dawn disclosed to view a greedy company of vultures and adjutant birds hard at work.

The 27th of June shone fiercely on a busy scene of men and women preparing to leave their frail home: some were hiding little relics of jewellery in the tattered fragments of their dress. For there was no distinction of dress now between rich and poor: all were bare-legged, for their stockings had gone to the ammunition-box. All were clad in short skirts and scanty underclothing, because they had torn up all their linen to serve as bandages.

Perhaps the greatest relief this morning was to be able to wash face and hands after three weeks' grime and dust and heat insupportable.

But in the Nana's tent his kinsmen and courtiers had been hearing Azimoolah's plans and arranging the parts each was to play in the coming tragedy. Tantia Topee, a Mahratta warrior, was in command of the troops to be employed. He was to order 5 guns and 500 picked shots to muster at the landing-place two hours before daybreak.

Certain rebel nobles were to present themselves with their retinue, and the cavalry were informed something of what was brewing. But, to the Nana's surprise, these sepoys came crowding before his tent, shouting indignantly against the treachery—a breach of faith that the gods might well resent. This was a little awkward, and promised a hitch in the Nana's arrangements which might spoil the day's entertainment.

The Maharaja came out and made the excited men a speech: "I assure you, my trusty sowars, that it is permissible to forswear at such a time as this: I tell you this on the authority of a royal Brahmin! For my part, if the object was to annihilate an enemy—and that enemy an unbeliever—I would not hesitate to take a false oath on burning oil or holy water."

The sowars bowed their heads and went apart to grumble: for they had known the white man's faith, and still possessed a conscience.

It was early when sixteen elephants and eighty palanquins were driven down to take the sick and wounded, women and children. More than two hundred were thus to be conveyed to the river. There were crowds of sepoys looking on indifferently: not one offered a helping hand as the wounded were borne along to the palanquins, and many a groan was forced from unwilling throats as the rude shaking jolted half-healed wounds.

The women and children were put on the elephants and into bullock-carts; the able-bodied walked down after them.

As soon as the first party had gone, the sepoys flocked in to examine and poke about for treasure.

"And did you dare to stand up against us with just this poor mud wall?" said one.

"Give me that musket," said another, catching hold of the barrel.

"You shall have its contents, if you like: but not the gun," was the stern reply.

The sepoys said they had lost a thousand men: they inquired after some of their old officers; and when informed that they were dead, seemed sincerely distressed. The Eastern mind is difficult to fathom. Major Vibart was the last officer to leave. Some sepoys of his old regiment insisted on helping him with his boxes, and escorted his wife and family down to the boats with many outward marks of respect.

The Suttee Chowra Ghaut, or landing-place, was within a mile to the north-west of the entrenchments. Here a ravine runs into the Ganges, which in summer is dry and lumpy, in the wet season is a boiling torrent. High banks and decayed fences and prickly pear stand up on either side as the gorge descends to the shore, where there is an open space 150 yards long and 100 deep. On the left of this as you face the river was a village, on the right a temple in good repair rises above the river on a little raised plateau, looking like an old-fashioned summer-house. A steep flight of steps leads down to the water, which is shallow and muddy for many yards.

Tantia Topee was there in the cold dawn of Saturday making his arrangements as the master of the Nana's ceremonies.

He placed a strong body of sepoys under cover of the village, and a squadron of troopers near the little temple: others were secreted behind some timber near the river. A field-piece was posted a quarter of a mile down the river, and on the opposite shore, facing the little ravine, stood two cannon with a battalion of infantry and some cavalry.

The heavy boats rested on the sandy bottom; the boatmen had had their instructions, and munched their cold rice and handed the pipe round, or said their prayers religiously. For was it not a religious ceremony they were going to share in—ridding the earth of a party of unbelievers in order to start life anew!

Before the procession of the victims arrived, thousands of townsfolk from the city thronged down to the landing-place. Curiosity brought some, and sorrow shone in the eyes of many a merchant who knew his best customers were going away.

Besides, was there not a fine spectacle to behold?—Azimoolah and the brothers of the Peishwa, and so many nobles glittering in jewels and gold as they rode proudly down and joined Tantia Topee on the Temple platform; a fine elephant, equipped with a state howdah, had been sent by the Nana for Sir Hugh Wheeler, his old and respected friend. The general was sensible of the attention: but it looked too much like a victorious leader sitting in triumph; and the poor old man, after seeing his wife and daughters safely mounted, called for a homely palanquin and was carried beside them.

The sepoys, as a rule, had no inkling of what was to follow: they talked freely to our men and peered about, finding only two bottles of liquid butter, a sack of flour, and, lying on quilts on the floor, eleven Europeans, evidently near death.

But already some of the rebels began to show a different temper. Lady Wheeler, just before mounting her elephant, had presented her ayah with a small bag of rupees for her constant fidelity. When the elephant moved off a sepoy relieved her of her treasure and dealt her a slash with a sabre: some sepoy servants who had been faithful to the last were rudely seized and carried off to death.

Colonel and Mrs. Ewart had started late, she on foot walking by the side of her husband's litter, which was carried by four native porters. As they came up to St. John's Church, seven or eight sepoys of the Colonel's own battalion stepped up, shouted to the porters and said, "Set down your load, brothers: stand back a while."

Then in taunting language they cried, "This is a fine parade, is it not? is it not well dressed up, eh?"

At once they set to and hewed him to pieces with their swords: then turning to Mrs. Ewart, who stood pale and trembling, they said: "Throw down whatever you have about you and go your ways: for you are a woman; we will not kill a woman."

Thereat she took out of her dress something tied up and handed it over to one of the sepoys, who instantly cut her down dead!

When the last of the garrison had entered the defile, a double line of troops formed across the mouth of the gorge and kept off any who wished to follow.

One sepoy was overheard to say, "They know not what is before them. Now let them repent of their misdeeds, and ask pardon of God."

Meanwhile the sight of the shining river had given

heart to many: the children openly rejoiced and thought all their fears and sufferings were over at last.

But to get on board was not so easy, for no planks were laid to serve as gangway: the Hindoo boatmen stood in their boats, silent, giving no help to men or women.

Standing knee-deep in the water, the British officers hoisted in the wounded and the women. The children, once on board, saw smoking plates of boiled rice, and were laughing merrily at the unwonted sight when the loud blast of a bugle came ringing down the ravine. Then occurred a dramatic scene which had been well prepared by Tantia Topee and his myrmidons.

The native rowers leaped into the water and hurried splashing to the water's edge: crack went the carbines of a hundred sowars: and before the Englishmen could handle their rifles, the straw roofs of the boats burst into flames from the red-hot charcoal which the boatmen had thrust into the thatch.

The guns thundered from the opposite bank, throwing grape amongst the startled fugitives: many girls leaped overboard and crouched beneath the prows, or waded out till the water touched their chins. The men set their shoulders to the sterns and sides of the boats and tried to push out into deep water.

Only three boats moved away, and of these two drifted across to the Oudh bank into the hands of the pitiless foe.

The third boat floated downstream almost unnoticed, for the smoke from the burning boats was spreading a pall over the scene. Into this boat some vigorous men had climbed: Vibart and Whiting, Ashe of the artillery, Delafosse and Bolton, Moore and Blenman, Glanville and Burney and a few others.

Sir George Trevelyan gives an account related by two Eurasian women, wives of musicians in the band of the Fifty-sixth:—

"In the boat where I was to have gone," said Mrs. Bradshaw, "was the schoolmistress and twenty-two misses.

THE MASSACRE OF CAWNPUR

The guns thundered from the bank, the straw roofs of the boats burst into flames, and many of the terror-stricken women leaped into the water and crouched beneath the prows. Only three boats could be moved, and of these two were captured by the enemy.

General Wheeler came last, in a palkee. They carried him into the water near the boat: I stood close by: he said, 'Carry me a little farther towards the boat.' But a trooper said, 'No, get out here.'

"As the general got out of the palkee, head foremost, the trooper gave him a cut with his sword into the neck; he fell into the water! Some women were stabbed with bayonets, others cut down. Little infants were torn in pieces: we saw it! . . . the school-children were burnt to death. I saw their clothes and hair catch fire."

There was more evidence of similar nature, very heart-rending and amply explaining the savage temper in which the news was received in England: where public meetings were held in every town, great or small; and a fierce requital was demanded. Tantia Topee stood on the Temple platform all this time and saw to it that none escaped.

With a motion of his hand he sent a few score sepoys into the water, like otter-hounds keen on the scent, to collect the girls that still crouched under the charred boats or in deeper water. With blows and shrieks for mercy, with tearing off ear-rings and rude pushing, one hundred and twenty-five were assembled near the landing-place and made to sit in the sand—a piteous company. There, in the heat of the morning, faint and desperate, they were made to abide, with sentries posted round: then they were marched back through the ravine and past the European bazaar, the chapel and racquet court. On either side surged a crowd of exulting natives, whose hands were full of silver and jewellery. Many of the ladies were barefoot and wounded, their clothes were covered with mud and blood and torn to tatters: a few children were naked: there were boys of twelve years of age, but no men in that procession of victims.

At last they emerged from the plain and were halted in front of the Maharaja's grand pavilion. The Nana glutted his eyes with the sorry sight, and then ordered them to be taken to the Savada house, a one-storied building to which was attached a small courtyard: here in two large and dirty rooms, furnished with cupboards, they remained until the final massacre; this was ordered perhaps by Azimoolah on hearing of the imminent approach of Havelock.

Let us now return to the escaping boat under Major Vibart. Mowbray Thomson tells us that after trying to push his boat out into deep water and finding it immovable, he and nine or ten others swam after the one boat which was drifting downstream. Close by Thomson's side were two brothers Henderson of the 56th Native Infantry: the younger soon went down from weakness, the elder was wounded in the hand by grape-shot, but managed with Thomson's help to reach Vibart's boat, which was stranded on a sand-bank on the Oudh side of the river.

Captain Whiting pulled them in terribly exhausted: all of the other swimmers sank or were shot in the water, except Lieutenant Harrison of the 2nd Light Cavalry and Private Murphy. Harrison had reached a small islet on the Cawnpur side, where he was attacked by three sowars armed with the tulwar: they had just cut down an English lady, and were bent on finishing off an English gentleman. But Harrison had his revolver at hand, and in spite of his late immersion it responded to the trigger; two sowars went down before him, the third turned tail and sought the water. Harrison then plunged in on the river side of the island and swam to Vibart's boat.

And now another boat came drifting down, but was struck by a round shot below water-mark and began to fill.

However, Vibart managed to take them off, and crowded his own boat so much that there was little room to work her with the spars they had. There was no rudder, and the boatman had taken away the oars: grape and round shot flew about the huddled fugitives from either bank, and on that 27th of June many were killed and thrown overboard.

Captain Moore, the cheery Irishman, was shot in the

heart while pushing off the boat: Ashe of the artillery and Bolton, the young officer who had ridden his horse over the entrenchment wall, were also shot. Burney and Glanville were cut asunder by the same round-shot that shattered Lieutenant Fagan's leg below the knee.

Mrs. Swinton, standing up in the stern, was knocked by a round-shot into the river. Her little boy, six years old, went up to Thomson and said, "Mamma has fallen overboard, Captain Thomson."

"Thank God, my little man, that He has taken your mother away: she will not suffer any more pain now, poor dear."

"Oh! why are they firing at us?" cried the child; "did they not promise to leave off?" History does not relate what became of that little boy.

They had no food to eat all through the long-drawn agony of that blazing day: at 5 p.m. they stranded again after a six miles' drift, and were attacked by a burning boat and lighted arrows; so that it became necessary to cut down the thatch and throw it overboard. Four more miles were made in the night. Next day Vibart was shot twice through the arm, Captain Turner had both legs smashed, Whiting was killed, Lieutenant Quin and Captain Seppings were shot through the arm, Mrs. Seppings through the thigh, Lieutenant Harrison was shot dead, and many others not named. At sunset a boat sent from Cawnpur with fifty natives well-armed grounded close to them on a sandbank: twenty British charged them, and instead of their finishing the Nana's massacre, they met their own doom.

Their boat was well supplied with ammunition, which was useful: but still our people had no food, and began to feel very faint and weary.

The next night a hurricane came on and set the boat floating; but as daylight came they found they had drifted up a side stream. At 9 a.m. Major Vibart directed Thomson, Delafosse, Grady, and eleven privates to wade ashore and drive off the sepoys who were firing at them.

This forlorn hope saved four lives: for, maddened by desperation, these fourteen men charged and cut through the sepoys, driving them back from the river: on their return they found their boat gone! The only chance now was to take flight anywhere: after retreating three miles they fortified themselves in a little temple, shot many assailants, but were smoked out: they dashed through the crowd outside, and seven reached the water, into which they threw their guns and then themselves.

As they swam more were shot: four approached the shore, but seeing some armed men standing near, they turned to swim away.

"Sahib! Sahib! why swim away? we are friends," they shouted.

They even offered to throw their weapons into the river to prove their sincerity. As one by one the Englishmen reached the shallow water, they fell exhausted—they had just swum six miles, their feet had been burnt in escaping from the temple: they only asked for a speedy death. But what were the natives doing?

Gently they drew the white men up on the dry sand, wrapped them in blankets, rubbed their bare limbs, and told how they were the retainers of the Rajah Dirigbijah Singh, of Moorar Mhow, in Oudh; this loyal gentleman treated the four men, Thomson, Delafosse, Sullivan, and Murphy, right royally and gave them each a piece of carpet to cover their bodies. Here they were hospitably entertained for a month, enjoying the simple fare of the Brahmins and the precious balm of unbroken sleep.

Three times during their stay the Nana sent word to the Rajah that he must surrender the white men: but the old chief took no heed: he was a gentleman indeed! It is pleasant to know that the English Government conferred upon him a handsome pension when the Mutiny was suppressed.

In course of time these four survivors of the Cawnpur massacre were taken across the river, and to their joy met a detachment of the 84th under Havelock.

They were only thirty miles from Cawnpur, marching in Havelock's rear and seeing on all sides the signs of recent battle.

Thomson went off alone, on arrival at Cawnpur, to see the place where they kept the flag flying for three weeks, and where so many loved ones were lying deep in the old well outside the mud walls. To his surprise, Dame Nature had covered up all the ghastly sights with a luxuriant growth of long grasses; as if she said: "Let the dead past go and be forgotten: be strong, quit yourselves as men; for there is always work to be done in a naughty world."

General Neill no sooner heard of the four survivors being in his camp than he sent for them and heard their story.

The two officers were given honourable posts; Delafosse lived to fight under Chamberlain in the Hindu Kush, Thomson to write his story of the Mutiny, "so told that it may be read by a Christian without horror, and by an educated person without disgust."

Murphy became custodian of the Memorial Gardens: Sullivan lived fourteen days in peace and safety, and then succumbed to an attack of cholera, being worn out by his privations and sufferings. A native spy told how Vibart's boat came back to the Ghaut at Cawnpur; sixty sahibs, twenty-five mem-sahibs and four children. "The Nana ordered the sahibs to be separated from the mem-sahibs and shot by the First Bengal Native Infantry." But they refused. However, some men of the Naduic regiment offered to kill them.

"So the sahibs were seated on the ground, and two companies stood with their muskets ready to fire. Then said one of the mem-sahibs (the wife of Dr. Boyes), 'I will not leave my husband: if he must die, I will die with him.' So she ran and sat down behind her husband, clasping him round the waist. Then the other mem-sahibs said, 'We also will die with our husbands'; and they all sat down, each by her husband. . . . The Nana ordered his soldiers to pull them away: but they could not pull away the doctor's wife, and she remained there. Then the Padre (Captain Seppings) asked leave to read prayers before they died. . . . After he had read a few prayers he shut the book and the sahibs shook hands all round. Then the sepoys fired: one sahib rolled one way, one another, as they sat. But they were not dead, only wounded. So they went in and finished them off with swords."

It is painful to read such things, but it is ungrateful to forget the heroes and heroines of those terrible days. They died for us and for England, and their brave example must surely nerve us, if ever the time should come, to scorn danger, suffering, and death, in defence of hearth and home.

In part from *Cawnpore*, by kind permission of The Right Hon. Sir George Trevelyan, Bart., and Messrs. Macmillan.

CHAPTER XIII

HAVELOCK AND OUTRAM: THE RELIEVERS OF LUCKNOW

SIR HENRY HAVELOCK, returned from his Persian campaign, was summoned to Calcutta, informed of the facts of the Mutiny, given the command of the Cawnpur district, and hurried off to Allahabad, for the Government still hoped to be in time to relieve Wheeler. As he led his column through the streets of that city in a drenching rain, the natives from the house-tops scowled and spat and cursed the foreigner.

It was the 30th of June when he reached Allahabad, and after organising his little force he set out for Cawnpur on the evening of the 7th of July. He had heard that Cawnpur had fallen, but Colonel Neill, who had done wonders at Benares and had saved Allahabad, was loth to believe the news, and Havelock hoped it was untrue.

With 1000 English infantry and 150 Sikhs, and taking his own son from the 10th Foot to be his aide-de-camp, Havelock pushed on to join Major Renaud, who had been sent on by Neill with 400 Europeans, 300 Sikhs, and 120 troopers. They made a forced march of twenty-four miles without stopping to rest. Then they halted for their well-earned breakfast, smoked, lay back under the trees, when with a shout some horsemen sent out to reconnoitre came in at a gallop; and well they might, for round-shot were bowling along the hard road close at their heels.

Drums beat the assembly, up jumped the soldiers, clutched their rifles and fell into line.

It was the Sabbath morn, but war takes no heed of

Sabbaths. Brigadier Havelock came up to the 78th and cried, "Highlanders, I promised you a field-day in Persia, but the Persians ran away. We will have that field-day now—let yonder fellows see what you are made of."

Captain Maude, R.A., was directed to place his 8 guns in front, behind were the men armed with the new Enfield rifle, while the horse guarded the flanks, volunteers the right, irregulars the left. The rebels' guns were the first to open fire, but when Maude began he soon silenced the enemy: then advancing within 200 yards of the rebel infantry, he poured in a withering fire.

Meanwhile the rebel cavalry rode up to our native troopers and said, "Comrades, leave these white men and follow us."

As they hesitated, Palliser sounded the charge: only three or four men rode after him. Palliser was unhorsed, but was rescued by some of his own men who had at first refused to charge. Our men galloped into Futtehpur after the fleeing rebels, captured 12 guns, much ammunition, and some silver. Twelve of our men died that day of sun-stroke.

After the battle the men enjoyed a rest in a mango grove; and the next day too they were allowed to lie idle and recoup themselves. Amongst the spoil an ominous find was that of many dresses of English ladies: that reminded them that they had no time to lose.

On the 14th, Havelock resumed his advance along a road strewn with properties cast aside by the rebels.

The native troopers who had behaved so badly in the last fight were disarmed and placed on duty as baggage guards: but they seized an opportunity, when some alarm occupied the troops, to plunder the baggage: they were then dismounted and dismissed.

Next day they found the rebels in force at Aoung: in dislodging them Major Renaud was killed—a skilled and gallant soldier; after a few rounds of Maude's battery the sepoys gave way and some guns were taken.

As our men were resting reports came that the enemy

had retired to a strong position, covered by a swollen stream, called Pandu Nadi: here there was a stone bridge.

"We must secure that bridge before the rebels destroy it," said Havelock: and the men had to rise and labour on.

Three miles' hot marching under an afternoon sun brought them to the bridge, intact, but guarded by two guns.

Maude was ordered up, and at his first discharge he smashed their sponge-staffs and they could load no longer.

The Madras Fusiliers and Highlanders dashed across the bridge, bayoneted the gunners, and Maude pounded the rest as they ran.

Once more they lay down for a night's sleep; but Havelock received a message that Nana Sahib with 7000 men was ready to oppose his entry into Cawnpur on the morrow; he was told also that 200 women and children were still held alive.

The news flew through the camp and cheered the weary fighters. "With God's help, men," Havelock exclaimed, "we shall save them, or every man of us die in the attempt."

"To-morrow we shall be in Cawnpur, and we will save the women and children," so said many an excited soldier that night.

They started very early and marched fourteen miles out of the twenty-two—then they rested; the day was fearfully hot and exhausting.

Barrow, sent on to get information, met two faithful sepoys who were coming to inform Havelock of the Nana's position at a spot where the road forks, a branch going off from the Grand Trunk road to Cawnpur.

The Nana, being sure the English would pass that fork, had measured the distance and trained all his eight guns on the spot. Therefore Havelock gave the men their dinners, and at half a mile from the fork turned off with most of his men to the right, while Barrow with the Fusiliers went straight on in skirmishing order. A thick grove concealed the main body until they were well to the right of the enemy. Before the guns could be brought round Havelock shouted to the 78th, "Now, my lads, go and take that battery."

With sloped arms and measured tread they swept on in grim silence through the iron storm that whizzed above them, till at 100 yards' range the word "Charge!" rang out.

Then with a cheer they dashed forward as the pipes skirled; not a shot was fired, so fiercely did they desire to use the bayonet, and in a few minutes they had climbed the mound and silenced guns and gunners.

"One more charge! take the big guns yonder!"

Again they dashed in and smashed up the enemy's centre, took the village and chased the rebels through the streets.

On the other wing the 64th and 84th had also forced back the enemy, one regiment racing against the other.

Havelock now thought the battle had been won—his men had marched twenty miles and fought a fierce battle; they fell down worn out; in a few minutes they again rose and mounted the low rise which separated them from Cawnpur.

As they reached the summit they saw the reunited forces of the rebels half a mile in front. In the centre was Nana Sahib, seated on an elephant, and native music was playing.

Three guns opened fire from their centre and a fierce discharge of musketry saluted the worn-out soldiers.

Havelock's guns were a mile in the rear, and their horses were done; he knew he must call on his infantry for one more effort. So he rode to the front on his pony—his horse having been shot—and said—

"The longer you look at it, men, the less you will like it. The brigade will advance, left battalion leading."

Major Sterling and Havelock's son led the 64th through round-shot and grape, charged and routed the foe.

Then to sleep on the bare ground—no tents, no food, no grog! but dimly in the short twilight they could discern the roofless barracks of Cawnpur, and they were well content.

Early next morning they heard a loud explosion—the Nana had blown up his magazine!

Tytler reported that the rebels had left the city and its environs, so they stepped joyously forth to rescue the women and children.

Alas! as they drew near the house in which they had been confined, they were told that all had been just massacred!

In a horror of silence they heard the awful news.

Many went into the rooms and courtyard, seeing the fragments of dress and hair, the children's socks soaked in blood, the marks on the walls of bullet and sword-cut. Some came out with oaths of vengeance, some with tears, some vowed they could never go near that spot again.

The number of victims counted by General Havelock's order as buried in the well was 118 women and 92 children.

It has been said that the walls bore on them pencilled messages: but a friend of the writer who was there with Sir Colin's force informs him that he saw none; they must have been added by soldiers visiting the house.

What was seen at Cawnpur, and what was told in England, explains, if it does not justify to all minds, the terrible vengeance which was taken: similar scenes had occurred at Meerut and Delhi and elsewhere, but nothing on so large a scale as at Cawnpur.

After one day's rest Havelock marched to Bithoor and burnt the Nana's palace, that chief having fled over the Ganges.

Havelock then designed and armed a fortified work commanding the Ganges, in which he left 300 men under Neill.

On the 25th July he crossed the river with some 1200 European troops, ten small field-pieces and a few Sikhs.

When he had fought his way but 15 miles towards Lucknow, Havelock had lost 170 men by wounds or sickness and had used up one-third of his gun ammunition: at this moment too he learnt of the mutiny at Dinapur and knew he could receive no reinforcements. In a moment of despondency he fell back, on the 31st, on Mangalwar, 5 miles from Cawnpur; thence he wrote to Neill and said he should need another 1000 men to reach Lucknow. To this letter Neill replied almost insultingly, which so stung Havelock that he advanced again, fought more battles, lost more men, and with the consent of his staff again fell back, and recrossed the Ganges on the 13th of August.

On the 16th he led his men out again to Bithoor, attacked 4000 rebels and took two guns.

Sir Colin assumed command of the army on the 17th August and at once telegraphed to Sir James Outram his hope that after Eyre's signal success the 5th and 90th regiments might go on to Allahabad in order to reinforce Havelock.

To Havelock he telegraphed: "The sustained energy, promptitude and vigorous action by which your whole proceedings have been marked during the late difficult operations deserve the highest praise. . . . I beg you to express to the officers and men under your command the pride and satisfaction I have experienced in reading your reports of the intrepid valour they have displayed."

There was no delay now in sending troops to reinforce; no more hesitation in councils, or keeping regiments at Calcutta. Sir Colin spared nobody, not even himself: the idle and the indifferent, the timid and the boastful, felt the lash of his anger and set to work in silence and dismay.

But for many weeks Sir Colin was unable to leave Calcutta, so important was it to organise a relief for Havelock.

We must now return to this hero, who had fought his way so gallantly to Cawnpur with so small a force at his disposal. On the 17th of August, the day after he had beaten 4000 rebels at Bithoor, Havelock read in the *Calcutta Gazette* that General Sir James Outram had been appointed to the command of Cawnpur.

Perhaps as he sat in his tent pondering on this news, his heart may have been wrung with a twinge of regret that he could not complete his duty of relieving Lucknow as general in command. For now Outram was coming to

OUTRAM AND THE TIGER

Outram had declared that he intended to kill a royal tiger on foot, at which his friends laughed. This was no idle boast, for on reaching the spot where a tiger was reported, he slipped from the howdah of his elephant, and armed with nothing but a Maratha spear, waited until the beaters should drive the brute out. With an angry growl it sprang out; the spear pierced its neck and broke off short, and the tiger was preparing for another spring, when a couple of shots from his friend Graham's gun drove it into the thicket.

supersede him at the critical moment, when reinforcements were beginning to arrive. Outram! His thoughts reverted to all he had heard of that brave soldier: how he had made a name for himself by his exploits in hog-hunting in Bombay, and had been chosen to lead a wing of his regiment when only a junior lieutenant, and was nicknamed "the little general," because of his inches. How for some years he was employed in keeping in order the Bhils, a wild hill-folk, and had killed many tigers and earned the gratitude of many an Indian mother.

Outram had declared that he intended to kill a royal tiger on foot, at which his friends laughed. This was no idle boast, for on reaching the spot where a tiger was reported, he slipped from the howdah of his elephant, and armed with nothing but a Maratha spear, waited until the beaters should drive the brute out. With an angry growl it sprang out; the spear pierced its neck and broke off short, and the tiger was preparing for another spring, when a couple of shots from his friend Graham's gun drove it into the thicket.

Then he smiled, possibly over the story so often told in camp, of Jemmy Outram rolling down a hill in the jaws of a tiger, drawing a pistol from his belt and shooting as he and the tiger went rolling over down the steep cliff. Outram, it was said, could hear the Bhils lamenting his death, and releasing himself from the dead beast, turned to the beaters and said, "Quiet, boys! what do I care for the clawing of a cat!" The Bhils treasured that sentence for many years: in those words tears and laughter met so closely together: they loved to tell it to their little sons and educate them for a life of hunting. Havelock did not care so much for hunting, but he recognised that India held too many vicious animals, and that a man who for sport had killed 200 tigers, with panthers, bears, hogs and buffaloes thrown in, was doing a good work for humanity. Outram, he remembered, had once had to deal with some queer-tempered camel-men from Cutch who had struck work. He assembled them—

some 2000—flogged the leaders and stopped the mutiny in a day.

Outram was at the storming of Ghuzni in 1839, and at Kabul, and at the siege of Khelab. Then, disguised as an Afghan, travelled far through a dangerous land to carry dispatches to Karachi: there he surprised his brother-in-law, General Farquharson, who only saw in him a dirty native in turban and slippers and native tunic.

"Well, my man, what do you want here?" said the suspicious general.

"I want a good dinner and a wash!"

"The devil you do! Then, who are you—an Englishman?"

"Why, my good fellow, don't you know Jemmy Outram?"

Then Havelock would remember how Outram came under Lord Ellenborough's censure, and how Lord Auckland defended him in the House of Lords, saying, "A more distinguished servant of the public does not exist than Major Outram."

Again, how at a dinner given in his honour when he was leaving Sind, Sir Charles Napier had called him "the Bayard of India, *sans peur et sans reproche.*"

Outram always spoke out freely when he thought things were wrong, as in deposing the Ameers of Sind, and he had helped in putting down bribery at Baroda.

He suffered and lost position by many of his chivalrous attacks on wrong done in high places. He was once sent to Aden, not the most pleasant abode: after Aden he was Resident in Lucknow. Then in a short Persian War he won the Grand Cross of the Bath. In 1857, Lord Canning telegraphed for him to Lord Elphinstone, "for we want all our best men here."

Outram arrived at Calcutta near the end of July 1857, and Lord Canning gave him the command of the divisions of Dinapur and Cawnpur. But when he heard how Havelock had gallantly and heroically led his small force through thousands of opposing rebels under Nana Sahib to Cawnpur, his chivalrous heart smote him that he should be superseding his old friend. As thus Havelock might have recalled some of the passages in his comrade's life, and feeling a little disappointed at not having the honour to relieve Lucknow, a telegram was put into his hands—it was from Sir James Outram: "I shall join you with the reinforcements, but to you shall be left the glory of relieving Lucknow, for which you have already so nobly struggled. I shall accompany you only in my civil capacity as commissioner . . . serving under you as volunteer." Here was a wonderful self-effacement! Outram was surrendering the general's share of the prize-money—and he was a poor man,—he might also be losing the chance of a baronetcy and a big pension; but he did what he thought right. And Havelock, who was a deeply religious man, no doubt thanked God for this act of Divine Providence, for all his life he had lived as the servant of the Most High God. From a small boy at Bishop-Wearmouth and later at Dartford in Kent, Henry Havelock learnt from his pious mother to take life seriously. At nine he went to the Charterhouse and made friends with Julius Hare and Thirlwall, the learned bishop to be of St. David's, with George Grote, the historian of Greece, and William Macnaghten of Kabul fame, and Eastlake, the artist.

When Napoleon escaped from Elba, the Danish blood in Henry Havelock urged him to enter the army. But it was not until 1823 that he got transferred from the Rifle Brigade to the 13th Light Infantry and sailed for Calcutta.

In 1825 he was serving with Sir A. Campbell in Burma, where he distinguished himself by coolness and daring, storming works, forcing a way through swamp and jungle, often knee-deep in water, struggling against malaria from Rangoon to Prome, mounting the marble steps of the king's palace with bare feet to witness the royal signature to the peace. His men, whom he had taught to pray and sing as well as fight, were called "Havelock's saints."

Then came experiences amongst the Afghans with Colonel Sale: Quetta, Candahar, Ghuznee called him, and then he had the honour of belonging to the brave garrison that held Jellalabad. Later, as lieutenant-colonel, he engaged in the Sikh War: Ferozepur, Aliwal, Sobraon saw Havelock often in danger, and often, as it seemed to him, miraculously preserved.

Often he was sneered at by empty-headed officers; but when danger to the Empire called for the best and truest men, Havelock was sent for, and, as we have seen, led his Highlanders of the 78th at Futtehpur and Pandu Nuddi and Cawnpur, marching in all that heat 130 miles in seven days, fighting four battles and taking twenty-four guns.

It was not until the 16th of September that Sir James Outram reached Cawnpur, bringing Eyre's battery of 18-pounders: the latter had crushed a body of rebels who were intent on cutting Outram's communications.

Havelock was now strong in artillery, having Maude's battery and Olphert's and Eyre's—the whole commanded by Major Cooper.

Leaving some 400 men to hold Cawnpur, the force of 3179 men set out through drenching rain on the 19th of September, and on the 22nd reached the bridge of Bunnee which was neither broken down nor defended. Havelock bivouacked for the night on the farther bank and fired a royal salute to hearten the defenders of the Residency: but it was not heard! On the morning of the 23rd, though Lucknow was only sixteen miles distant, they could hear no booming of guns. Doubtless, the sepoys were saving up their resources to meet the relieving force.

After a good breakfast, they marched on till they came near the Alumbagh, when the guns made play right and left and the 5th Fusiliers stormed the wall: the 78th and Madras Fusiliers followed, and in ten minutes the Alumbagh was cleared. As Outram was cantering back from the pursuit near the Charbagh bridge, a dispatch was brought him. Outram galloped to Havelock and, baring his head, shouted to the soldiers, "Hurrah! boys—Delhi is at last in our hands." Cheer after cheer rose as the news went round:

and, though no tents were up and no supper forthcoming, they made merry, cheered by their late success and by the splendid news.

On the morrow, after leaving the sick and wounded under Major M'Intyre of the 78th in the Alumbagh, at half-past eight the advance sounded, Maude's battery in front; and Outram pushed forward to the right to clear the Charbagh garden, while the main body lay down till Maude's guns had done their work on the earthen rampart, seven feet high, which defended the bridge. But the sepoys were firing under cover and had made havoc of Maude's gunners, so that Maude himself and his lieutenant, Maitland, were serving the guns themselves.

"I say!" shouted Maude to Havelock's son, who was on horseback near, "I can't fight these guns much longer—can't you fellows do something?"

Young Havelock rode at once to Colonel Neill and suggested he should charge the bridge.

"I can't take the responsibility in the absence of Outram: he will be round soon—no, I really can't do it."

But Outram had been detained in his flank movement: the position was critical, something *must* be done.

Then the valiant son of a valiant father tried a daring ruse: young Havelock rode to the rear out of sight, then came galloping back, rode up to Neill and, saluting him, said, as though the order had come from his father, "You are to carry the bridge, sir."

Then Neill gave the order to form up: Havelock, Tytler and Arnold and twenty-eight men made for the barricade. Then a hurricane of missiles opened upon them.

Arnold fell, shot through both thighs. Tytler's horse was killed, and he himself was shot through the groin.

Only young Havelock and a private named Jakes were unhurt: Havelock on his horse waved his sword and called on the main body to come on: Jakes stood by his side, loading and firing as fast as he could. As Mr. Malleson writes: "There they stood, the hero officer and the hero private, for fully two minutes exposed to the full fire of the enemy; and they stood unharmed!" Then with a wild cry the Madras Fusiliers stormed the barricade and bayoneted the rebel gunners where they stood.

By storming this fortified bridge they had won the entrance to the city. As it grew towards evening, Outram proposed a halt for the night, but Havelock decided for an attempt to reach the Residency.

Meanwhile, the beleaguered garrison had been painfully and pleasurably excited all day: hearing the boom of big guns, and the sharp crackle of the rifle-fire.

On 25th September about 11 a.m. they saw how agitated the natives were in town: at 1.30 they saw many leaving the city with bundles on their heads: their bridge of boats must surely have been destroyed, for they perceived many swimming their horses across the Goomtee. Yet still the rebels kept up a heavy cannonade.

At 5 p.m. the Minié-bullet began to whiz over their heads; then they knew their friends were near.

But would they be repulsed? their hearts asked for anxiety. It is growing dusk, but they can hear and see the red-coats fighting their desperate way through street and alley.

Suddenly, all pent-up feelings burst forth like a broken weir in a succession of mad, delighted cheers.

From pit and trench and battery, from behind sand-bags and on shattered roofs, and even from the dim hospital men rose to cheer. The wounded crawled forth to wave a hand, ladies fell on their knees and wept with many a prayer of thanksgiving for deliverance from the unspeakable horrors that had threatened them.

Quickly the defences were thrown down, and Havelock and Outram and many a hero of lesser note stepped over into the grounds of the Residency that had been held so staunchly for eighty-seven days. "And ever above the topmost roof our banner of England blew."

Only a portion of the force entered the Residency that

night: many lay on the ground and slept peacefully after their toils.

We had 196 killed and 535 wounded; of the latter about 40 were stabbed in their dhoolies or litters on their way to the Residency.

After a brief conference it was decided that no attempt should be made to withdraw the women and children to Cawnpur: if it had cost them so much to cut their way in, what might it not cost to break through the thousands of sepoys outside? In fact, Lucknow had been reinforced, not relieved.

Outram and Havelock and the men had done all that men could do: but they had been given an absurdly weak force. People at Calcutta had not yet realised how strong the rebels were in numbers, equipment, discipline and artillery.

So Outram and Havelock remained in Lucknow: the first thing was to find room for the increased force. With this view the palaces along the winding river were strongly occupied under the command of Havelock. M'Intyre of the 78th with 250 men fit for duty and others nearly convalescent, held the Alumbagh. The rebels could not now fire into the Residency from close quarters, and they made no more desperate assaults: they had enough to do in repelling sorties and counter-mines from the British posts.

Outram was busy repairing the defences and erecting new batteries during the six weeks which followed.

On the 9th of October they heard of Greathed's column relieving Agra, and of Sir Colin's proposed march to relieve Lucknow.

Then Sir James looked about for some one who could carry a message and plans of the city for Sir Colin's information. But he could not bring himself to ask any one to incur a risk so great, and which promised almost certain death, as hostile masses surrounded them on all sides and guarded every avenue.

But Outram's anxiety reached the ears of Thomas

Henry Kavanagh, a civil office clerk, and he at once volunteered for the duty. Kavanagh is certainly one of the heroes of the Mutiny, and we must devote a few lines to his memory.

At first Outram thought the tall Irishman unfitted for the disguise he proposed; for he was fair and ruddy, and his hair glittered like red gold. But Outram found he could speak the patois of the country like a native, and he learnt how brave he was. This moved Outram, for he loved a brave man.

So Kavanagh had his hair cut short and stained with lamp-black, as well as his face, arms, hands and legs. He dressed himself as a badmâsh—a native cut-throat—and set out one dark evening on the 9th of November, attended by a faithful native who had been employed as a spy on various occasions, Kunonjee Lal.

Both Sir James Outram and Colonel Napier wished him God-speed, and Captain Hardinge, as he squeezed his hand, murmured, "Noble fellow! you will never be forgotten."

He passed out from the Residency feeling he was a hero. But the very first thing he had to do was to strip and go through a stream carrying his clothes on his head.

The chill took away all heroic feelings for a time. They had to dress under a grove of trees, cross the Goomtee twice by bridges, and answer several challenges from native sentries. Through the streets they tramped without notice, and on reaching green fields where every plant was fragrant they enjoyed the new surroundings after months of nasty smells: they ate fresh carrots and chatted merrily for five miles.

Then Lal said, "I have lost my way, sahib."

They were in the Dilkoosha Park, and it was occupied by the enemy!

But they got through safely and spoke to several peasants in the fields. Wet shoes and sore feet troubled Kavanagh; he often fell and hurt himself: once a woman got out of bed to show them the way. By three o'clock they reached a grove of mango trees and heard a man singing. As they drew near he called out a guard of sepoys, who began to ask a torrent of questions. These men they satisfied, and their next adventure was to fall into a jheel, or swamp, when they had to wade waist-high for two hours.

After a rest they crossed a plain, dodged more sentries, met villagers fleeing with their chattels on buffaloes from the terrible English soldiers: then they slept for an hour.

After this as they entered a grove, "Who comes there?" was uttered in native dialect. Another sepoy guard?

No! there were too many voices! Lal thought they must be British.

"This sahib is an English officer," he stammered in his fright.

Silence! suspicion! incredulity!

Then the Sikh commander came forward and shook hands with Kavanagh, and he knew that after all his perils and fears he was safe! "Rash! very rash! but plucky!" said the Sikh, and gave him two sowars as escort to the camp.

Lieutenant Goldie of the 9th Lancers gave him dry clothes, and Captain Dick of the 29th Foot lent him his Burma pony and showed him the way to Sir Colin's tent. What a relief it was to feel safe!

The full account of Kavanagh's perilous journey has been given by him in *How I Won the Victoria Cross* (Ward, Lock & Co.).

We have seen how Sir Henry Norman met the disguised messenger at the entrance of the tent, and suspecting him of some treachery, half drew his sword before Kavanagh cried, "I come from Lucknow—from Outram and Havelock—with important plans of the city for Sir Colin."

Sir Colin was immensely glad to see him, and spent some hours in his company working out his route so as to avoid the narrow streets which had proved so costly in Outram's case.

Kavanagh, who knew the city well, remained with Sir Colin's force and directed the advance. The Home Government rewarded this Irishman with the Victoria Cross and some substantial gifts. He died in St. Thomas' Hospital in 1883.

The success of Sir Colin Campbell in safely withdrawing the women and children from Lucknow was saddened by the illness and death of the gallant Havelock. Dysentery had worn him to a shadow, but he had tried to do his duty to the last.

He died in the Dilkoosha Palace as the army was retiring, and General Outram had only a few minutes to spare, to bid his old comrade a last good-bye.

Sir Colin, in a general order, conveyed to the army his last tribute: "His march of this year from Allahabad to Cawnpur, his frequent victories gained over immensely superior numbers, when he was nearly without artillery and cavalry . . . concluded by the onslaught and forced entrance into Lucknow, have established a renown which will last as long as the history of England."

CHAPTER XIV

SIR COLIN CAMPBELL: THE HERO OF THE QUEEN

THIS famous Scot was born in Glasgow on the 20th of October 1792: he was not a Campbell by his father's side, but a Macliver: and though his father was a carpenter, yet Colin Macliver was an aristocrat by birth. His splendid fight for recognition and promotion is one of the proofs of the value of hereditary qualities.

Colin's grandfather, the Laird of Ardnave, in the island of Islay, west of the Clyde, had forfeited his estate by taking part in the Forty-five rebellion: thus the Maclivers had come down in the world. His mother, Agnes Campbell, was a daughter of a respectable family who had settled in Islay two centuries ago with their chief, the ancestor of the Earls of Cawdor.

Colin was the eldest son, and had one brother and two sisters: his uncle, Colonel John Campbell, took an interest in the boy, and after Colin had spent a few years at the High School in Glasgow the colonel removed him to Gosport—the Royal Academy.

When only fifteen and a half years old Colin was taken by his uncle to be introduced to the Duke of York at the Horse Guards. The Duke, supposing the boy to be "another of the clan," as he remarked, entered him for a commission in the 9th Regiment of Foot as Colin Campbell.

Upon leaving the Horse Guards the boy said: "Uncle, the Duke has put me down by a wrong name."

"No, laddie: the name of Campbell will be a rare good name to go by in the army: dinna fash yourself aboot it at all." Thus it was that Colin Macliver was always known as a Campbell.

On the 26th of May 1808, Colin received his commission of ensign, and within five weeks he was promoted to a lieutenancy in the same regiment. Colin's after promotions were not so speedy, for that was the time of winning promotion by a long purse, or by interest with noble families: the boy did not possess these advantages, and only very slowly did he emerge from obscurity.

Thus Lord Raglan was a colonel at twenty-seven; Colin Campbell did not attain that rank until he had served twenty-seven years: bitterly did he feel the promotion over his head of inferior soldiers who had never heard a shot fired in warfare.

It was a stirring time when Colin Campbell first joined the British Army: Napoleon had placed his brother Joseph on the throne of Spain; Junot was ruling in Lisbon under Napoleon's orders; but the Spaniards misliked the attention, and, calling on England for help, they rose in arms against their foreign master. The Portuguese followed suit, and Wellesley had just sailed from Cork to the Peninsula in July 1808 for six years' hard fighting before they succeeded in driving the French armies over the Pyrenees.

Campbell was posted to the 2nd battalion of the 9th, commanded by Colonel Cameron, whom he soon learnt to like and admire. They took ship at Ramsgate on 20th July, and Campbell reports in his journal for the 19th of August, "lay out that night for the first time in my life": this was on a sandy beach at the mouth of the Maceira. We may note that all through his life Colin Campbell preferred to bivouac in the open with his men and live on the same fare as they did: this was one secret of his popularity. On the very first day after landing, Campbell's battalion was under a fierce fire from Laborde's guns at Vimiera. Campbell's captain, an officer of years, seeing the extreme youth of the Scottish boy, called him to his side, took him by the hand and led him by the flank of the battalion to the front, where he walked with him up and down the front of the leading company for several minutes in full view of the enemy's artillery, which had begun to open fire on our troops. He then let go the hand of the fifteen-year-old boy and told him to join his company. The captain intended to give the youngster confidence, but the lesson might have had a different result.

However, Sir Colin in after years, when he told the story, added: "It was the greatest kindness that could have been shown me at such a time, and through life I have felt grateful for it."

After the battle of Vimiera and Junot's defeat the French agreed to leave Portugal by the Convention of Cintra, and Campbell was transferred to the 1st battalion near Lisbon: he now was under Sir John Moore, and after the advance to Salamanca was in the terrible retreat to Corunna with Soult in pursuit, in the middle of winter. One officer and one hundred and forty-eight men of his battalion died on the road from exhaustion, or were made prisoners: Sir Colin used to relate how he had to march with bare feet for some time before reaching Corunna, as the soles of his boots were completely worn away. When he got on board ship he could not take off his boots, as from constant wear the leather stuck so closely to the flesh of his legs that he was obliged to steep them in hot water and have the leather cut away in strips—a process rendered painful by the coming away of pieces of skin. The battalion on its return was stationed at Canterbury. In six months' time they joined the forces of the Earl of Chatham which were preparing to advance up the Scheldt, attack Antwerp, and destroy the French fleet moored under its walls.

Under General Montresor the 1st battalion landed on the island of South Beveland, opposite that of Walcheren. While waiting for the fall of Flushing over one-sixth of our troops died of malarial fever: the expedition was a costly failure, and Colin Campbell, as well as hundreds of others, brought away the seeds of "Walcheren fever," which assailed them at periods to the end of their lives. After this Campbell was sent back to the 2nd battalion, then stationed at Gibraltar, and fought in a severe engagement at Barossa (1811), under Sir Thomas Graham. As all the other officers were wounded, this boy had to command the two flank companies, and gained some praise. In 1813, Campbell was, to his delight, under Lord Wellington on the lower Douro, when with 70,000 men he turned the French positions and drove them towards the Pyrenees.

He writes, after a long pursuit of the enemy on the 18th of June: "The ground on which we skirmished was so thickly wooded and so rugged and uneven, that when we were relieved . . . I found myself incapable of further exertion from fatigue and exhaustion, occasioned by six hours of almost continuous skirmishing."

Campbell, we must remember, was not yet twenty-one years old. His next battle was Vittoria, in which the French lost guns and treasure, stores and papers, and many Frenchmen retired in rags with bare feet. Then came the investment of San Sebastian, situated on a peninsula jutting out into the sea: here Campbell distinguished himself in the capture of a redoubt and convent and was mentioned in dispatches. Later, in a hopeless attempt to storm through a breach, Campbell was twice wounded, but still pressed on.

Napier in his *History* writes: "It was in vain that Lieutenant Campbell, breaking through the tumultuous crowd with the survivors of his chosen detachment, mounted the ruins — twice he ascended, twice he was wounded, and all around him died."

Campbell's wounds prevented him from sharing in the glory of the last and successful assault on San Sebastian: but the hospital could not keep him long; for he and a brother-officer, hearing that a battle was imminent, deserted from hospital and limped after their regiment, getting a lift now and then from commissariat wagons, till they waded the

Bidassoa, and with the 9th invaded France, assailed the steep Croix des Bouquets and won the position.

Napier writes: "At this moment Colonel Cameron arrived with the 9th Regiment, and rushed with great vehemence to the summit of the first height." At last the French, appalled by the furious shout and charge of the 9th, gave way, and the ridges of the Croix des Bouquets were won as far as the royal road.

Colin commanded the light company in front, and was again severely wounded: this occurred on the 7th October 1813.

His colonel reprimanded him for his breach of discipline, but he could not refrain from a word of praise for his gallantry. On the 9th of November, Colin Campbell was promoted to captain, without purchase, in the 60th Rifles.

He returned home with the strongest recommendations to the Horse Guards; but he was "nobody" at present, and instead of getting staff employment, took a temporary wound-pension of £100 a year, which helped him in his straitened circumstances. For a time Colin found a home with his uncle, Colonel Campbell, who interested himself in trying to procure his nephew a staff appointment in Holland, but in vain.

Seeing no prospect of serving in Holland, Campbell applied for leave to join his regiment in Nova Scotia, where a force had been collected in view of hostilities against the United States. But his wounds incapacitated him for duty, and he left Halifax in July 1815 for London: here he renewed his pension, and was advised to seek health in the south of France.

After some months' stay at Aix he rejoined the 60th at Gibraltar, and remained there until, in November 1818, his battalion was named for reduction, and Captain Campbell was transferred to the 21st North British Fusiliers, serving at home.

In April 1819, Campbell embarked for Barbados, whither the 21st Fusiliers had preceded him: here he was under the command of Lord Combermere, to whom he was warmly recommended by Lord Lynedoch, his ever-constant friend.

The years from 1819 to 1826 were passed by Colin Campbell in the West Indies, first in Barbados, then in Demerara. The climate and a vigorous constitution enabled him to shake off much of the Walcheren fever, and he enjoyed the pleasant society of the islands. When General Sir Benjamin d'Urban succeeded General Murray, Campbell became brigade-major, and the two officers lived in the closest intimacy and friendship.

In November 1825, Campbell purchased his majority: a friend in the colony lent him £600, and he borrowed £200 from his agents. As he was sending his father £40 every year, the expense of a field-officer's outfit fell heavily upon him: he once or twice thought of throwing up the service in despair, as many a good and poor officer had been compelled to do before; but, luckily for his country, he listened to the advice of his friends, pocketed his Scot's pride and accepted his friend's loan of £600. Campbell now had to leave Demerara and join the depôt in England. General Shadwell describes his appearance from a portrait taken at this period.

"A profusion of curly, brown hair, a well-shaped mouth and a wide brow, already foreshadowing the deep lines which became so marked a feature of his countenance in later years, convey the idea of manliness and vigour. His height was about five feet nine, his frame well-knit and powerful; to an agreeable presence he added the charm of engaging manners, which, according to the testimony of those who were familiar with him at this period, rendered him popular either at the dinner-table or in the drawing-room."

Fair, curly-haired, pleasant-mannered, and known to be brave, even to rashness—no wonder the slender-pursed officer made his way amongst those who valued the man above his clothes.

Once when dining with Dr. Keate, the Eton headmaster,

a guest suddenly asked Colin Campbell in a pause of the conversation—

"How did you feel, sir, when you led the forlorn hope at San Sebastian."

With a little sarcastic laugh the soldier replied—

"Very much, sir, as if I should get my company if I succeeded."

His interrogator could get no more out of the model major, and regretted his somewhat blunt inquiry.

After a few months' service in Ireland, Colin Campbell was able, through the kindness of a relation on his mother's side, to purchase an unattached lieutenant-colonelcy.

On the 5th October 1832, Lord Fitzroy Somerset wrote to say that on his lodging £1300 in the hands of his agents, Lord Hill would submit his name to the King. So, after serving for twenty-five years on full pay, this exceptionally good officer was enabled to buy his promotion!

But what of those officers who had no rich friends to help them? George Bell of the Royals, a friend of Colin's, possessed the Peninsular War medal, with seven clasps for seven pitched battles. He had since fought in India and Burma: but whereas Campbell was a lieutenant-colonel in 1832, Bell was still a captain in 1839! As Campbell had no duties, being unattached, he went off to Antwerp, to watch the siege conducted by Marshal Gérard. He kept an accurate journal of the operations for the Horse Guards, and was thanked by Lord Hill. When Antwerp and the Dutch capitulated, Campbell went to live in Marburg, and studied German.

In 1834 he was back in London, asking for a regiment, and always being politely put off: his means were small, his hopes low, his expenses too great; yet he felt he must be near the Horse Guards.

In his journal he writes: "It has been a sickening time to me; and what makes it more disagreeable is the little appearance, even after twelve months of misery, of such a termination as would be satisfactory." But his time came in May 1835, when he was offered the command of the 98th.

From Captain Henry Eyre, Colonel Campbell learnt the minutest details concerning this regiment: he resolved to train his regiment on the principles laid down by Sir John Moore and practised at Shorncliffe: by this method the officer grew to be the friend and protector of his men: gradually they became so intimate, and trusted in each other's honour so confidently, that the men would follow their officers willingly on the most desperate ventures.

Yet Campbell was no gentle sentimentalist: he was never slow to wrath when events stirred him; and sometimes, indeed, his anger blazed out, and his Highland blood boiled and his grey eyes flashed dangerously for very little incitement.

We have seen already how he savagely rebuked the officer at the Cawnpur bridge for saying, "We are at our last gasp." Another occasion of like sort was when, in the last attack on the rebels before Lucknow, a famous colonel came to him flushed with victory and carrying a flag he had torn from the grasp of the foe. Sir Colin turned fiercely on the gallant officer, and shouted, "D—— you, sir! what business have you to be taking flags! go back to your men."

The staff officers looked wistfully at the poor colonel, as he retired crestfallen and surprised: they pleaded for him after he had gone, and the anger vanished and passed into a more generous mood. That evening Sir Colin asked the colonel to dine with him in his tent, and begged his pardon for his hasty rebuke. Stories like these teach us more about a man than many pages of subtle analysis.

But the slack officer and the drunken soldier found no sympathy in this hot-blooded chief: for he never spared himself and he expected all to do their duty without fail. He insisted on economy in the officers' mess, knowing that the expenses of a soldier's life often led to gambling or resignation.

For more than two years the 98th served in the northern

district of England, and it was during this period that Colin Campbell taught his men to advance firing in line—a difficult movement with the old muzzle-loader, and one which he found useful in later days.

In December 1841, the 98th embarked on the *Belleisle* for China, 800 strong: they were all in good health, but the ship was overcrowded, and on joining the force under Sir Hugh Gough in their red coats and thick European clothing, the hot sun struck them down, and cholera and fever turned them into invalids. Within ten days of landing at Chin-kiang near the river estuary, fifty-three men had died, and the ship was becoming a floating hospital.

In a letter to his sister written in December, the colonel says: "The regiment has lost by death up to this date 283 men, and there are still 231 sick, of whom some 60 will die."

In those days less attention was paid to health than now: but the Japanese have shown us how important it is to shield troops from the incompetence of men in authority: we have still much to learn. At the end of 1842 Campbell became commandant of Hong-Kong: here he learnt that he had been made Companion of the Bath and Aide-de-camp to the Queen. Later he got leave to remove the remains of his sick regiment to the island of Chusan, where the air was bracing. Campbell kept his men busy and active, with sham fights in the open country: but it was long before they could strike off the effects of the disease. Ague made the colonel irritable and melancholy: after a year and a half in Chusan he wrote: "I have only one thought and one wish left, and that is for repose; for my spirit has already been sufficiently broken by disappointment; and as all whom I wished to please have sunk into the grave, success or miscarriage in the struggles of professional life have become empty sounds."

In July 1846, Campbell received a letter of thanks from the Chinese Commissioners for his kindness and liberality towards the Chinese, and in his journal of 24th July writes: "Took a walk on shore in the evening—my last walk in

Chusan, where I have passed many days in quiet and peace, and where I was enabled to save a little money, with which I hope to render my last days comfortable. I have been able also to assist others to a great extent: altogether I have every reason to be grateful to God for sending me to such a situation."

The 98th landed at Calcutta in October 1846, and marched to Dinapur, where the colonel heard he was appointed brigadier to command at Lahore. It was a great wrench to leave the regiment, and his health was drunk at mess with warmth and cordiality.

On his way to Lahore, Campbell met the Governor-General, Lord Hardinge, who described Henry Lawrence, the Resident in the Punjab, as "the king of the country, clever and good-natured, but hot-tempered." The two hot-tempered men became great friends.

But Campbell had not been long at Lahore before the rebellion of Moolraj broke out at Multan, and then the Sikh War occurred. At Chilianwallah, while Campbell was leading a charge on the Sikh guns, a gunner rushed at him, tulwar in hand, and gave him a deep sword-cut on his right arm. Before this the Sikh gunner had fired and apparently missed. But next morning Campbell found that the bullet had smashed the ivory handle of a small pistol which he carried in his waistcoat pocket, and had also damaged his watch.

The pistol and the watch saved Colin Campbell for other fights. At the end of this campaign Campbell heard from Sir Charles Napier that he had been promoted to be a Knight of the Bath. "No man has won it better: may you long wear the spurs." The next three years Sir Colin was Warden of the N.W. Frontier, having under him the 98th and 61st.

In dealing with the turbulent tribes Sir Colin leaned to the side of mercy, for he hated burning villages and exterminating families. Lord Dalhousie, that imperious Governor-General who took all knowledge for his province, and could not brook any to cross his wishes, sent a formal censure of Sir Colin to Peshawur. "You have manifested over-cautious reluctance in advancing against the Swat marauders."

Sir Colin wrote to Sir William Gomm, who had succeeded Napier as commander-in-chief: "I have come to the conclusion that I should be wanting in what is due to myself, were I, after what has passed, to continue in this command. . . . There is a limit at which a man's forbearance ought to stop."

And to Sir Henry Lawrence, Sir Colin wrote: "I have put a restraint upon myself, of which at one time in my life I should not have been capable: I feel it is safer for me, and better for the public service, that I should not have longer to continue the effort. Remember me to John: he must not quarrel with me." Lord Dalhousie in his pride had accused Sir Colin of placing "himself in an attitude of direct and proclaimed insubordination to the authority of the Governor-General in Council."

What Archibald Forbes calls "the barbed and venomous insinuation" which underlay the words "over-cautious reluctance" was modified a little by Lord Dalhousie's dispatch in which he acknowledged Sir Colin's "personal intrepidity and sterling soldierly qualities."

Lord Gough was censured for losing so many men against the Sikhs; Sir Colin for taking measures to preserve his men! Sir Charles Napier wrote Campbell a sympathetic letter, casting ridicule on the attempt of Dalhousie to direct a frontier campaign from Calcutta: "You have saved your column, and for this you are abused . . . it was a foolish, ill-judged and most unmilitary operation, and I said all along that the Government were lucky in having a real soldier to command it, and save their army. You have done so, and I think you have every reason to be proud of having, like a wise commander, conducted an ill-judged operation in a masterly manner."

General Napier's kind letter gave the wounded brigadier

great comfort, and he thanked his friend for the expression of approval from one whose opinion was to him "almost like the Creed." On his return to England Sir Colin resigned the command of the 98th, and went on half-pay.

He was sixty-one, and longed for a rest after forty-four years' hard service: but it was not to be, for England and France had formed an alliance in defence of Turkey against Russia; and in March 1854 war was declared.

Lord Raglan was appointed to the command, and Sir Colin was nominated to a brigade command.

With Major Sterling his brigade-major, and Captain Shadwell his aide-de-camp, he embarked for Constantinople on the 3rd of April. Here he learnt that he was appointed to the Highland Brigade, which consisted of the 42nd, 79th, and 93rd regiments. This was the first time that Campbell, a Highlander himself, had commanded Highlanders. But the men took to him at once, regarding him rather as the chief of a clan than an ordinary commanding officer.

In August 1854 they embarked at Varna for the Crimea. In writing to his sister about the Alma, Sir Colin says: "Here I lost my best horse—a noble animal. He was first shot in the hip, the ball passing through my sabretasche, and the second ball went right through his body, passing through the heart. He sank at once; Shadwell kindly lent me his horse, which I immediately mounted."

He did not tell her how he had led three battalions against twelve Russian battalions, the élite of the Tzar's troops: but he did tell his friend, Colonel Eyre, something of the struggle, the firing while advancing in line, the marching over rough ground, the successive attacks, and the emotion of Lord Raglan when the battle had been fought and won.

"He sent for me: when I approached him I observed his eyes to fill and his lips and countenance to quiver. He gave me a cordial shake of the hand, but he could not speak. The men cheered very much . . . they had behaved nobly.

I never saw troops march to battle with greater sang-froid and order."

Kinglake tells us that as the Brigade of Guards was about to cross the river on Campbell's right they were exposed to fire of artillery, and some officer shouted, "The Brigade of Guards will be destroyed! Ought it not to fall back?"

The Highland blood flew up, and Sir Colin replied, "It is better, sir, that every man of Her Majesty's Guards should lie dead on the field than that they should turn their backs upon the enemy."

This is Kinglake's version: but those who knew Sir Colin remarked that his language would have been stronger and franker.

On the 16th of October, Lord Raglan gave Sir Colin the command of the troops and defences covering Balaclava harbour, the British base of operations: 1200 marines landed from the fleet in the harbour held the line of batteries: the 93rd were in camp at the head of the gorge, and an exterior chain of redoubts was garrisoned by Turks; but they had only nine guns to work with. On the 23rd, General Laprandi led 24,000 Russians to assault these redoubts: after a gallant resistance the Turks fell back and rallied on either flank of the 93rd.

As the Russian cavalry charged against Lord Lucan's division, one body consisting of some four hundred men turned to their left and charged the 93rd. This charge Sir Colin awaited calmly in line—"the thin red streak tipped with a line of steel." Sir Colin was quite conscious that the protection of the post depended on his kilted men, with a few guns of the marine artillery; as he rode along the face of his regiment, he told his men how grave the occasion was. "Remember, there is no retreat from here, men! You must die where you stand."

A loud and cheery answer warmed his heart: "Ay, ay, Sir Colin; we'll do that and a'."

The cavalry charge was no sooner repulsed by the 93rd

than they stood spectators of the Scots Greys—the heavy brigade—slashing their way fiercely through the grey-coats of the Russian troopers. How intense was their gaze, as, panting from their recent exertions, they followed the movements of the great mass of Russians, dividing, meeting, wavering, and then breaking into clusters before they turned their horses' heads and fled in wild disorder.

Scarlett's troopers heard the ringing cheer, the wild yell of delighted mountaineers—as they rode back in triumph.

Then Sir Colin rode forward to greet the Greys and congratulate them.

"Greys, gallant Greys!" he cried, "I am sixty-one years old, and if I were young again I should be proud to be in your ranks."

A general order from the commander of the forces was read, in which Sir Colin and the 93rd Highlanders were thanked for the brilliant manner in which they had repulsed the enemy's cavalry.

Sir Colin's anxiety night and day was so tense and continuous that he only took sleep by snatches, and he was ever going round in the dark and examining the posts and redoubts.

On December 5th the Russian field-army withdrew from the vicinity of Balaclava, and then Sir Colin undressed and went to bed.

But in his dreams he started up and shouted, "Stand to your arms!" startling the officer who shared his room.

The French General Vinoy and Sir Colin became great friends, and worked together loyally on many occasions: for Sir Colin could speak French fluently.

In the terrible winter that followed, when our troops were ill-housed and ill-clothed, it was Lord Raglan who got all the blame in the English papers. As to this Sir Colin wrote to Colonel Eyre: "I am disgusted with the attacks that have been made upon dear Lord Raglan. God pity the army if anything were to occur to take him from us!"

THE HERO OF THE QUEEN

In May 1855, Sir Colin was disappointed by the removal from his command of the Highland Brigade, which was now sent on the expedition to Kertsh. A second disappointment was his in the Highland Brigade not having been chosen to take a prominent part in the final assault on Sebastopol.

Sir Colin acknowledged the noble defence made by the Russians, their skilful withdrawal from the city, and their care of our wounded in the great Redan. "Indeed," he says, "before the Russians left the Redan some of our wounded were carefully dressed by them and placed in safety from the fire of our own shells."

Sir Colin had saved Balaclava by his unremitting exertions and skilful formation of trenches and redoubts: officers averred that it was he and his Highlanders who won the battle of the Alma; yet the newspapers at home were clamouring for the promotion of younger men, and Lord Panmure, the War Minister, yielded to the ignorant clamour, and, through General Simpson who had succeeded Lord Raglan, offered Sir Colin Campbell the Malta command.

So a second time the brave and cautious Scot was requested to give up his command. He was now by virtue of seniority second in command, and Simpson was about to retire.

The irascible old general felt the slight and winced under the blow, but before he left the Crimea he carried out one more cautious scheme in the face of authority.

General Parke, who commanded the 72nd Highlanders, tells us: "The example he set us all of every military quality, pre-eminently that of care and forethought in all that appertained to the welfare of those under him, can never be forgotten."

He goes on to say that the Highland Division in the autumn of 1855 was encamped near the south shores of the Crimea, but still under canvas; the cold was increasing, and the men would suffer.

Sir Colin heard of a ship laden with huts having come into harbour, and he at once rode over to headquarters and applied for them.

"No transport available—very sorry—but if you can obtain transport, your application may be entertained."

"Vary weel!" thought the canny Scot, and galloped off to his camp, ordered out all his regiments in fatigue-dress and marched them down to Balaclava.

Piece by piece the brawny Highlanders carried the huts upon their shoulders, to the astonishment of many a smart linesman: captain and subaltern, sergeant and private—all shared alike in the work with right goodwill and merry quip: in a very short time these Northerners were comfortably hutted for the winter.

Then, with a moving speech of "Farewell" to his men, Sir Colin sailed for England on 3rd November, and three days later Sir William Codrington was nominated to the chief command.

"I have come home to tender my resignation," said Sir Colin to his friend Lord Hardinge, now commander-in-chief, and Lord Hardinge, we may be sure, gave him his warmest sympathy.

There was another who had watched his career with admiration and valued his services more highly than her Ministers.

Queen Victoria promptly invited General Campbell to Windsor. There both the Queen and the Prince Consort received him with such gracious attention that all soreness, all angry feeling was dispelled from his mind, and he frankly spoke out: "Your Majesty, I am willing to return to the Crimea and serve under a corporal if you wish it."

So off he went again to the Crimea, staying at Paris long enough to be presented to the Emperor and Empress, and to have a pleasant evening with his Crimean friend, General Vinoy.

Once more he was given the Highland Division, but in

April 1856 peace was proclaimed: Sir Colin told his troops he was going home and should never serve any more. In this changing world a "last farewell" often leads to a renewing of love.

In part from General Shadwell's *Life of Clyde*, by kind permission of Messrs. Blackwood.

CHAPTER XV

LORD CLYDE: THE SAVIOUR OF LUCKNOW

IT was not until 11th July that tidings of the death of General the Hon. George Anson reached the War Office.

On that afternoon Lord Panmure sent for Sir Colin Campbell and offered him the chief command in India.

"I accept it," said Sir Colin, not in the least surprised.

"When will you be ready to start?" said Lord Panmure.

"To-morrow! I can get my outfit in Calcutta."

Sir Colin was sixty-five; his soldiers called him "Old take care!"

Lord Dalhousie and Lord Panmure had both deemed him too cautious; but when Britain was in danger, the Queen pointed to the man.

Sir Colin left London by the night train after being bidden to Buckingham Palace. In his journal he wrote:

"Her Majesty's expressions of approval of my readiness to proceed at once were pleasant to receive from a Sovereign so good and so justly loved."

In Paris he took breakfast with his "dear old friend General Vinoy"; and reaching Marseilles on the 14th July, he embarked on the *Vectis*, which was awaiting him with its steam up.

On the 13th of August the new commander-in-chief landed at Calcutta. General Sir Patrick Grant met him, and Lord Canning invited him and his military secretary, Major Alison, to stay at Government House.

We may here quote a few lines on Sir Colin from Holme's history of the Mutiny: "He had not the wonderful dash, the power to put everything to the hazard for a great end . . . which belonged to some other well-known leaders of that time. Yet for any work requiring methodical and precise movements, extraordinary care for details, few were better fitted. . . . No commander-in-chief more acceptable to the mass of Anglo-Indian officers could at that moment have been selected. Many of them already knew his appearance well—his strong spare soldierly frame, his high rugged forehead crowned by masses of crisp grey hair, his keen, shrewd but kindly honest eyes, his firm mouth with its short trim moustache, his expression denoting a temper so excitable yet so exact; so resolute to enforce obedience yet so genial; so irascible and so forgiving."

As Sir Colin had to wait at Calcutta until 27th October, he had time to gather up the threads of what had occurred. We know from previous chapters most of the events: Havelock, with less than 2000 men, had fought his way from Allahabad to Cawnpur, but arrived just too late to save the women and children. Then his gallant attempt to relieve Lucknow failed in August, and he had to fall back on Cawnpur.

But the country between Calcutta and Cawnpur was seriously disturbed: Allahabad, placed on a tongue of land at the junction of the Ganges and the Jumnah, had been the scene of a revolt of sepoys on the 6th of June. Many officers were shot, and the rest, with sixty-five invalided white soldiers and some sepoys, took refuge in the fort.

Fortunately the senior officer on the spot, Lieut. Brasyer, who had been promoted from the ranks for gallantry in the Sutlej campaign of 1846, saw from the looks of the sepoys in the fort what he must do. He promptly, with the help of some Sikhs, disarmed the rebels and drove them from the fort.

Allahabad was saved by Colonel Neill on the 12th of June, though he had only a few men under him. Thus one of the most important cities in India was saved by

Brasyer, still only a lieutenant, and Neill of the 1st Madras Fusiliers, both true heroes of the Mutiny.

But there were two other weak points between Calcutta and Allahabad: namely, Dinapur, 344 miles distant from Calcutta, and Patna, which was twelve miles nearer to the capital.

The commissioner, William Tayler, had preserved the province from revolt by his splendid energy and foresight.

Colonel Malleson says in his *History*: "His services have never been acknowledged, he has been treated with contumely and insult, but he contributed as much as any man, in that terrible crisis called the Indian Mutiny, to save the Empire."

We must not forget William Tayler when we recall the brave heroes who fought for Britain and her Empire in those troublous days.

There were 3000 disaffected sepoys at Dinapur, and Tayler asked the authorities at Calcutta if he might disarm them. It was most important that this should be done, because reinforcements could not be sent to Havelock with this danger left in the rear.

Lord Canning, Sir Patrick Grant, and Mr. Halliday, Lieutenant-Governor of Bengal, hesitated. The leading merchants sent a deputation to Canning, stating that a favourable opportunity now occurred for disarming the sepoys. Canning listened, and curtly replied, "I cannot comply with your request."

Later they threw the responsibility of the disarming on General Lloyd; if he thought it desirable, he might take that step!

On the 25th of July, Lloyd took away their percussion caps. Three hours after the sepoys broke out into open mutiny and started westward in the direction of Arah. No attempt was made to stop them.

They marched to Arah, opened the gaol, plundered the treasury and hunted for Europeans. But Vicars Boyle, a civil engineer, had provisioned and fortified his house, foreseeing the catastrophe which Canning and his advisers had neglected to prevent. With fifteen Englishmen and fifty Sikhs, sent by William Tayler, this heroic band resisted sternly on the 27th, 28th, and 29th; then came a lull in the fighting: the sound of firing was heard in the distance! But Dunbar, sent by Lloyd with 415 men at Taylor's instigation, had fallen into an ambush, and only fifty-three were left alive.

The effect of this repulse at Patna and Dinapur was alarming: the whole province would rise and all would be massacred.

But another unknown hero started up, Major Vincent Eyre of the Artillery. This man had served in the first Kabul war and had been kept there a prisoner: since then he had served in Gwalior and Burma. He was bringing a battery on a steamer from Calcutta to Allahabad, and had reached Dinapur on the evening of the day on which the mutineers had gone off to Arah.

Next day he went up the river, persuaded Captain d'Estrange to bring 150 men of the 5th Fusiliers, and started for Arah.

Thereby he risked his commission, for his orders were to proceed to Allahabad, and a march to Arah was fifty miles out of his way. But Eyre risked all that, and with 220 men and 3 guns and 40 gunners he set out on the 31st of July, a fortnight before Sir Colin landed at Calcutta, and at his first halt the news came to him of Dunbar's defeat. That made no difference: next day they came within six miles of Arah, and found the rebels entrenched in a wood.

By fierce bayonet charges and flank movements and good gun-fire, the British at last drove the enemy from cover. Eyre pressed on, hoping to be in Arah that night: but a raging torrent stopped them, and they spent the whole night in making a causeway. Next morning they crossed the torrent, entered the city and rescued the brave little garrison, which for eight days had defied an enemy fifty times more numerous than themselves.

But some of the rebels had fled to the stronghold of Kenwar Singh, a disaffected landholder: this fort Eyre stormed and captured on the 11th of August.

In a moment the despair of the British residents in West Behar was changed into unexpected relief, hope, and even triumph. Such is the magic of brave deeds done by a heroic soldier.

Eyre's action was of course upheld by the Indian Government: what would have been dealt to him if he had been unsuccessful, we better not inquire. For William Tayler, who had done so much to save his province, was removed from his office and ruined; he had advised his subordinates to bring all their men and treasure to Patna before Vincent Eyre's arrival: and was deemed at Calcutta to have been acting too much on his own initiative!

But the failure of the Government to disarm the three regiments had wasted a month and prevented Havelock from reaching Lucknow with any chance of success.

Sir Colin must have been encouraged by the stories that came to Calcutta of British pluck and patient resistance in many quarters: but he was full of business troubles, buying up stores and sending small reinforcements to Allahabad.

The men went by bullock-train, which took ninety daily: they had their knapsacks and blankets with them, ammunition and rifles. They travelled day and night, halting only for two hours at noon. Food was scanty, but the men were eager to get to the front.

"I am delighted with Lord Canning," wrote Sir Colin; "he has never looked black at any event which has occurred. He is such a nice person to do business with. Very clever and hard-working . . . with the highest courage, so simple and gentlemanly; and so firm and decided that I cannot be too thankful for the good fortune which has placed me under such a chief."

In October, Sir Colin received a letter from Sir John Lawrence, in which he wrote: "We have indeed had a terrible storm: and it is only, I am persuaded, by the mercy of God that a single European is alive on this side of India. At one time I began to think that all must be lost. We have now, as far as I can judge, weathered the gale; but until the troops arrive from England, our position must continue to be precarious . . . I only know that Havelock has done nobly. In fact he and his troops have exceeded all our hopes and expectations. I was rejoiced to see that Outram did not supersede Havelock . . . my brother's death has indeed been a great calamity. There were few, perhaps none, who would have proved more useful with his counsel and experience than he."

On the night of the 27th of October, Sir Colin, attended by the headquarters staff, left Calcutta by rail for Ranigunj.

Then he went on by carriage-dâk up the Great Trunk Road, and a terrible catastrophe nearly occurred.

For as they drove along some peasants held up their hands and cried out, "Stop, sahib! sepoys all in front!"

"Nonsense!" said one of the officers, "I can't believe that."

"There they are, sahib; some of them on elephants."

Then the Englishmen saw through their glasses nine elephants crossing the road about 1000 yards ahead.

Sir Colin was in the second carriage, and word was sent to him to stop, as some 400 mutineers were ahead.

The carriages in the rear heard an exaggerated rumour and a panic seized the drivers, who turned round to flee: one carriage was upset in the act of turning. Two officers got upon country ponies and galloped back for the nearest detachment.

All the time Sir Colin was quietly tracing the route of the mutineers on the map. Fortunately these gentlemen had no idea they were so near to the commander-in-chief and continued calmly on their way. The headquarters staff prudently drove back some miles, and then with a proper escort retraced their steps in the cool of the evening. So what might have been a tragedy came to be regarded as a comic interlude. At Allahabad, Sir Colin heard that Outram could hold out in Lucknow till the end of November: this gave him some satisfaction and a few spare days to complete arrangements. On 3rd November they reached Cawnpur, and remained a few days to forward the Engineer park.

But to a cautious general like Sir Colin, who liked to make war according to rule and principle, the state of affairs was very disadvantageous. For his line of communications from Allahabad to Cawnpur was threatened by the Gwalior Contingent and other rebel bodies who were concentrating at Calpi on the Jumna, forty miles only from Cawnpur. He knew that his first duty should have been to clear this line of communication; but the call of Lucknow seemed imperative, and he had no alternative but to leave Cawnpur open to attack by superior numbers. However, he did all that was possible to strengthen the post of Cawnpur, as it covered the bridge of boats, his only line of retreat from Lucknow. Early on the morning of the 9th, Sir Colin left Cawnpur and reached the camp of Buntera after a forced march of thirty-five miles. Here he met his old friend, Hope Grant, and placed him in divisional command of the force.

On the morning of the 10th, Kavanagh came into camp with his attendant native: and some hours were spent in working out the safest route to the Residency. It was resolved to give the city a wide berth this time and swerve away to the right. A letter written in Greek character was sent to Outram: "I have come only to hand out the wounded, women and children." Outram was to make all preparations for their departure on the 16th. In the afternoon Sir Colin reviewed his troops in brigades, addressing each separately: as we have stated before, when the war-worn, anxious commander had reviewed the 9th Lancers, the Sikh horsemen in their loose dress and red turbans, the 8th and 75th Queen's worn with fighting, with never a word or cheer from any—he rode on to his old Crimean friends, Highlanders of the 93rd, a massive body of veterans in tartan and waving plume: and then there burst forth such a rapturous welcome as took all the lines from his face and gave him strength for his mission.

"Aye, aye, Sir Colin; we'll bring the women and bairns oot o' Lucknow, or we'll leave oor ain banes there."

We will not dwell at length on the fortunes of war in this second relief of Lucknow: it has been given in a former chapter. On the morning of the 14th of November they reached the Dilkoosha Park, and then on to the Martinière College they forced their way helped by Travers' heavy guns.

Next day, by the advice of Kavanagh, Sir Colin chose a long détour to the right, approaching the Secundrabagh by the open ground near the river.

The latter part of their way lay through a narrow lane, where the cavalry got jammed, and Sir Colin rode to the front and thrust them in his impetuous way into the side alleys of the village: then he ordered up the 18-pounders to batter a breach in the south-west bastion of the Secundrabagh.

While three companies of the 93rd were clearing the Serai of the enemy, the rest of the infantry were lying down behind an embankment. At the end of an hour a Sikh native officer, without waiting for the order, sprang up sword in hand, his men following. The Highlanders followed, and it became a race who should get into the Secundrabagh first. Some say that Sir Colin called to Colonel Ewart, "Ewart, bring on the tartan," and then they dashed from behind the bank.

Many were killed as they crept through the narrow breach, and for hours the conflict raged; 2000 sepoys were found slain. We must remember that these soldiers had recently seen Cawnpur and the house of massacre, and had heard all that gruesome story. So they never dreamt of taking prisoners: the only penalty was death. After the Secundrabagh came the Shah Nujeef, a great mosque and tomb: this was held so strongly in spite of Peel's gun-fire that once more Sir Colin had to call upon his Highlanders. But a high wall loopholed brought them to a standstill, and the fire of the rebels was making havoc with the regiment and Sir Colin's staff when Sergeant Paton of the 93rd came running up to Colonel Hope saying, "I have found a breach, sir, near the river."

Sergeant Paton was the hero of the Shah Nujeef. It was by his plucky examination of the defences that the mosque was taken. The relief of the Residency, which before had been very uncertain, now seemed assured. The men lay down to rest and sleep, and next day, the 17th, Captain Wolseley, the Field-Marshal, attacked and took the mess house, and Lieutenant Roberts, V.C., our Field-Marshal and honoured General, raised the British flag on the top of the Motee Mahal, the signal that our troops were near the Residency.

It was now that Outram and Havelock crossed an open space half a mile wide intervening between the Motee Mahal and the Residency, though they were exposed to fire from the Kaiserbagh. Indeed three of their staff were wounded during the transit. Warm greetings were exchanged, and plans quickly proposed.

Sir Colin was firm in his resolve to waste no time in getting back to Cawnpur to meet the Gwalior Contingent and guard the bridge across the Ganges. But, said he, we must take back the wounded, the women and children, and the garrison. Five days were occupied in making preparations, and the whole British force simply held the positions they had won, like a vast outlying picket.

At midnight of the 22nd the garrison filed out from the Residency in the deepest silence. The rebels never suspected what was doing; before dawn they had all reached the Martinière in safety.

We have already seen how Sir Colin hurried back to the bridge, crossed the Ganges, and heartened Windham's garrison by his presence. It was a narrow escape for both forces. Windham had been beaten back to his fortified camp at Cawnpur by Tantia Topee, after a march of six miles down the Calpi Road to attack the rebels. On the morrow Windham saw the bungalows at Cawnpur all in flames, and the clothing and stores left by Havelock's force being burnt.

Sir Colin was only just in time to prevent the bridge of boats from being destroyed by placing Captain Peel's heavy guns to cover the crossing. He placed his convoy of women and children near the riddled walls of Wheeler's encampment, and spent two days preparing for the dispatch of his large convoy to Allahabad. He sent them off on the night of the 3rd of December, and then turned his attention to the 25,000 rebels in front of him.

These rested their centre on the town, being separated from the British force by the Ganges Canal. Their right was covered by limekilns and mounds of brick; their left rested on the Ganges.

Sir Colin had with him 5000 infantry, 600 cavalry, and thirty-five guns; with this force he attacked the rebels on the 6th of December.

During the days of waiting our men had been chafing and fretting at the delay, while the enemy kept bowling round-shot into the camp. But the cautious Scot was making victory secure for them, planting heavy gun batteries to command the canal bridges.

Early in the morning Sir Colin called the commanding officers together and explained his plans with clearness from a written paper. All knew that only one week's supplies of food were left in camp, and that no more could be procured unless the rebels were beaten! But the men were like greyhounds straining on the leash!

Greathed was directed to make a false attack on the centre, whilst Walpole, Hope, and Inglis turned the enemy's right. These latter drove the rebels from mound to mound despite a fierce resistance. At length they reached a bridge strongly fortified and held by artillery. There was a long and terrible struggle, the 4th Punjab Rifles and the 53rd gallantly attempting to carry the position. All of a sudden a rumbling was heard, and up came William Peel and his sailors, dragging a heavy 24-pounder, placed the gun on the bridge, and opened fire.

The British cheered again and again as the rebels fell back under the storm of shot: and then with a shout Highlanders, Sikhs, and 53rd dashed at the foe and drove them back in wild disorder.

At this moment Lieutenant Bunny, H.A., rode back at a gallop and shouted to Captain Bourchier, "Come along; they are bolting like the devil."

Away rattled the battery of field-guns along the Trunk Road. The infantry made way for them, as if so many fire-engines were coming, and after galloping a mile and a half they saw the rebels' camp, and at four hundred yards poured round-shot into the flying masses.

Major Turner rode up and ordered, "Go to grape distance."

Again the battery limbered up and at two hundred yards range poured a shower of grape into the camp.

Bourchier writes: "The men were yelling with delight. They actually stood upon the gun-carriages as we advanced. The drivers cheered, and such a scene of excitement was never known." Then Sir Colin himself rode up to the battery and said, "Well done, my men, well done. Now go hot in pursuit of the rascals."

"Hurrah! Hurrah! we are on their track. Gun after gun is passed and spiked, cartloads of ammunition lie strewed along the road; Pandies are bolting in all directions."[1]

Without a check that battery pursued for two miles, Sir Hope Grant and his staff riding in the dust behind.

Four times they came into action after that, to clear front and flank. Then General Grant said, "We are getting too far away from our supports. Halt! Wait till the cavalry come up."

[1] Bourchier's *Eight Months' Campaign*, Smith Elder & Co.

The cavalry had been taken by their guides far too much to the left, and only arrived late. But ten minutes' rest for the horses did good service; for, highly trained though they were and in racing condition, the pace had been killing. With lowered heads and frames shaken by the quick panting of exhausted lungs they awaited the next call upon their stamina and muscle. And the gunners rubbed them down and spoke cheery words to them.

Presently a small cloud of dust was seen on their left coming nearer and nearer: it is lost in a grove; soon the head of a cavalry column appears—they arrive: a quick order is given. Like lightning the horsemen spread over the plain at a gallop and in skirmishing order; Sir Colin is riding at the front. One might have thought it was a fox-hunt, and indeed more than one fox did break cover, and the men merrily roared out a "View halloa": so they rode on for fourteen miles, catching whom they could and making many prizes.

So at last came the defeat of that Gwalior Contingent that had given Sir Colin so much anxiety and nearly wrecked his plans. Sixteen guns, 350 cartloads of ammunition, huge stores of grain, tents, bullocks, etc., fell into our hands.

The return to Cawnpur was rendered almost comic by an offer made to the men of three rupees for every bullock the men could bring in. So the guard left at Cawnpur saw three or four pairs of bullocks tied at the tail of each gun, while the Lancers were driving their prisoners before them in hundreds, lowing as they went.

The next few weeks were spent in defeating rebel rajahs in Rohilkhand; but Lord Canning strongly insisted on Lucknow and Oudh being brought to subjection before any other attempts were made to sweep Rohilkhand.

By the 23rd of February 1858, Sir Colin had collected near Bunnee, 17 battalions of infantry, 28 squadrons or cavalry, 54 light and 80 heavy guns.

Outram at the Alumbagh had been left alone for some time after the last severe handling by Sir Colin of the sepoys at Lucknow. But the Maulavi, one of the chief authors of the Mutiny, was now in Lucknow, and made two or three attacks which Outram repelled, though it was said that the rebels had 100,000 men to Outram's 4000.

We need not dwell again on the storming of Lucknow, which was carried out so gallantly with the help of Outram at the cost of 800 of all ranks. At this time Sir Colin received a letter from the Queen written by her own hand, thanking him for his devotion, and the troops for their gallantry.

After his next clearance of Rohilkhand in June, Sir Colin retired to Allahabad, where he found a letter from Lord Derby: "Her Majesty deems the present a fitting moment for marking her high sense of your eminent brilliant services by raising you to the dignity of a peer of the United Kingdom."

Sir Colin was disposed to run restive at strange titles, but was at last reconciled to the honour: though he continued to sign his letters to friends as before C. C., and not Clyde.

When he met the 93rd, of which he was colonel, the first time after becoming Lord Clyde, he called the pipe-major to the front. John MacLeod saluted, saying, "I beg your pardon, Sir Colin, but we dinna ken hoo tae address you noo that the Queen has made you a Lord!"

The chief replied, with a touch of humorous sadness, "Just call me Sir Colin, John, the same as in the old times: I like the old name best."

Mr. Russell relates a story of Lord Clyde—an incident which he witnessed in the campaign in Central India in December. It was dark and cold: the men had made blazing fires of straw and grass in houses lately occupied by Nana Sahib's followers.

"At one of these fires, surrounded by Beloochees, Lord Clyde sat with his arm in a sling (his horse had fallen with him) upon a native bed. Once he rose to give an order, when a tired Beloochee flung himself on the crazy charpoy, but was jerked off by an indignant comrade with the loud exclamation, 'Don't you see, you fool, that you are on the Lord Sahib's charpoy?' Lord Clyde broke in, 'No—let him lie there; don't interfere with his rest,' and himself took his seat on a billet of wood."

It was not until June 1860 that the old general was able to sail home, after taking a touching farewell of Lord Canning. Everybody now, from the French Emperor to the Court of the City of London, was eager to welcome the man who had saved India at the cost of the fewest lives possible. There was no more talk of being over-cautious, or too old: honours were poured upon him: in November 1862 he was promoted to the rank of field-marshal. His last appearance at the head of troops was on Easter Monday 1862, when he commanded 20,000 men. His health had begun to fail, and he died at Chatham on the 14th of August 1863, and was buried in Westminster Abbey.

Fifty years of arduous service had raised him from a carpenter's son to the peerage, but he always remained a simple, God-fearing Scot, beloved by the rank and file of his army.

CHAPTER XVI

SIR HUGH ROSE AND JHANSI: THE AVENGER OF CAWNPUR

AMONGST the heroes who fought, schemed, or held command during the Indian Mutiny the fame of Sir Hugh Rose, Baron Strathnairn, is not so well known as many who did far less than he.

Lord Derby, speaking in the House of Lords, 19th April 1859, said: "In five months the Central India Field Force traversed 1085 miles, crossed numerous large rivers, took upwards of 150 pieces of artillery, one entrenched camp, two fortified cities and two fortresses, fought sixteen actions, captured twenty forts."

One historian has described Sir Hugh Rose as "far in advance of any of the other commanders in genius, tact, judgment and energy." He recovered Central India, from the borders of the Western Presidency to the Ganges, acting in a difficult country entangled with wild jungles, hills and forests, and studded with forts strongly defended. He pressed on relentlessly, allowing the enemy no breathing time; and without his strenuous support, Lord Clyde's campaign would have required another two years of fighting to end the Mutiny.

Hugh Henry Rose was born in Berlin in the year 1801. His father was Sir George Rose, G.C.B., British Minister at the Prussian Court: here young Rose was educated and instructed in the rudiments of the military art.

In 1820 he entered the British Army, and serving in Ireland with tact and ability during the Ribbon disturbances, was rewarded by receiving his majority at an early age.

Later, he served in Malta, being in command of the 92nd Highlanders; and, when cholera broke out among his troops, Colonel Rose visited every man who fell ill and buoyed the sick up by his cheerful and sympathetic manners.

For his services with Omar Pasha's Brigade in Syria against Mehemet Ali and the Egyptian army, he received a sword of honour, and was made a Companion of the Bath. Frederick William of Prussia also sent "his former young friend" the Cross of St. John of Jerusalem. In his case, no doubt, powerful friends and money helped Rose to rise quickly from the lower ranks of officers to the higher. Soon after, he was appointed British Consul-General in Syria. It was no easy post at that time, because Christian Maronites and Mahommedan Druses were constantly flying at one another's throats. On one of these occasions, in 1841, Rose galloped between the opposing lines, held up his hand and stopped the conflict.

At another time he saved the lives of 700 Christians, and led them safely to Beyroot, walking himself most of the way, so that his horse might be at the disposal of any over-tired woman.

In recognition of these services in Syria, Lord Palmerston in 1851 appointed Colonel Rose to be Secretary of Embassy at Constantinople. During his time here, when acting as Chargé d'Affaires in the absence of Lord Stratford de Redcliffe, he learned that the Russians were demanding that the Sultan should sign a secret Treaty, giving to the Czar the protection of all the Christians in Turkey.

The Grand Vizier came to the colonel and said, "We must sign the secret Treaty to-night unless you can summon the British Fleet to Turkish waters."

"I will write to Admiral Dundas and point out the gravity of the situation," said Colonel Rose.

Soon after sunset the Porte's chief Dragoman visited Colonel Rose at Therapia and informed him that Prince Menschikoff had presented his demand for their signature, but that relying on the approach of the British Fleet they had refused it.[1]

Here was a firm and able man acting on his own responsibility and stopping the panic which was endangering the independence of the Ottoman Empire. If Colonel Rose had been backed up by Her Majesty's Government, there would probably have been no Crimean War.

When that war was declared on the following year, Colonel Rose was appointed Queen's Commissioner with the French army, having the rank of brigadier-general.

Rose distinguished himself both at the Alma and Inkerman—was recommended by Marshal Canrobert for the Victoria Cross.

He received the thanks of the French general and of Lord Clarendon for his tactful address and helpful advice tendered to the French commanders, and on his return home was made a Knight of the Bath and a Commander of the Legion of Honour.

So far General Rose had shown himself full of activity and resource: he never spared himself, if he seldom spared his subordinates: perhaps he was prone to be impatient of others' defects, and did not consider men's feelings when he had fault to find. But his officers and men ever found him just and generous.

The Duke of Cambridge having given General Rose a division in the Bombay Presidency, that general reached Bombay in September 1857, and was at once placed in command of a field force with instructions that he was to march to Kalpi through Central India and thus relieve the pressure on Lord Clyde.

At that time the Gwalior contingent held Kalpi, while the brave and pitiless lady, the Rani of Jhansi, was holding a large tract of country, comprising 1600 square miles, round her fortress, and was the mainspring of the Mutiny.

It is necessary to say a few words about this Indian

[1] *Clyde and Strathnairn, Rulers of India,* by General Sir O. T. Burne (Clarendon Press).

heroine, who with the Nana Sahib and the Maulavi, or "learned man" of Oudh, seem to have conspired together to rouse the sepoys to mutiny. The Nana, as we have seen, was made our enemy by being unjustly treated, as he and his friends thought, by Lord Dalhousie.

It was much the same brusque treatment which turned a gracious and gifted Indian princess into an implacable Fury.

Her husband died childless in 1854, and according to Hindoo law the Rani possessed the right to adopt an heir. This right Lord Dalhousie curtly refused and proclaimed that Jhansi had lapsed to the Company.

The Rani argued eloquently against this, pleading the services rendered by the rulers of Jhansi to the British in the past.

It was all in vain: the little fiery Scot brushed away her arguments and her pleadings, little thinking what grave consequences were to follow, and what was the power of an injured woman. The Rani of Jhansi, burning to revenge this insult, yet nursed her anger quietly until the seizure of Delhi warned her that the time for action was come.

Then, in June 1857, she won over the sepoys stationed at Jhansi, and persuaded the English officers and their families to accept her protection; they were 67 Englishmen with their wives and children. A solemn procession was formed of these victims, headed by ulemas and fanatics and followed by the leading townsfolk: as they paced along these natives sang verses of the Koran, and repeated the refrain, "No mercy shall be shown to Giaours."

There walked the Resident, Captain Skene, doubtless knowing the bitterness of the hour, if the children did not. When they reached the ruins of an old mosque the procession was halted. The men were carefully separated from the women and children; the Afghan mercenaries and sepoys kept the ground lest any should escape, and the butchers of the city were bidden to go in and hack the doomed unbelievers to pieces.

It was this massacre which prompted General Rose and his men to strain every nerve to reach and capture Jhansi's strong fortress.

Sir Hugh Rose's force consisted of two brigades—the first under Brigadier Stuart of the Bombay army; the second under Brigadier Stewart of the 14th Light Dragoons.

There were many deficiencies to be met: supplies were scarce; the batteries were short of horses and men; the siege artillery was very inefficient for making breaches. But Sir Hugh Rose made every one hurry up, in spite of heat and fever; he began by punishing revolt in Indore and early in January started for the relief of Sagar.

On the 7th of January it was found necessary to disarm the Bhopal contingent. We can quote from an unpublished diary written by Lieutenant J. Bonus of the Royal Engineers: "As I command the sappers and miners I went to a council to discuss the disarming. . . .

"About 7.30 a.m. of the 8th, the infantry and cavalry of the Bhopal contingent were ordered to march through the camp, to the surprise of those not in the secret. The dragoons and artillery were at stables, and the 3rd and 24th were strolling about. But no sooner were the contingent gentlemen clear of camp than a change came very rapidly over the scene. In a few minutes the dragoons were mounted and the guns horsed. The infantry fell in armed with ball. Great must have been the surprise of the late mutineers to see cavalry, guns and infantry between them and their village.

"The contingent infantry were ordered to pile arms; which they did. They were then marched some fifty yards from their arms, and the 3rd Europeans marched up to the piles.

"Next the cavalry were ordered to dismount, when their horses were led away. But these men on being ordered to give up their swords, refused. Mayne asked for a company of Europeans to compel obedience. But the brigadier said, 'I'll give you something better than that.'

"He at once ordered the artillery to prepare for action in front of the dismounted men. 'Trot, march'—'action right'—'with grape load!'

"No sooner was the order given than the mutineers put down their swords. Each man had his uniform stripped off."

Often the men began their march at 2 a.m. Once the headman of a village was impudent to an officer and received two dozen lashes. Bathing and snipe-shooting relieved the monotony of the march at intervals, and alarms of sharpshooters in the jungle kept men awake.

On the 24th they sighted Rhatghur at 2 p.m. on the top of a steep hill. Between them and the fortress was a river with a stony bed, which the horse artillery and dragoons had to cross. They were under fire from the enemy concealed amongst trees at the foot of the hill.

On the 25th, General Rose and his staff went on a reconnoitring expedition, as was his wont; for he liked to discover for himself the best way of attacking a stronghold.

On the 26th, the guns and howitzers shelled the fort until dark.

On the 27th, Lieutenant Bonus was ordered to examine a round tower near the walls, but when it had been seized it was found useless, and the men were withdrawn.

On the 28th, a battery was opened on the face of the fort which soon made considerable breaches.

On the 29th, up at 7 a.m. While at breakfast news came that the fort had been evacuated during the night. I walked into the fort through a breach and saw over the place. There were very few bodies about, and very little loot, merely some ponies, camels and horses. The rascals had escaped down an almost vertical precipice by the aid of ropes. Two had been killed in the descent. We shall never catch these fellows; they always manage to get away. They did the same thing before; they will never wait till the breach is practicable. It was an awful cliff down which they escaped."

Lieutenant Bonus was left to blow up the gates while

the Force marched for Barodia, a strong village in a dense jungle.

Here the Rajah of Banpur was entrenched and lost 500 men in the resistance he made. Captain Neville, R.E., who had gone untouched through the Crimean War, was killed by a round-shot close to the general.

The besieged garrison at Sagar had been shut up for eight months anxiously expecting relief, and feeling sick at the delay: but at last they heard Sir Hugh Rose's guns bombarding Ratghur; then a rider came and signalled that relief was coming. The investing force melted away and Sir Hugh's troops on 3rd February marched through the city in a long line.

The natives stared in wonder at a European regiment and the 14th Dragoons and the siege-guns drawn by elephants—while the ladies and children of the garrison officers waved a glad and thankful welcome.

"The Europeans in Sagar were uncommonly glad to see us. The Bengal 31st Native Infantry was there and, wonderful to say, had not mutinied!

"We had a fine time there: our dandies went peacocking, but they could only muster one tall hat among them, so they took that in turns! On the 6th, we had a grand parade . . . the general said, 'I don't believe you have a full dress among you.'

"On the 9th we had to cross the Beas: I was extremely astonished to find an excellent suspension-bridge over the river. Considering that we were in the jungle this was an extraordinary sight. The man who built this bridge dug up the iron on the spot, smelted it and forged his bars then and there. All honour to him! he was a clever fellow. The heavy guns and elephants were directed to cross the river by a ford; but it is said that they crossed the bridge.

"On the 10th I had a weary day—in the saddle with Sir Hugh till 8 p.m.: there was some skirmishing and we had a few men wounded. To wind up, Sir Hugh asked me to dinner—a kind cruelty!"

Some 25 miles east of Sagar was Fort Garhakota, where the mutinous 51st and 52nd Bengal Regiments had established themselves. This was taken on the 13th February after a hot march through dense jungle.

Lieutenant Bonus says: "The enemy evacuated the fort in the night: things had been made rather hot for the rebels with the big howitzer: our shells had killed many men—the place has large supplies of food."

Then follows in the diary a sad story, in which Lieutenant Dick, Royal Engineers, shows a rare chivalry, to be rewarded only by arrest and loss of his command.

"25th—A most unhappy incident has occurred just now: a native of the Bombay Sappers and Miners named Maun was tried on the 22nd by a native district court-martial on the charge of attempting to pass out of Fort Garhakotah a camel laden with sugar, ghee, rice, flour and one matchlock—with intent to injure the Prize Agents. The man was found guilty and sentenced to fifty lashes.

"Dick, who now commands the Sappers, believed that a great injustice had been done by this finding and sentence; he wrote to the brigade-major and advised the sapper to appeal to Brigadier Stewart for a new trial by a European court. Accordingly when Maun was paraded for punishment on the 24th he appealed to the brigadier for a fresh trial.

"The brigadier was furious and dismissed the parade, saying to Dick, 'We may thank you for this, Lieutenant Dick.'

"Soon after the parade Dick was placed under arrest and I was placed in command of the Sappers.

"Maun was tried by a general European drum-head court for mutiny and disobedience of orders: he was found guilty, sentenced to seven years' hard labour and to be marked with the letter M: also to forfeit all property to Government.

"This morning, 25th, Maun was flogged before the whole brigade. The impression made upon me by the whole unhappy business is that the authorities behaved with exceeding harshness, even cruelty! I doubt very much whether Maun was guilty in the first instance: I gather that he had nothing to do with the loading of the camel, that he did not know what was on it: he was casually asked by a soldier to take the camel outside the fort and complied in all innocence!"

We may state that two separate accounts written by surgeons and published agree with this: the surgeon on parade refused to brand the letter M on Maun.

"27th—Dick has been reprimanded before all the officers of the Brigade, released from arrest but deprived of his company. The command was offered to me, but I refused it on the ground that duties as Assistant Field Engineer occupied all my time. Goodfellow also declined: Fox of the Madras Sappers accepted the command. . . . Dick is in very low spirits."

The diary now describes the taking of a small fort, for Sir Hugh's energy omitted nothing: the forcing of a pass through the hills and the jungle fights and retreats: a hungry day with no food and plenty of strong language when the tents were at last pitched.

"5th March—To-day the first bugle was sounded at 3 a.m.: I cannot imagine why the general insists on turning out the men at this dreadful hour!

"6th—Dick and I made a plan of Marowra fort: then we shot twelve couple of snipe and two brace of quail."

Sir Hugh pressed on to Jhansi, often marching all night, taking a fort here and blowing up the palace of an insurgent there, until they came near Jhansi on the 20th.

The fortress stands on a high rock and is built of solid masonry, guns peeping from every elevation.

The city is four and a half miles in circumference and is surrounded by a massive wall, eight feet thick: 11,000 men formed the garrison, and the brave lady who inspired them took no mean part in the defence: for she and other women assisted in repairing the havoc made in the defences by the hot fire of seventeen days. Sir Hugh Rose was engaged from sunrise to sunset, reconnoitring and placing the siege batteries, as he had no plan of the city or map of the country. To the east of the city was a picturesque lake and a palace of the old rajah's: on the south side were the ruined cantonments of the British troops.

Sir Hugh never wasted a moment. He wrote to Sir Colin: "The great thing with these Indians is not to stay at long distances firing: but after they have been cannonaded, to close with them."

Day and night a heavy fire was kept up on the fort and Mamelon, and the native women in the city were ever busy working at the repairs. By 30th March the defences of the fort and city had been dismantled and the enemy's guns mostly disabled.

Sir Hugh made arrangements to storm Jhansi on the next day, but news came of the advance of Tantia Topee with a large force of 20,000 men: flags were flying from Sir Hugh's observatory, a signal of danger, and an immense bonfire on the Jhansi side of the river Betwa was received with shouts of joy from the walls.

Sir Hugh might well have quailed under such a danger, but he at once resolved to fight a general action with the new foe while he still pressed on the siege of Jhansi. During the evening of the 31st he moved all the men he could spare to meet Tantia Topee.

Next morning Tantia Topee made a vigorous attack, feeling certain of an easy victory over the few English.

But Captain Lightfoot's battery and the charge of the 14th Light Dragoons forced the enemy to break and retire in confusion. Then they fired the jungle: but through smoke and fire our field battery galloped and opened fire as the Indians were recrossing the Betwa: the pursuit was continued until dark, and stores, siege guns and materials of war fell into our hands: Tantia Topee had lost 1500 men and was in full retreat for Kalpi.

Meanwhile the fire on the breach was redoubled, and

Sir Hugh determined that, whether the breach were practicable or no, Jhansi should be taken on the 3rd of April.

On the evening before, Sir Hugh sent for Lieutenant Dick, and said: "You have rendered yourself liable to a court-martial, sir: but I have heard of your high promise and good qualities and I cannot subject you to a punishment which would be ruinous to your career and deprive you of the honour of the assault. I therefore pardon you, and I know you will do your duty to-morrow."

General Bonus, then Lieutenant, says in his diary:—

"On the night of the 2nd April orders came round very late, but neither Dick nor I was detailed for any duty. We both, however, decided that we would be in the game somehow.

"3rd April. At 2.30 a.m. the sappers left camp with Brown, Fox, Goodfellow, Meiklejohn and Dick. I did not move until 4 a.m. and then went down to the right attack, where I found the staff in the advanced battery. The ladder party with Fox and Brown was just approaching the wall, and it was very plain that things were not going well. I ran out and joined the party to help as far as I could.

"Fox and I managed to get a double ladder placed, but with much difficulty: for the ground was very rough, the wall high, the ladder heavy and too short, and the fire of the enemy incessant and well directed.

"As soon as the ladder was ready, I called to the Europeans of the storming party to follow me, and mounted: but only one man would at first venture. He and I went up side by side on the bamboo double ladder. At the top we had an unpleasant time; as many men on the wall as could crowd in front of us hacked away at us. But they were so anxious to protect themselves with their shields that they could hardly see what they were doing: my sword was chiefly used to ward off their cuts, and I was so busy with my right hand that I quite forgot the revolver in my left.

"The soldier alongside of me used his bayonet freely, but I don't think he did much damage. However, this

THE STORMING OF JHANSI

Lieutenant Bonus, supported by only one man, mounted a double ladder of bamboo, and for some time was hacking, thrusting, and parrying blows, until a rebel with his clubbed rifle hurled him to the ground. Although he had a revolver in his left hand he was so busily engaged that he forgot to use it.

little game soon came to an end. I was dimly conscious of a man well to my left who clubbed his musket, swung it round his head, and the next instant it was fireworks and black night with me.

"The first thing I realised after I fell was that some one was standing over me, saying, 'Poor fellow! he's done for!'

"However, though I could not move a limb, I felt that I was not 'done for,' and soon I managed to crawl behind a low bit of wall, when I lay still till I could look about me.

"I was half-blind with blood and felt as if every bone in my body was broken . . . it was clear that the escalade had failed, and that there was very sharp fighting going on inside the walls."

Lieutenant Bonus, owing to his being stunned, was not able to record what was the effect of his plucky attempt to gain the wall; but Colonel Malleson writes in his *History*: "The rampart they had to escalade was very high and the scaling-ladders were too short. Thanks, however, to the splendid gallantry of three officers of the Engineers, Dick, Meiklejohn, and Bonus, and of Fox of the Madras Sappers, they succeeded in gaining a footing there. Just then Brockman, from the left attack, made a timely charge on the flank and rear of the defenders. Their persistence immediately diminished, and the right attack made good its hold."

These young officers led the way at the cost of life or limb: for the men seemed to hang back at first, not liking the look of the place with its awkward climb. Lieutenant Dick, on putting his foot on the step of another scaling-ladder, said to a brother-officer, "I never can be sufficiently obliged to Sir Hugh Rose: tell him how I have done my duty."

He ran up the ladder, received several shots and fell down mortally wounded: such was the end of a chivalrous officer who had imperilled his career to save an Indian private.

Meiklejohn, who had spent part of the night before in writing to his mother, feeling certain that he should be killed in the storm of the morrow, no sooner gained the top than he was dragged from the ladder by the Afghan mercenaries and hacked to pieces so as to be unrecognisable. Though the escalade had partially failed, yet it served to draw a body of the garrison away from the other escalade. Fortunately the assault was more successful on the left, and the general entered the breach, fought his way from street to street and from room to room of the palace.

The next day, 4th April, the rest of the city was taken and occupied: in the evening the Rani sent for her horse to the fort ditch, and was let down from a window into the saddle, and so fled to Kalpi, having her little stepson in her lap.

For seventeen days and nights our men had never taken off their clothes nor unsaddled their horses!

Sir Hugh Rose wrote: "No recollection of the revolting murders perpetrated in that place could make our men forget that in an English soldier's eyes the women and children are always spared. So far from hurting them, the troops shared their rations with them."

The capture of Jhansi had cost us 343 killed and wounded, of whom 36 were officers. The rebels lost about 5000 men. But Sir Hugh gave the enemy no rest: he stormed Lohari and Kunch and fought such a battle at Gulauli on the 22nd of May that the rebels dispersed, broken and dispirited.

Thus in five months Sir Hugh Rose had traversed Central India, stormed many fortresses, won several victories, and re-established British authority in a most important province.

"It was impossible to have done this better than Sir Hugh Rose did it. As a campaign his was faultless."

It only remained to catch the de Wet of the Mutiny—Tantia Topee: but he for more than nine months eluded all the forces sent to intercept him: he was supreme in fighting and running away: the only native who developed a genius for war.

At length he was compelled to hide in the jungle and was betrayed by a rebel chief, Man Singh, at midnight on the 7th of April 1859. Tantia Topee was taken to Sipri, tried by court-martial and hanged on the 18th of April.

Such was the end of this able guerilla leader: but we must not forget that this was the man who organised the massacre at Cawnpur, and gloated over the deaths of our women and children. Sir Hugh was appointed commander-in-chief first of Bombay, then of India, made Field Marshal and Baron Strathnairn. He died at Paris at the age of eighty-four and was buried at Christchurch Priory, Hants.

Clyde and Strathnairn. Clarendon Press.
Malleson's *History of the Indian Mutiny*. Seeley, Service & Co.